P9-CKY-232

Jim Beckwourth

**BLACK MOUNTAIN MAN
AND WAR CHIEF OF THE CROWS**

Jim Beckwourth

BLACK MOUNTAIN MAN
AND WAR CHIEF OF THE CROWS

By ELINOR WILSON

University of Oklahoma Press
Norman

Library of Congress Cataloging in Publication Data

Wilson, Elinor, 1914–
  Jim Beckwourth, Black Mountain Man and War Chief of
The Crows.

  Bibliography: p.
  1. Beckwourth, James Pierson, 1798–1866. I. Title.
F592.B3975   917.8′03′20924 [B]   72–931
ISBN 0–8061–1012–0

Copyright 1972 by the University of Oklahoma Press, Publish-
ing Division of the University. Composed and printed in Norman, Oklahoma, U.S.A., by the University of Oklahoma Press.
First edition.

To
Evalyn and Alexander Summers

Preface

To a child growing up in Trinidad, Colorado, playing at the foot of the equestrian statue of Kit Carson and climbing the slopes below "Simpson's Rest" were diversions taken in stride. The old tales about Carson, the Bents, and the Baca family were standard lore, but not without a magic to stir the imagination even of children. The Spanish Peaks and the Sangre de Cristo Range, Raton Pass, Taos, and Santa Fe were intriguing names, as were Pueblo and Hardscrabble and Fort Garland. One could not help knowing that exciting history had been built around them. But in all those years, I cannot remember ever having heard the name of James Beckwourth.

When, at last, as an amateur historian, I began to learn a little more about these people and places, I came across constant references to Jim Beckwourth, but at a certain point there arose a blank wall—very little was known about the man, other than what he himself had recorded. Almost every historian of the fur trade and the West referred to Beckwourth, sometimes quoted him and checked his dates, and passed him off as a great liar. And that was all.

But for one who had also been brought up on nineteenth-century novelists who never liked to leave a story incomplete in its least detail, this was not enough. If the man deserved notice, why could we not know a great deal more about him?

I hope that this work will act as an inducement to much more research into the life of a man who contributed richly to the development of the West. Jim Beckwourth's life was spent in the company of men who are recognized as true pioneers. His explorations, his work in the mountain fur trade, his knowledge of Indians and their ways, his very human search for "renown," all make him a proper subject of interest to the historian.

Beckwourth was a courageous, intelligent, independent pioneer who exemplified the spirit of his day: there might be something on the other side of the mountain and he would go and see. That in each instance he "tried it out" and, disillusioned, moved on, speaks for his refusal to settle for the ordinary and for his enduring belief in the charm of life and its endless new invitations.

Acknowledgments

Countless kind and patient foster parents of this book can be found from Massachusetts to Missouri to Oregon. They range from temperance societies to members of California's famous E Clampus Vitus and from the staffs of historical societies and libraries to individual scholars. All have my deepest gratitude, as have such great authors as Dale L. Morgan, Harrison C. Dale, Nolie Mumey, J. Cecil Alter, and many others.

I am particularly indebted to John Barr Tompkins, of The Bancroft Library, whose pleasant responses to my requests always included an offer to do even more and, usually, resulted in his having to do just that. Assistant Archivist Joseph Snell of the Kansas State Historical Society contributed much to my knowledge of Jim Beckwourth's later life. James de T. Abajian, currently compiling a bibliography of Afro-American materials for the Friends of the San Francisco Public Library, took time from his busy schedule to give me significant direction to journal materials. David Lavender directed me to important newspaper and other sources.

Librarians across the country took the trouble to set me straight on difficult questions. In California, Mrs. Marion L. Buckner, The California Room, San Diego Public Library, was always gracious and helpful; Mrs. Thelma Neaville, Marysville City Library, which has one of the best indexes to local history to be found anywhere, was of inestimable assistance. Mrs. Ernstlee Henshaw, our local San Diego County Librarian, patiently ordered book after book, then packed them up and carried them to the post office to mail them off again. In Quincy, Mrs. Dorothy Egbert of the Plumas County Library was extremely helpful in locating valuable records.

I am indebted to Mrs. Alys Freeze, Head of the Western History Department, Denver Public Library; to Mrs. Virginia Lee Starkey and Mrs. Alice L. Sharp of the State Historical Society of Colorado; to the staff of the Pioneers' Museum, Colorado Springs; to the librarians of the University of Colorado, Boulder; and to Susie Henderson, at the Museum of New Mexico, Santa Fe.

The staffs of the California State Library, Sacramento, the Newberry Library, Chicago, the National Archives, the American Antiquarian Society, the Virginia State Library, the Missouri Historical Society, the State Historical Society of Missouri, the Western Historical Manuscripts Division of the Library of the University of Missouri and the Berkshire County Historical Society of Pittsfield, Massachusetts, all provided much-needed information and they did it so graciously that much of my guilt for constantly plaguing them was eased.

Mrs. Guido Ramelli, who has lived on the old "Beckwourth Ranch" for many years, and her neighbors, Mr. and Mrs. Leonard Baier, were hospitable and most kind in granting interviews, in permitting photographs to be made, and in introducing me to some of the lesser-known details of the area of Beckwourth's Pass and Trail.

I am grateful to John Covert for presenting me with a copy of Letts' *California Illustrated*; to my sister, Alice Mueller, for many editorial suggestions; to Blanche Hanes Fish, who did a great deal of research for me in Denver and whose help on several research trips was of great value.

My gratitude to my husband, Orlando, and to our daughter, Patricia, must be expressed. They have willingly accompanied me on research trips through northern California. Together we have followed Beckwourth's western trail, as far as was feasible, from New Mexico and Colorado, through Wyoming, up into

Wind River country, and along the Snake and the Green rivers. We also searched out what we thought would have been a likely spot for Jim's first terrifying encounter with western Indians on a scalp hunt. In addition, Patricia has assisted in typing and in innumerable other ways.

Finally I must thank the two friends to whom this book is dedicated—friends who made their every vacation and their every visit to a library an occasion to look for "something else" on Beckwourth. Their cheerful encouragement will always be remembered.

With such friends and such help, responsibility for error can lie only with me. I accept it fully.

ELINOR WILSON

Poway, California
January 18, 1972

Contents

Illustrations

Maps

Jim Beckwourth

BLACK MOUNTAIN MAN
AND WAR CHIEF OF THE CROWS

I

"The Gaudy Liar"

Young men on American frontiers of the 1820s were as adventurous and daring as in any age and they had one great advantage over the generations that succeeded them: adventure lay at their back door. They needed only to head up the Missouri or out across the plains toward the mountains or famed "Mexico" and they were immediately challenged, tried, and fulfilled.

When farsighted and fortune-hunting entrepreneurs of the fur trade set their hopes on the Rocky Mountains, they brought out restless runaways, reckless lawbreakers seeking a haven, and young and hardy hunters who, perhaps, had an eye to profit and a hope of returning to a farm and a settled existence. All these, as well as numerous nondescript men willing to work—and work hard—for a mere living, poured into the West. Fortunately, the names of many of these *engagés* and trappers are known. They are remembered not because they were great men individually, but because their deeds were incidental to the accomplishments of the giants of that era: Thomas Fitzpatrick, Kit Carson, Jim Bridger, the Sublettes, Jedediah Smith, Louis Vasquez, to name but a few.

The principal mountain men provided materials for the weaving of legend and myth. From the headwaters of the Missouri to the adobe-lined plazas of Taos and Santa Fe, they and their lesser-known comrades roamed the valleys, trapped the streams, and drifted down roaring rivers in crude bullboats, getting to know every inch of their chosen land. They knew every Indian tribe and just about what to expect of each. They lived under the open sky or in Indian lodges and sometimes in fortified trading posts. Buckskin shirts, leggings, and moccasins, fringed and

3

decorated by Indian squaws, provided a practical yet picturesque costume. If they did not marry Indian women, most of them nevertheless found a welcome in an Indian lodge.

The lives of the mountain men fascinated the stay-at-homes in the East, who could never hear enough to satisfy their avid need for vicarious excitement, danger, and exotic romance. Contemporary accounts were eagerly snatched up and published in books and newspapers; still later, reminiscences transformed these men into superheroes. Inevitably, fabrications embroidered the sturdy cloth of their real lives, but also sometimes left a hero looking somewhat less than noble.

Such was the fate of James P. Beckwourth, who, long before he dictated his memoirs to Thomas D. Bonner,[1] had become famous in the mountains and across the plains. He was partner, comrade, or employee of every mountain man of importance. He traded, fought, and lived with Indians for nearly fifty years. He was courageous to the point of folly; his adventures far exceeded those of many of his contemporaries.

Jim Beckwourth was a figure suited to the making of western legend. He stood six feet tall, was muscular and strong, quick and lithe. His long black hair reached to his waist; his eyes were very dark and could flash in anger. Many mistook him for a Spaniard, perhaps for a half-blood Indian. All who knew him in the 1850s recalled that he was very open, free, and of a kindly nature, loving song and merriment. His vitality was remarkable, his judgment excellent, and his knowledge of Indian ways superb. Beckwourth loved to talk and he did so at the least opportunity. But he was no bore—his audiences were attentive, for his voice was clear and musical and his stories well arranged. "His language was much superior to that usually heard in the Rocky Mountains in his day."[2]

Jim Beckwourth took to Indian costume as though born to wear it. On occasion he dressed in elaborately beaded and embroidered buckskin, braided his hair into long rolls, or tied it at

4

the neck with a gaudy ribbon. He loved personal ornaments: gold chains, buttons, even earrings—his ears were pierced in several places.

All the old mountaineers rode horseback well, but Beckwourth enjoyed performing such dangerous feats as racing bareback at full speed, leaning over until his hair swept the ground. Of course he was an expert shot and could handle dagger, lance, and bow.

Yet, with all this, James P. Beckwourth has been frozen into a historical role that has precluded the kind of investigation given to the lives of Carson, Bridger, Joe Meek, and many others with whom he worked and lived.

For Jim Beckwourth was a "liar."

Once this sobriquet was fastened upon him, it was accepted by all. Jim's role frequently became that of providing comic relief in histories of other men. There arose a convention of having a little fun with Beckwourth, not making the mistake, however, of removing the odious label, for it provided splendid opportunities for the light touch or an amusing aside. Jealous or aspiring writers of the past often libeled him—probably no other man has been so brutally and repeatedly damned as a liar as he —yet in many instances it can be shown that the authors could not possibly have known their subject.

Early historians, in the main, wrote Jim off as a scoundrel, though not all of them used such virulent terms as those of Francis Parkman, whose information was secondhand but in a form that suited his malevolent mood: "Jim Beckworth, a mongrel of French, American and Negro blood . . . is a ruffian of the worst stamp, bloody and treacherous, without honor or honesty; yet in his case the standard rules of character fail, for though he will stab a man in his sleep, he will also perform the most desperate acts of daring. . . ."[3] Years after having formed this conclusion, according to Bernard De Voto, Parkman penciled a note to the preface of his own copy of the *Life and Adventures*: "Beckwith is a fellow of bad character—a compound of white and black blood, though he represents otherwise."[4]

Hubert Howe Bancroft grants that Beckwourth was a "famous hunter, guide, Indian-fighter, chief of the Crows, and horse-thief. No résumé can do justice to his adventures, [but not] the slightest faith [can] be put in his statements."[5]

Although Hiram M. Chittenden was capable of delivering a severe tongue lashing on occasion, he spoke of Beckwourth with restraint and mildness: "[He] belonged to a class without which the history of those times would lose much of its spice and variety —he was one of those 'charming liars' . . . who are delightful to listen to for the very enormity of their misstatements." Still, Chittenden cautioned, "The whole work is replete with fable, and there is probably not a single statement in it that is correct as given."[6]

Dale L. Morgan's knowledge of the West and the fur trade was something more than encyclopedic. Having become sympathetic to the spirit of those times, he was tolerant of Jim: "Most joyfully a member of the party was James P. Beckwourth, 'the gaudy liar.' To be a gifted liar was as much a part of mountain honor as hard drinking or straight shooting. Embroider your adventures, convert to your uses any handy odyssey, and spin it all out in the firelight, the only sin the sin of being dull."[7]

Beckwourth's contemporaries were, with some exceptions, less kind. Racial prejudice inspired much of what earlier writers said about his life. It is clearly apparent in the words of Francis Parkman, who could look down his nose at almost anybody but who especially could not abide the thought of a "mongrel" of mixed blood. Such popular "historians" as Frank Triplett and Charles Christy, whose works are thoroughly discredited today, were merciless in fostering the already well-known tales about Beckwourth's color and his prevarications. Triplett published accounts of "old Jim's" exploits and put in his mouth language so obviously not his that William E. Connelley all but flung the word "liar" at Triplett himself.[8]

A more serious charge could be brought against Charles Christy, who headed a chapter of his reminiscences "Nigger Jim Beckwith," and then proceeded to reveal Jim's background thus: "Jim was born in that section of the United States where they spell Afro-American with a double g. He was a half-breed French-negro slave. His mother was a full-blood negress, one of the slaves belonging to [Pierre, Sr.] Choteau [sic], and as to Jim's paternity, it was generally believed Choteau himself was answerable."[9]

There is much, much more: the "pickininny" was traded off by Chouteau to a Mississippi river pilot named Jim Beckwith, who bestowed his own name on the boy. From then on the slave was called "Nigger Jim" to distinguish him from Pilot Jim! Later, Jim was "sold to Alex Culbertson, president of the American Fur Company, who took 'Nigger Jim' to Fort Owens on the Yellowstone." The fact that Culbertson was not president of the company and that Fort Owen was across the divide from the Yellowstone did not disturb Christy; he was a collector of much more interesting information and he could scarcely wait to brand Jim as a "past master of the art of Ananias." "I knew Jim intimately and he was the biggest liar that ever lived. . . . As a single-handed liar, Jim had no superior or equal," Christy recalled.[10]

Reminiscences are notorious traps for the unwary, but in the happy days before documentation any error or fantasy, once in print, could be passed along from book to book, each new author embellishing it in colorful, gossipy detail. And, says William Connelley, "to secure a remunerative piece of work in competition with their fellows, [the old pioneers] did not hesitate to speak in disparaging terms of the ability and reliability of those who might be preferred over them."[11]

James Beckwourth has not been without respected defenders,

however; among them can be listed William E. Dellenbaugh: "Captain Chittenden is rather too severe, it seems to me, for Beckwourth appears to have been a frontiersman hardly surpassed in dexterity and skill by Bridger, Carson, Fitzpatrick, Jedediah Smith, or any of the others of that masterful band, but as he was believed to be of partly African blood, this put him at a disadvantage, especially with writers of the slave-holding states, who would consider him impudent to rate himself high."[12]

William Connelley asked of his readers an appropriate recognition of Jim's achievements:

Few men equaled James P. Beckwourth, and he lived in the age of great men. The West owes him a debt it would be hard to pay for leaving such a record of his adventures on the plains and mountains. This work will come to be one of the great authorities; not that all it contains can be relied upon, but that it is mainly true, and that it is a record of a life spent in the Great West, the record being made by the man himself. . . . So far as I know, this is the first appeal for justice to the memory of James P. Beckwourth. I make it because I believe in the worth of the man. . . .[13]

Colonel Henry Inman also attempted to deal fairly with Jim Beckwourth:

I never saw Beckwourth, but I have heard of him from those of my mountaineer friends who knew him intimately. I think he died long before Parkman made his tour to the Rocky Mountains. Colonel Boone, the Bents, Carson, Maxwell, and others ascribed to him no such traits as those given by Parkman, and as to his honesty, it is an unquestioned fact [that] Beckwourth was the most honest trader among the Indians of all who were then engaged in the business. As Kit Carson and Colonel Boone were the only Indian agents whom I ever knew or heard of that dealt honestly with the various tribes, as they were always ready to acknowledge . . . so also Beckwourth was an honest Indian trader.[14]

8

Lewis H. Garrard's delightful account of his travels in 1846, when he was seventeen, has a freshness and appeal seldom found in the journals of older men. He left an amusing, clear-sighted picture of life around Bent's Fort and in Taos and Santa Fe, as well as of the harrowing dangers of the Santa Fe Trail. Garrard and his companion came across Beckwourth one evening on the trail and Jim stayed to visit a while.

In Santa Fe last winter, Beckwith kept the best furnished saloon in the place—the grand resort for liquor-imbibing, monte-playing, and *fandango*-disposed American officers and men.

He was a large, good-humored fellow; and while listening to the characteristic colloquy, I almost forgot that he was of a race who, in the much boasted land of liberty, are an inferior, degraded people. With their *caballada*, we found a horse of Mr. St. Vrain, which we drove to our own band, without a previous by'r leave or a single compliment to Jim's honesty. Hatcher thought the party was on a horse-stealing expedition, to which propensity, however, in the mountains, small blame should be imputed.[15]

Beckwourth does not specifically mention this meeting with Garrard and Hatcher, but he may have been referring to it in this passage: "At the time I met my informant [that he had been charged with aiding the Indians to steal horses], I had an order from Captain Morris, of the United States Army, in my pocket, authorizing me to pick up all the government horses that I might find in my rambles, and bring them in; but up to the time that I was informed of the charges against me, I had found but one horse, the property of Captain Saverine [St. Vrain], and it I had restored to the owner."[16]

Another young man, who met Beckwourth only shortly before his death, found him and his comrades

worthy of the reputation and regard in which they were held

9

by the soldiers of the frontier, and I venture to say that we knew them best. They were brave, resourceful and kindly. They were, as their primitive life in the open demanded, rough in dress and demeanor, yet very attractive in both. Physically, in their peculiar and unique costume of buckskin, they were, except the Indians, the most picturesque and interesting characters of that almost unknown territory spreading out west of the Mississippi, which was in those days as pregnant with legend, mystery and romance, as the Sargasso Sea. They were the West personified, from Bowie to Bridger, and a living blank contradiction to the shallow doctrine that the "tailor makes the man." In speech they were blunt, straightforward and honest. . . . They neither feared nor shrank from any danger, yet they were cautious and discreet, but confident. . . .

Nor were they the debauchees that some fantastic writers would lead us to believe. They were not prohibitionists nor were they drunkards. . . . Their life was as open as the immense territory over which they roamed. They were the poorest material for the making of hypocrites I ever met. . . .[17]

With that benediction, let us take a closer look at the "gaudy liar."

Sir Jennings and "Miss Kill"

That James Pierson Beckwourth was sired by Sir Jennings Beckwith, grandson of Sir Marmaduke Beckwith of Richmond County, Virginia, and son of Sir Jonathan is now generally acknowledged. Apart from settling forever the speculation as to Beckwourth's paternal nationality ("Irish overseer" has been the favorite label applied to his father), this information also helps to explain some aspects of Jim Beckwourth's character and behavior.

The Beckwiths of Virginia were prominent men—prosperous, civic minded, and proud to trace their ancestry back to Sir Hugh de Malebisse, one of Duke William's warrior-knights at the Battle of Hastings. In 1226, Hugh's descendant, Sir Hercules de Malebisse, married Lady Beckwith Bruce, daughter of Sir William Bruce of Uglebarnby and heiress to an estate called Beckwith. Sir Hercules kept the Malebisse escutcheon and took the name of his wife's estate. This lady, for her part, could also trace her ancestry to a Norman knight, Sir Robert Bruce, founder of the line that produced King Robert I, "the Bruce of Bannockburn."[1]

Sir Jennings's ancestors in England continued to achieve recognition. The first baronetcy was bestowed on Sir Roger of Aldborough, Yorkshire, in 1681. Sir Roger's wife was Elizabeth Jennings (or Jenings), daughter of Sir Edmund Jennings, Knight. Their first son, also named Roger, succeeded to the title. He was High Sheriff of County York in 1706; a year earlier he had held the post of mayor of Leeds. This man had two sons, both of whom died unmarried, and a daughter, the sole heir. The title, therefore, at Sir Roger's death in 1743, went to his younger brother Marmaduke, born in 1687.[2]

Sir Marmaduke Beckwith came to Virginia shortly after 1700 and was apprenticed as a scribe in the office of the Secretary of Virginia. His relative, The Honorable Edmund Jenings, President of the Council of Virginia, wrote to the Justices of Richmond County in 1709 that Marmaduke "had bin bred up in the Secretary's Office [at Williamsburg] under Mr. Thacker above these three years and I doubt not both in respect of his Capacity and diligence will merritt your good opinion."[3] This recommendation aided Marmaduke in attaining the post of county clerk, an office he held until his death in 1780.[4]

Marmaduke enjoyed considerable prosperity, particularly during middle life, and built handsome homes for himself and his sons. His own Richmond County house, "Belvoin," was located a few miles north of present-day Warsaw, Virginia.[5] A short distance away is the beautiful Mt. Airy, an estate continuously occupied since 1740 by the direct male line of the Tayloe family. It was here that Jennings Beckwith died. It can be assumed that Sir Marmaduke's house was comparable to Mt. Airy in size and richness.

Marmaduke's title fell to his second son, Jonathan, who could surely have served as prototype for every Heathcliff that ever lived. Wild, passionate, determined to have his will, Jonathan might have been perfectly at home roaming the lonely Yorkshire moors. He quarreled with everyone who attempted to balk him, not excepting his own father, his brother, and his nephews. But the overweening, primary quarrel was with Richard Barnes, father of Rebecca, whom Jonathan was determined to marry. Such a quarrel was it that a quarter of a century later members of Richard's household remembered it and its consequences vividly.[6]

Tucked away among the ancient court documents is a paragraph, partially scratched out as being, apparently, irrelevant to the litigation that resulted from this dispute but of uncommon interest to the student of James P. Beckwourth's life: "Sir Jonathan Beckwith was summoned . . . as a witness and proved that one Morgan Williams had told him . . . that there was a track of two men or one from a *beaver trap* of Sir Jonathan's that was stolen."[7] Perhaps Jonathan preferred roaming the forests, fishing the rivers, and trapping beaver to visiting horseraces and gaming tables, diversions very popular in his day.[8]

At his own death in 1796, Jonathan Beckwith left a handsome estate. Several horses, numerous sheep, oxen, and cattle comprised the livestock and all kinds of farm equipment were listed. There were rich household furnishings, including mahogany tables, desks, chairs, fourteen family portraits, and much fine silver—tea and coffee services, as well as flatware. And, of course, there were slaves—thirty-four in number.[9]

The Beckwith family was related in one way or another to many distinguished early Virginians. The names of Harrison, Dade, Alexander, Butler, Hooe, Posey, Mason, and many others appear frequently in Beckwith-connected genealogies. There is ample evidence that Jonathan's and Rebecca's children contributed handsomely to the political, cultural, professional, and military life of their day. All, that is, except Jennings, who may have been "the vagrant of the family," as James P. Beckwourth once said of himself.

Jonathan's eldest son began well enough. At the age of nineteen, Jennings Beckwith was "Recommended as Captain of the Company lately Commanded by Captain Randall,"[10] at a court held on June 4, 1781. Whether he attained a higher rank in the American Revolutionary forces is not known, but his service record, social position, and family background could have qualified him for promotion before the end of the war.

Nothing is known of Jim Beckwourth's mother, although she has been variously described as a "full-blood Negress," as a mulatto, and as a quadroon. A recent study of Beckwourth's life states that Jim was born of a mixed union and names Jennings as his father, adding that "reliable sources indicate that his mother, known only as Miss Kill, was probably a slave."[11]

The primary source for this assertion is Paul Beckwith's book, *The Beckwiths*. But Beckwith states flatly that Jennings Beckwith *married* a Miss Kill; there is no talk about mixed unions, or mulattos, or slaves.[12] The fact that Paul Beckwith identified Sir Jennings's wife in this fashion merely indicates that he knew very little about that branch of the family.

One of the "gentlemen justices" of the court that recommended Jennings Beckwith's commission as captain in the Virginia militia was William Miskell, son of Henry Miskell, a prominent plantation owner and man of wealth. In a will dated October 31, 1760, Henry devised to William and "to the heirs of his body lawfully begotten the plantation whereon I now live and the half of the land that is contained within this track adjoining."[13]

William Miskell, who was to receive his father's plantation, was born in Richmond County, March 5, 1729. He married Elizabeth Samford and died intestate in 1790. A division of his property was made equally between five of his six children. One of these was a girl, Catherine, who had married Jennings Beckwith in 1787, the bond being dated April 12.[14]

In the often difficult to decipher script of the nineteenth century, someone must once have recorded that Jennings Beckwith "married a Miskell." The transcription of this statement by someone not familiar with the Beckwith genealogy could easily lead to the unfortunate error of rendering the name as "Miss Kill."

As early as 1794, Jennings and Catherine Beckwith disposed of land inherited from William Miskell. They had also received several Negro slaves, but no further record of them has been found. In January, 1800, Jennings Beckwith sold 310 acres of land in Lunenburg Parish, Richmond County. This property, called "Winders," was inherited from Sir Jonathan. At that time the law required the wife of a grantor to enter into and acknowledge deed for land. Catherine's name does not appear on the document. While this is not proof positive of her death before that date, no other document indicates that she was living at a later date. Indeed, other circumstances indicate that Sir Jennings left Richmond County about this time, although he did not set out immediately on the long trek to Missouri.[15]

Jennings Beckwith was definitely a resident of the District of St. Charles, Louisiana Territory, as early as September 7, 1809. On that date he, with Samuel Griffith and François Lesieur, was appointed by the judge of the Probate Court as appraiser of the estate of one George DeLapp.[16] A letter was advertised for Jennings in St. Louis on November 2 of that same year.[17] Jennings's signature appears on a memorial to a board of commissioners that met late in 1809 to ascertain and adjust titles to lands in the Louisiana Territory.[18]

By August, 1810, Beckwith had bought land not far from Portage des Sioux, on "The Point," below St. Charles. With the Mississippi River forming the northern and the Missouri the southern boundary, the property consisted of about 1,150 arpens (not quite two sections, or 1,280 acres).[19] This primitive tract comprised an isolated backwoods settlement, exactly the kind of environment that suited Jennings Beckwith, who seemed to be seeking anonymity and seclusion. (He never took an active role in the social or political life of St. Louis or St. Charles, as he could have done by virtue of his background.)

Jim Beckwourth's "howling wilderness" must have been just that. Heavily forested with ash, cottonwood, pawpaw, hickory, elder, elm, and hackberry trees, some of the land on The Point had to be cleared for crops. The Beckwiths joined with neighboring families in erecting a blockhouse for their common protection against Indians.

Jim says there were thirteen children, but Jennings Beckwith's descendants are difficult to trace.[20] To the children who went to Missouri there is some lead through early newspaper advertisements. Paul Beckwith says that one son, Edwin, was supercargo on a merchant vessel lost at sea.[21] It was supposedly captured by pirates, who murdered those aboard. The St. Louis paper carried notices of the arrival and departure of the steamboat *Belvedere,* which plied the Ohio and Mississippi rivers. The captain was E. Beckwith. There was also a Captain Jacob Beckwith of the *Phoenix* on the upper Mississippi in the years 1823 through 1825. Other notices of Beckwiths living in the St. Louis–St. Charles area occur in the *Missouri Gazette, Missouri Republican,* and in the St. Charles census.[22]

Paul Beckwith knew of only four of Jennings Beckwith's children. He mentions Richard M. B.; Edwin; Malbis, who died in Frederick (now Clarke) County at the "Retreat," a cousin's home;[23] and an elusive "T. W." Beckwith says that Richard M. B. was born in Jefferson County, West Virginia, enlisted in the army in 1813, and died in 1818 while in St. Louis visiting his father, who was "with the Indians of the Far West."[24]

There is a touch of mystery to this story. Here is a young Virginian of perhaps twenty-five years making a visit to St. Louis and dying there. It is known that he was married and had at least two children.[25] Yet no official or newspaper record of his death has been found either at St. Charles or at St. Louis. Many years later, in the early 1900s, a man in Colorado caused Francis W. Cragin to write this:

> Dick Beckwith bro. of Jim B. Their father was a Virginian. Edward B (64 years old=son of Dick B now lives Colo Spgs   Dick and Jim were born in Va. (either "Glosster" or "Caroline or Norfolk county) Dick died in 1869 or 70 in Waco, Tex, aged betw 78 & 79 yrs. . . . [A later note adds] Jim Beckwith had two bros. Richard (probably the oldest unless Jim was) and one who was a doctor and 2 sisters, Laura and Rebecca, who before the Civil War were living in Baton Rouge, La. All the bros were [fighters?]. (Statem[ent] of his nephew Edward Beckwith.)[26]

James Haley White, who had lived in St. Louis as a youth, had some recollections regarding Jim Beckwourth's family.[27] His memoirs were written in the year of his death, at the age of seventy-seven. Fading memory and the reading of western lore mingled to produce accounts, not always totally correct, of the mountain men he had known. Among other errors, he had Jim going to the mountains with General Ashley's first expedition of 1822. He must, however, have known Beckwourth at one time.

White was fourteen when he came to St. Louis on May 11, 1819. He declares positively that he met Jim at that time and that Jim was apprenticed to John Sutton in May of that year. Beckwourth, however, says that he was apprenticed to George Casner, not Sutton. This seems to be substantiated by the fact that Casner had lived in St. Charles and probably knew Jennings Beckwith.[28] It happens, also, that Casner and Sutton had dissolved their partnership early in February, 1819. It can be assumed that Jim had departed Casner's blacksmith shop before James H. White appeared on the scene.

According to White, Jim "was born of a mulatto woman and a white father." Jim's "proclivities were low," and he was boastful and untruthful. There were three other children in the family: one of these was a barber, one a house servant, and one, "Winney," a "woman of the town." There was a woman in St. Louis called "Winey" Beckwith—Jennings had given her her freedom before 1819[29]—who later became a property owner, having purchased a lot lying in "Julie C. Soulard's First addition to the City of St. Louis . . . on the east side of Columbus Street."[30] The name of "Winey" (for Winifred) was popular with the Beckwiths and the Miskells.

In 1824 Jennings Beckwith also freed Lurana, "a mulatrix age about seventeen,"[31] but nothing further regarding her appears in the court records of St. Louis. (Jim Beckwourth recalled a sister named Louise; he later called her "Lou," which may have been a shortened version of Lurana.)

A number of arguments can be made in favor of Jim's legitimacy. Photographs do not indicate that he was darker than many swarthy frontiersmen and there is nothing Negroid about his features. His hair was wavy but not kinky, and in one photograph it appears heavy and almost straight. Moore's statement that there was nothing in Beckwourth's appearance to indicate Negro ancestry and the fact that several others did not remark that he was a mulatto (unless they wrote their memoirs years after they had already absorbed the legendary tales about him) are significant.

It was not customary to send the children of slaves to school; aside from all other considerations, they were generally too valuable as "hands" on the farms and plantations. Yet Beckwourth says that he had a few years' schooling, and while he has frequently been labeled "illiterate," it is now known that he could write a legible hand.[32] His spelling is no worse than that of many of his contemporaries; it is not likely that he learned it around the evening campfires in the mountains. While Jennings Beckwith was not a wealthy man,[33] literacy was part of his heritage. It is reasonable to assume that he sought for his son the rudiments of education; it is not so easy to believe that he would brother to educate a chance mulatto offspring. All these factors lead to the conclusion that Beckwourth's mother may have been a quadroon, probably fairly light-skinned. Jennings's behavior seems to indicate that he formed a long-term alliance with her, based on affection, and that she lived openly with him as his wife, at least in Missouri. In the remote backwoods area that was Jennings's choice, her children probably grew up in an atmosphere free of the burdensome stigma that would have plagued them in the South.

Jim Beckwourth's manner, his speech, and his outlook all seem to indicate that he was brought up under the tutelage of Jennings, who imparted to him some of the qualities of a gentleman—qualities that were noted by all impartial observers in later years.

Nevertheless, it can now be stated with finality that Jim Beck-wourth was technically a slave, although it is apparent that he was not so treated by his father, and that he enjoyed considerable freedom to come and go as he pleased. When Jim finally decided to leave for the mountains, Jennings Beckwith made certain that he went as a free man: on three separate occasions Jennings "personally appeared in open court and acknowledged the execution of a Deed of Emancipation from him to James, a mulatto boy."[34] He could scarcely have shown a greater parental affection.

While it may never be possible to identify Jim Beckwourth's mother with certainty, it can scarcely be doubted that his father was Jennings. The following obituary was written for the sire, but much of it could just as appropriately have served for the son:

> Sir Jennings Beckwith. Died at Mount Airy, Richmond County, on the 13th of November, Sir Jennings Beckwith, son of Jonathan and grandson of Sir Marmaduke Beckwith, Baronet, aged 72 years. Sir Jennings was the *Leather Stockings* of the Northern Neck. Much of his life had been spent wandering in the *Far West* on hunting excursions with the Indians and of late years he would live with men as would fish with him in summer or fox hunt in winter. Within the last twelve months he had slept on the river shore in the sturgeon season and had been in at the death in search of sport, and had insuperable objections to spending time profitably—consequently he lived poor but respectable and esteemed by many friends, who regret and sincerely mourn his death.[35]

A Youth in Missouri

"I was born in Fredericksburg, Virginia, on the 26th of April, 1798." This is the first sentence in James P. Beckwourth's memoirs.[1] Unfortunately, Beckwourth must be shown straight off as being in error—mistaken, not lying. The tax records of Fredericksburg, Virginia, from 1787 to 1807, at no time show the name of Jennings Beckwith, whereas those for Frederick County carry Jennings's name from 1799 through 1804.[2] Jim must be forgiven; because of the similarity of names, the city and the county to the north were not infrequently confused—and he was long removed from any knowledge of that area.

Jennings Beckwith owned 215 acres of land in Frederick County in 1801 and the name of Francis Beckwith appears for the next five years as owner of 215 acres, presumably the same farm. By 1806 the name of Beckwith disappeared from the land-tax lists of Frederick County, and does not occur again.

Of even more interest are the Frederick County Personal Property Tax Rolls.[3] In 1799 and 1800, Jennings Beckwith owned ten slaves and three horses, surely not a great estate. It appears that he was dissipating his share of the great Beckwith properties and that his resources had by now all but disappeared. By 1803 Beckwith is shown to have had one slave and one horse as taxable property. It is likely that he had left someone on his property as caretaker and had already started on his journey to the West by that year. The Beckwith ménage may have moved even farther north—into Maryland—before making its way west to Missouri.[4] For Jennings Beckwith, the first years of the new century seem to have marked a distinct break from the past and from his family. This, together with several other factors, leads one to wonder if

T. D. Bonner's date for Beckwourth's birth is not in error by about two years. It seems more likely that the event occurred in 1800.

If Bonner's date of 1798 is correct, several curious gaps occur in Jim's story. For example, Jim says that he was sent to school in St. Louis "when about ten years of age" (i.e., about 1808) and that he continued there for two years.[5] But there was only one school in St. Louis up to that time and it is not quite clear whether it was operating in 1808. On the other hand, assuming 1800 as the correct year, the picture becomes much clearer, for in 1809 and the following year at least four schools opened in St. Louis.[6] One of these schools opened on May 7, 1810, and continued until June, 1814, when its master took to the study of law. If Jim attended this or another school until 1814, other parts of the puzzle fall into place. For example, Beckwourth says his nineteenth year ended his indenture and he also mentions the partnership of Casner and Sutton, which was dissolved on February 3, 1819,[7] having lasted only three months. It seems unlikely that Jim would refer to this association if he had fled Casner's blacksmith shop in 1817, which would be the case if Bonner's date is followed.

Also, if Jim was born in 1798, some five years of his life are unaccounted for. What was he doing between 1817 and the summer of 1822, when he went to Fever River? Some writers think he may have gone with Louis Vasquez on a trading jaunt,[8] but there is no proof of this and certainly Beckwourth does not mention it in his memoirs. There still remain at least two years of Jim's early life that have not been traced, but it is very possible that his memory telescoped them into the brief period he describes in his book. "I went home to my father," says Jim, and perhaps he remained there longer than he seems to imply.

Two final arguments in favor of the 1800 birthdate exist. First, the Frederick County Personal Property Tax Rolls show that in 1801 Jennings Beckwith was taxed for *twelve* slaves, whereas for the two prior years he had owned ten. Jennings may have brought Jim and his mother to the Frederick County plantation in that year. Second, a few months before Beckwourth's death an Oroville, California, newspaper carried a short item about him:

> Jim Beckwourth—This notorious and somewhat ancient trapper and pioneer of Butte County, whose "adventures" were published in book form some years ago is still pursuing the business which has made him famous—that of trapping. He is now 66 years of age—that is, when we saw him last in '55 he had a silver dollar, of the coinage of 1800, on a rawhide string, which he wore around his neck, that, as he said, marked his year of birth.[9]

Jim Beckwourth's memory of his childhood in Missouri was sketchy: he recalled the conditions of living—the insecurity, the constant alarms, the need for community defenses against treacherous Indians:

> The settlers or inhabitants of four adjoining sections would unite and build a block-house in the centre of their possessions, so that in case of alarm they could all repair to it as a place of refuge from the savages.
>
> It was necessary to keep a constant guard on the plantations, and while one portion of the men were at work, the others, with their arms, were on the alert watching the wily Indian. Those days are still fresh in my memory, and it was then I received, young as I was, the rudiments of my knowledge of the Indian character, which has been of such inestimable value to me in my subsequent adventures among them.[10]

Jim's passing recollection of playing with other children in the backwoods settlement was soon obliterated by the memory of his coming upon the mutilated bodies of his playmates, murdered and scalped, as were their parents, by marauding Indians. Beckwourth thought this gruesome event occurred about 1809.

Early documents concerning Portage des Sioux support the assertion that the settlers lived in fear of such slaughter, but it is extremely unlikely that Jim saw any "massacres" before 1810, and it was not until 1812 that settlers along the rivers were seriously threatened.[11] In the years between 1805 and 1809 only nine men were known to have been slain by Indians in the St. Charles area.[12] This number, considering the conditions of the frontier and the foolhardiness of some of the victims, is not alarming.

During the War of 1812, the Indians of the area frequently wavered between allegiance to the British and a neutrality that would allow them to benefit from the "presents" and supplies offered by the United States. Plundering, horsestealing, and common theft were prevalent all along the Mississippi Valley. Settlers' claims poured into William Clark's Office of Indian Affairs in St. Louis; they cited everything from destruction of crops to the loss of an ax. One Callahan reported the loss of all his family possessions—clothing, furniture, tools, and animals, as well as a pair of knitting needles.[13] By 1813 the situation had become so threatening that a company of rangers was formed at Portage des Sioux to patrol a triangle from Portage to Cuivre to St. Charles and back. One of the leaders of this patrol was Nathan Boone, son of old Daniel, who had settled in the area many years earlier.[14]

On July 16, 1813, William Clark, Superintendent of Indian Affairs, requested from all agents under his jurisdiction a report on "the disposition situation and number of Indians" within the boundaries of their agencies; he also desired to know the number of citizens killed or made prisoners since April 1, 1810. Within a few days several of the agents had responded. Thomas Forsyth reported that the "Potawatomies, Kickapoux and other tribes towards Lake Michigan, may be considered to be hostile towards the United States. . . ," but he also thought that with proper handling they could be brought back into the fold. Isolated instances of murder and theft were reported by John Johnson, agent of the Sac and Fox tribes, and by their interpreter, Maurice Blondeau.[15] No agent mentioned the horrible massacre that Jim recalled from his boyhood, but the St. Louis newspaper of that day hinted at such outrages.

The party of Sacs and Foxes at Captan Gray [Captain Gray's] is considerable. I advised them to remain on an island near Captan Gray until his arrival, and all go on to the Portage des Sioux together, agreeably to your orders; I knew if they went to St. Louis it would be useless to them and troublesome to you. . . . On Sunday last 155 canoes arrived at Portage des Sioux where Governor Clark held a council with them. They have hitherto and continue to show every mark of neutrality in the present contest. This part of their nation who have joined the British wished to come in, but they would not receive them, as it would commit them with the United States. These wretches have gone to Prairie de Chien . . . they have taken a decided part with the British. . . . Our army will now meet an enemy in every savage band, and . . . that vengeance they have so long merited, will fall on them with redoubled fury. *For the shades of our unsuspecting farmers, their innocent wives and children cry loud for revenge.*[16]

Jim Beckwourth also recalled a large body of hostile Indians assembling across the Mississippi:

This was at Portage de Soix, and about two miles from my father's house; and their intention was to cut off all the white inhabitants of the surrounding country. . . . The settlers collected, crossed the river, and after a severe engagement defeated the Indians with great loss and frustrated their bloody purposes.

The Indians soon after appeared in great force opposite St. Louis. Blondo [Blondeau], an interpreter, was dispatched across the river to them, to inform them . . . that the people of St. Louis were provided with numerous "big guns mounted on wagons. . . ." They credited Blondo's tale and withdrew their forces.[17]

As if in further support of Jim's memory, the *Missouri Gazette* stated that some 1,500 Sacs and Foxes had gone to their wintering grounds: "besides those contained in 155 canoes which ascended the Missouri on Monday last, near 500 warriors crossed over by land, accompanied by Blondeau, their interpreter."[18]

A recently published old document, well flavored with pithy phrases and phonetic spelling, tends to confirm Jim's story. William Van Burkleo, Indian fighter, trapper, and pioneer, had lived in the St. Charles area as early as 1797; he settled on The Point about 1811. Having bought land at one dollar per arpen, paid for with two hundred bushels of corn at fifty cents each, and having purchased his wedding suit "of cheap quality" for $75 worth of peltry and venison, Van Burkleo considered that Fortune had smiled

> ontill the fawl 1812 when the Indien war broke out when my good luck turned to bad luck some time abought the first of October in the night I was warned to be at Portage de Soux the next morning by sun up armed and aquipt for thier was a grate bodey of Indiens at the south of Alinois . . . the company met and was mustered by Capt. Samuel Grifeth[19] and was ordered up the Mississippi near the mouth of Alinois whare we stood gard that day and night and the next day with thought aney thing eate except a few apples we got at Portage. . . .[20]

Van Burkleo returned to his farm to obtain provisions. That very night the Indians attacked his home and shot both Van Burkleo and his wife as they lay sleeping. Although he was severely wounded, this sturdy frontiersman held off the Indians until daybreak, when he sent his young brother-in-law for assistance. The wounded man and his wife were later taken to her brother, "Dr. Fallis," in St. Louis, where they remained under treatment for months. But this was not all: "My house was burned down a few nights after we was shot . . . with everything that we had and from that my fence tuck fire and burned one hole string of it and I lost my hole crop which was about 30 acrese of corn and all my truck they shot one hors and stole two. . . ."[21]

Such experiences toughened Jim for other troubles. His departure from Casner's blacksmith's shop was as dramatic as many of his later adventures and perhaps occurred under the same motivation: he could not submit to arbitrary and high-handed direction. It also involved the first of a long series of "affairs of the heart."

> When I had attained my nineteenth year, my sense of im-
> portance had considerably expanded, and, like many others of
> my age, I felt myself already quite a man. Among other indis-
> cretions, I became enamored of a young damsel, which, lead-
> ing me into habits that my *boss* disapproved of, resulted finally
> in a difficulty between us.
>
> Being frequently tempted to transgress my *boss's* rules by
> staying from home somewhat late of an evening, and finding
> the company I spent my time with so irresistibly attractive that
> I could not bring myself to obedience to orders, I gave way to
> my passion, and felt indifferent whether my proceedings gave
> satisfaction or otherwise. One morning I was assailed by my
> principal in language which I considered unduly harsh and
> insulting, and on his threatening to dismiss me from his house,
> I was tempted to reply with some warmth, and acknowledge
> that his doing so would exactly square with my wishes.[22]

A violent quarrel involving a "one-armed constable" followed. Jim, the temporary victor, nevertheless went into hiding for three days and then attempted to ship on board a keelboat headed for Fever River. Casner, feeling his responsibility, intervened. The recalcitrant romantic was sent home to his father, who, with his customary indulgence, finally bade "God speed" to his son. Jim could not resist adding that Jennings also loaded him down with cash and gifts.

That Beckwourth did go to Fever River in 1822 has been con-firmed.[23] Moreover, his account of the expedition led by Colonel Richard M. Johnson carries internal evidence that he was part of that group. Beckwourth mentions, among others, Messrs. January and Kennerly, and he seems familiar with the military installa-tions along the way. Jim relates that after nine days' parleying a treaty was concluded; the actual date of signing was September 13, 1822. The lead mines of Fever River were now officially opened to the white man's exploitation.[24]

Moses Meeker says quite definitely that it was Colonel James Johnson, brother of Colonel R. M., who fitted out the expedition to Fever River, but he confirms Beckwourth's statement that a military escort was provided for the party:

Col. James Johnson and others arrived on the Fever river (now Galena), about the 5th day of July, 1822. Anticipating opposition from the Indians, he had procured an order from the Secretary of War to Col. Morgan, commanding the troops on the Upper Mississippi, to meet him with a force sufficient to overawe the Indians. Detachments of troops were ordered from Fort Edwards, Fort Armstrong, on Rock Island, and Fort Crawford, at Prairie du Chien, Col. Morgan's headquarters. The Sac and Fox Indians had determined to resist their land-ing, but found that resistance would be in vain from the de-monstrations made by the government troops. The Indians afterwards informed me, that they, by virtue of necessity, con-cluded to let the white man work with them.[25]

In August, 1823, Moses Meeker took a census at Fever River. "There were seventy-four persons, men, women, and children, white and black . . . Colonel Johnson had four black men with him, one of whom was James P. Beckwourth, afterwards a moun-taineer [of] notoriety."[26] Moses Meeker made this statement when in his seventies, long after he had heard of the exploits of Jim and knew that he was identified as a mulatto. Unfortunately, Meeker's journal for that period had long since burned; there was no way to check his day-to-day observations against his recollections. Other sources say that James Johnson took "slaves" to Fever River, but there is no evidence that Jim Beckwourth ever was "hired out" as a slave.

The Indians in the Fever River area were troublesome at times, but while the settlers protected themselves by living in "companies," Jim was out getting acquainted: "The Indians soon became very friendly to me," he recalled, "and I was indebted to them for showing me their choicest hunting grounds."[27]

What were Indians to Jim? He was young and cocky—not belligerent, but well able to take care of himself. And, like his father, he loved to roam the forest and to be in at the kill. If Indians happened to be there first, Jim simply joined them. And so he stayed on at Fever River, hunting, sometimes also mining for lead when there was nothing better to do.

A man of Beckwourth's temperament and background could have enjoyed the Fever River of that day. But for the villager, it was a different story. Perched high above the stream, the little settlement was reached by climbing ladders placed against the muddy banks. The best of houses was a log cabin, crudely built, with the roof held down by green oak logs. Many of the settlers were sheltered by tents during the summer and in winter made their homes in abandoned mine shafts in the hillsides.[28] Illness was rampant; scurvy, typhoid fever, and ague took their toll, and it was not long before the residents began to get nervous about public reaction to the name of their village. In 1826 they renamed it Galena, after first having attempted to rationalize the word "fever" (*fèvre*) as deriving from the French *fève*, meaning "bean." These worried citizens could have set their minds at ease, for *fèvre* had nothing to do with either beans or fever. It was simply "*un ancien nom du forgeron,*" an old-fashioned word for metalworker or smithy. And very appropriate it was, under the circumstances.[29]

Jim Beckwourth suffered no ill effects from his eighteen-months' adventure. But, having made enough money to feel himself "to be quite a wealthy personage," he decided to return home. His visit paid, "a disposition to roam farther" led him to board a steamboat to New Orleans. The pattern of his life was taking shape: restless, longing to travel, eager for adventure and "renown," he never stayed long in one place, never settled down to one occupation.

The journey to Louisiana ended with an attack of yellow fever and the adventurer fled once again to the shelter of his father's house. But not to remain for long. In the summer of 1824, General William H. Ashley was organizing an overland expedition and he was looking for recruits. Jim, "being possessed of a strong desire to see the celebrated Rocky Mountains, and the great Western wilderness so much talked about," seized the opportunity to go along.[30]

Mountain Man

Only frustration and confusion can result from any attempt to follow Beckwourth's account of his first trip to the mountains. Chart and calendar as one will, it is impossible to unscramble his dates or reconcile them with the events described. All that is reasonably certain is that Jim departed Fort Atkinson in General William Ashley's party on November 3, 1824. This we learn not from Beckwourth, but from General Ashley.[1] But, according to the *Life and Adventures*, Ashley had previously attempted an overland expedition with a party of twenty-nine hunters and trappers, of whom Beckwourth was one. The group reached the "Kansas village, situate[d] on the Kansas River," from whence, said Jim, he and Moses ("Black") Harris were sent ahead to obtain horses from the Republican Pawnees, thought to be some three hundred miles distant.

Having failed to find the Indians and without sufficient food to sustain themselves for any length of time, the two men tried to make their way back to the settlements—specifically to Curtis and Eley's post at the mouth of the Kansas River.[2] After many a hair-raising moment, and on the very brink of starvation, Jim and Harris were found by friendly Indians, who fed them and then escorted the two weary travelers to safety. Having thoroughly recovered his strength as the guest of Curtis and Eley, Jim proceeded downriver to the fur depot established by Francis G. Chouteau for Berthold, Pratte and Chouteau.[3] After a good look at the ice in the river and knowing the difficulty of travel at that season, Beckwourth hired on with Chouteau to spend the winter packing furs at a salary of $25 a month.

This certainly could not have taken place in 1822, for Jim

Beckwourth was on Fever River in that year; nor in 1823, for in June of that year General Ashley was far up the Missouri unsuccessfully defending himself and his men and goods against the Arikaras. The weeks following that debacle were spent in rearranging Ashley's plans to meet his partner, Andrew Henry. Still later, he and his recruits joined Colonel Henry Leavenworth in a punitive expedition against the "Rees." Almost immediately following the attempted chastisement of the Indians in mid-August, Ashley sent two overland parties to the mountains, one under Andrew Henry, and the other led by Jedediah Smith.[4] Beckwourth, if Moses Meeker may be believed, was still in Fever River in August of 1823.

It is evident that Jim was familiar with Curtis and Eley's post, and also with Chouteau's. Yet he could not have become acquainted with them while a member of Ashley's 1824 party; at least, it would seem an out-of-the-way stop, for "Ashley did not even use boats to get his outfit to Fort Atkinson. Pack mules and horses served from the time he left the settlements."[5]

It may be that upon leaving Casner's household in 1819, prior to going to Fever River, Jim headed west either on his own or with some small trading or trapping company. A few slight clues pointing to this possibility are worth examining.

Louise Barry says that probably "when Curtis and Eley were granted a one-year license on July 20, 1822 . . . their 'large house' already stood upon the banks of the Missouri." Apparently, the two men had become partners in summer or fall of 1820. Similarly, Chouteau's fur-depot was established in 1821, just in time to be available to the purpose of tracking down Jim Beckwourth.[6]

Jim, in reminiscing about his emotional reaction to the horrors of starvation, recalled that his thoughts had turned to his last encounter with Mr. Casner, the blacksmith. "The extremities I had been reduced to had so moderated my resentments that, had I encountered my former *boss*, I should have extended my hand to him with ready forgiveness."[7] (Whether Mr. Casner would

31

have been equally generous to his erstwhile apprentice is another question.) But surely, if Jim's ordeal had occurred in 1824, the 1819 quarrel would have been too distant in time to be of primary importance; if, on the other hand, Jim had but recently struck out alone, an impulse to return to security would seem natural. Also, Jim reveals that following this adventure he experienced a strong desire to stay with his father—a wish more appropriate to a youth than to a man of twenty-four years.

Although no one seems to have placed Moses Harris as an *engagé* on the Missouri River prior to 1822, it can be conjectured that he was in the area before that time and that Beckwourth may have known him. Whatever the time of the adventure may have been, and whatever the identity of the companion, the sufferings of the two men are so vividly told that one must believe that they actually occurred . . . sometime, somewhere.

Dale L. Morgan has concluded that Jim was speaking of events of 1826 when Jedediah Smith abruptly left the usual trail to the West and headed north, evidently in search of horses. Morgan deduced that Harris and Beckwourth were sent ahead to determine whether or not the Grand Pawnees were encamped to the north.[8]

Still, Beckwourth recalled several details of the summer and fall events of 1824 prior to Ashley's departure—Thomas L. Fitzpatrick's return to the mountains to bring in the general's furs, for example. This knowledge could, of course, have been picked up around the campfires and probably was part of common mountain lore. Harrison C. Dale, however, accepts Jim Beckwourth, along with Robert Campbell, as members of Fitzpatrick's party.[9]

One *can* feel sure of Jim's presence in the fall expedition, however; his account of the journey is strikingly similar to General Ashley's "Narrative." Ashley recorded that

on the afternoon of the 5th, I overtook my party of mountaineers (twenty-five in number), who had in charge fifty pack horses, a wagon and teams, etc. On the 6th we had advanced within ——— miles of the Grand Pawney's when it commenced snowing and continued with but little intermission until the morning of the 8th. During this time my men and horses were suffering for the want of food, which, combined with the severity of the weather, presented rather a gloomy prospect. . . . On the 22nd of the same month we found ourselves encamped on the Loup fork of the river Platt within three miles of the Pawney towns. Cold and hunger had by this time killed several of my horses, and many others were much reduced from the same cause. On the day last named we crossed the country southwardly about fifteen miles to the main fork of the Platt, where we were so fortunate as to find rushes and game in abundance, whence we set out on the 24th and advanced up the Platt. . . .[10]

Jim Beckwourth remembered these details:

On our arrival at the upper camp . . . we found the men, twenty-six in number, reduced to short rations, in weakly condition, and in discouraged state of mind. They had been expecting the arrival of a large company with abundant supplies, and when we rejoined them without any provisions, they were greatly disappointed. . . . We numbered thirty-four men, all told, and a duller encampment, I suppose, never was witnessed. No jokes, no fire-side stories, no fun; each man rose in the morning with the gloom of the preceding night filling his mind; we built our fires and partook of our scanty repast without saying a word. At last our general gave order for the best hunters to sally out and try their fortune. I seized my rifle and issued from the camp alone.[11]

Shortly afterward, on this disheartening search for mere sustenance, James Beckwourth learned a little something about self-denial, though he did not practice it at the moment. Jim, off by himself in the rushes, killed a teal duck and devoured it, despite the fact that his comrades were famishing. The account of this episode manifests an intensely human quality, both in Jim's behavior and the resultant sense of shame. But, of all the meals he ever ate, this one he enjoyed the least and remembered the longest. A self-laudatory note creeps into his remarks, yet it is evidently true that from then on Jim Beckwourth "never refused to share my last shilling, my last biscuit, or my only blanket with a friend. . . ."

Happily, he had no sooner completed his lonely feast than he brought down a fine large buck he had sighted across a narrow deer trail. Before returning to camp he also bagged three good-sized elk. "The game being all brought into camp, the fame of 'Jim Beckwourth' was celebrated by all tongues," was our hero's immodest description of his reception.

Raging storms cut across the plains during nearly the whole of General Ashley's trip. Only a man as determined as he to win a fortune in furs would have set out at that time of year; forage and game were difficult to find and fuel was practically non-existent. At the critical moment a party of Pawnee Loup Indians came to the rescue. Descriptions given by Ashley and Beckwourth again coincide very closely. General Ashley writes:

> [The men] had undergone an intense suffering from the inclemency of the weather, which also bore so severely on the horses as to cause the death of many of them.
> This, together with a desire to purchase a few horses from the Loups and to prepare my party for the privations which we had reason to anticipate in traveling the next two hundred miles, (described as being almost wholly destitute of wood) induced me to remain at the Forks until the 23d December, the greater part of which time we were favoured with fine weather, and notwithstanding the uplands were still covered with from 18 to 24 inches of snow, the Valleys were generally bare and afforded a good range for my horses, furnishing plenty of dry grass and some small rushes, from the use of which they daily increased in strength and spirits.[12]

Jim's memory told him this:

A severe storm setting in about this time, had it not been for our excellent store of provisions [the deer and elk killed previously by Jim?] we should most probably have perished of starvation. There was no game to be procured and our only resource was the flesh of horses which died of starvation and exposure to the storm. It was not such nutritious food as our fat buffalo and venison, but in our present circumstances it relished tolerably well. . . . When the storm was expended we moved up the river, hoping to fall in with game. . . . It was mid-winter, and every thing around us bore a gloomy aspect. We were without provisions, and we saw no means of obtaining any. At this crisis, six or seven Indians of the Pawnee Loup band came into our camp. . . . They invited us to their lodges. . . . The Indians . . . spread a feast. . . . Our horses, too, were well cared for, and soon assumed a more rotund appearance.[13]

Thus Beckwourth, with other novices, had an introduction to the tribulations of winter travel on the western plains. It was perhaps more difficult there than in the high Rockies, where shelter from the wind could sometimes be found "under the mountain," or in caves and woods.

General Ashley had elected to follow the South rather than the North Fork of the Platte, believing that better forage and wood were available there. Leaving the South Fork somewhere near present Greeley or Longmont, Colorado, he then followed up the Cache la Poudre or Big Thompson rivers and thence to the headwaters of the North Platte, over a most difficult terrain and in dreadful weather. Snow fell so steadily that General Ashley often failed to note it in his diary.[14] When at last his party succeeded in reaching the Laramie Plains they were still faced with a long and difficult search for the "Shetskedee," as Green River was then called.

The Ashley men, both those with the general and others already in the mountains, performed feats of exploration and sur-

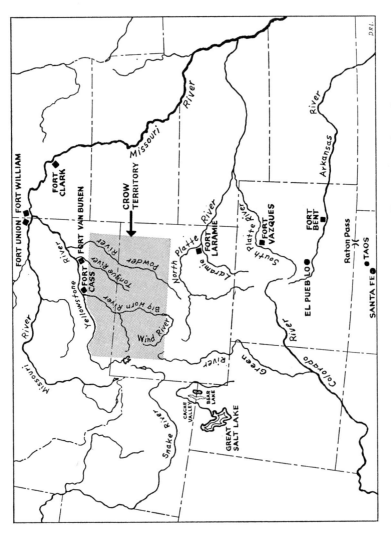

FORT WILLIAM

FORT CLARK

FORT UNION

FORT VAN BUREN

CROW TERRITORY

FORT CASS

Missouri River

Yellowstone River

Powder River

Tongue River

Big Horn River

Wind River

North Platte River

Platte River

FORT LARAMIE

Laramie River

South Platte River

FORT VAZQUES

FORT BENT

Arkansas River

EL PUEBLO

Raton Pass

SANTA FE

TAOS

Missouri

Snake River

Bear River

Green River

Colorado River

CACHE VALLEY

BEAR LAKE

GREAT SALT LAKE

D.R.I.

Region of Beckwourth's Mountain Adventures, 1824–48

vival that winter which would challenge sportsmen for generations to come. Working in icy streams at dusk and dawn; sleeping on the ground, the only mattress a few boughs and often not even that; eating anything that came to hand, frequently stringy horse-meat; forced to become pack animals through the loss of these horses—still the Ashley men toiled on. Their leader, not much given to praise of his employees, was impressed, nevertheless, and he recalled that "they did [a certain difficult assignment] with alacrity and cheerfulness as well as all other services required at their hands; indeed, such was their pride and ambition in the discharge of their duties, that their privations in the end became sources of amusement to them."[15] Beckwourth voiced the thought that were the general "now living, he would recollect the hardships and delights we experienced in this expedition."[16]

And delights were soon to come: the exquisite beauty of clean streams tumbling and roaring beneath snow-laden boughs, flashing back at a brilliant sun, or resting now and then in placid pools, rich with beaver. Canyon walls rising in grandeur above the rivers made a man know he was as nothing in time and space, yet challenged him to prove he was *somebody*. Rolling away from the canyons, rank after rank of mountains enclosed delicate hidden meadows which offered a precious contrast to rugged gorges and hazardous shelf-like trails. One approached the overbearing jagged peaks only with the utmost respect. Sunrises would be remembered forever, and night skies offered such fascination that only the most callous could fall asleep without pausing to study them in wonder.

Warren Angus Ferris remembered those days and nights: "In this country, the nights are cold at any season, and the climate perhaps more healthy than that of any other part of the globe. The atmosphere is delightful, and so pure and clear, that a person of good sight has been known to distinguish an Indian from a white man, at a distance of more than a mile, and herds of buffalo may be recognized by the aid of a good glass, at even fifteen to eighteen miles."[17]

Finally, "spring, with all its beauties" would set the seal: Jim and his comrades would be caught up in the magic of mountain life and they would never again be ordinary men, content to live in the pale centers of civilization. For General Ashley, however, another magic called: fortune, public acclaim, the role of political leadership. The general was willing to risk his life for the means to realize his ambition, and when he had succeeded, the mountains would see him no more.

In addition to helping him in his quest, Ashley's men, and others who were working their way north from Santa Fe and Bent's Fort, were collectively opening up a land that would eventually welcome thousands of land- and gold-hungry emigrants. The mountaineers were becoming the geographers on whom the future Corps of Topographic Engineers would rely for guidance. They were the pathfinders without whom *the* Pathfinder, John Charles Frémont, might never have attained his sobriquet. Still later, the United States Army would rely on these mountain men as guides and interpreters, and even as commanders in seemingly endless Indian wars. And Jim Beckwourth, in looking back, also looked slightly down his nose at the tenderfeet who were swarming into the West:

> When I recurred to my own adventures, I would smile at the comparison of their sufferings with what myself and other men of the mountains had really endured in former times. The forts that now afford protection to the traveler were built by ourselves at the constant peril of our lives, amid Indian tribes nearly double their present numbers. Without wives and children to comfort us on our lonely way; without well-furnished wagons to resort to when hungry, no roads before us but trails temporarily made; our clothing consisting of the skins of animals that had fallen before our unerring rifles, and often whole days on insufficient rations, or entirely without food; occasion-

ally our whole party on guard the entire night, and our strength deserting us through unceasing watching and fatigue; these are sufferings that made theirs appear trivial, and ours surpass in magnitude my power of relation.[18]

It is this sense of theater that plays havoc with Beckwourth's veracity. In relating his experiences with General Ashley he introduces all the elements of popular entertainment. He sees himself as a hero in conflict with a ruthless and unreasonable overlord—the general. Jim's innate nobility invariably allows him to perform a magnanimous service in return for insult. Pride forces him at last to threaten withdrawal from the party, but he has earned the respect of his arrogant leader: has Ashley not been saved three times from certain death by this same Beckwourth? True merit is recognized at last: Jim is offered leadership of a trapping party. With modesty—and an eye to the future: he does not wish to risk such responsibility just yet—the hero declines.

The "gaudy liar" earned his not very flattering title from his account of the Ashley expedition. Beckwourth, for example, says he was first to lay eyes on the Shetskedee. General Ashley merely notes in his diary that on Sunday, April 19, 1825, he and his party "traveled west 6 miles over a broken sandy country & came to the Sketkadee . . . pleasant weather—game scarce. . . ." In memory, Jim Beckwourth saw "on its banks . . . acres of land covered with moving masses of buffalo." And later, "We all feasted ourselves to our hearts' content upon the delicious, coarse-grained flesh of the buffalo, of which there was an unlimited supply." General Ashley, on the other hand, recorded on April 20 that his men had been two days without anything to eat and that they were unhappy about it.[19]

One of Jim Beckwourth's "whoppers" concerns his alleged rescue of General Ashley from the "Suck" of the Green River. The Ashley Diary and "Narrative," as well as Beckwourth's own account, all attest to the impossibility of this episode having occurred as Jim described it. General Ashley, having decided to carry the trade goods and other burdens downriver to a place of rendezvous, divided his force into four units, one to be headed by himself and the others by James Clyman, Zacharias Ham, and Thomas L. Fitzpatrick. Beckwourth himself says that he was in "Clement's" (Clyman's) party, which was set north toward the headwaters of the Green, while General Ashley and his nameless adventurers were hurtling through the lower canyons toward the Uinta Basin.[20] (That General Ashley *was* rescued from drowning is clear from his diary. Don Berry has this comment: "In his account James P. Beckwourth does say the general was no swimmer, which the general's diary confirms. It should be admitted, however, that until Dale Morgan's identification of the Ashley diary, historians had scoffed at the idea of Ashley's shipwreck entirely; James P. Beckwourth was right and they were wrong."[21])

James Clyman and his small band had their first encounter with hostile Indians while encamped in a canyon on "Le Brache" Creek, a beautiful beaver-laden tributary of the Green River, so named for the man who lost his life on that occasion. The Indians (perhaps Blackfeet, but the novice trappers did not attempt to identify them) were sixteen in number and, at first, outwardly friendly, though brash and audacious in poking about the camp and in handling the trappers' guns, even at one time stacking and carrying them off a short distance. The white men became suspicious and moved down the stream toward the open country through which it flows before reaching the river. They did not reach the prairie before the attack came. The third night, while all except Le Brache, the guard, were lying down, a cry for help and the report of a gun brought them to their feet.

> We were all up in an instant. An Indian had seized my rifle, but I instantly wrenched it from him, though I acknowledge I was too terrified to shoot. [An unusual admission for Beck-

wourth.] When we had in some measure recovered from our sudden fright, I hastened to Le Brache, and discovered that a tomahawk had been sunk in his head, and there remained. . . . He was a corpse in a few moments.[22]

The trappers learned some valuable lessons from this unfortunate event. They would be on their guard in the future.

The poor victim's body was left where it fell and was never recovered. Although the stream today is called LaBarge Creek, in honor of Joseph LaBarge, father of Captain Joseph LaBarge of Missouri steamboat fame, it seems unlikely that the trappers called it so. They were much more inclined to name streams and sites for their comrades or the events that befell them: Pierre's Hole, Horse Creek, and Cache Valley are examples. Probably the dead man's name was La Branche or something similar—Bonner could never get his French correct—and should have been retained as a designation for this stream.

Jim Beckwourth told his tales—true or not—many times before they saw print. Such stories bore repeating; they found their way into distant camps, all the way from Fort Laramie to Santa Fe, from Bent's Fort to California. The taking of the Blackfoot fort described in Chapter VI was told to Francis Parkman, who recorded it in 1846 with the comment that he had heard it too often to doubt that it had occurred under Beckwourth's leadership.[23]

Alonzo Delano, whose gossipy pen found ample material in California, recorded another of Jim's stories from this period. The tale concerns the "Blackfoot wife," who, Jim says, was bestowed upon him in gratitude for his opening a trading post for the Indians in their country. Jim dates the event in 1827 while he was under the direction of William L. Sublette, who with Jedediah Smith and David Jackson, had bought out General Ashley's interest in the fur trades. Within a few days there were family problems: the girl had joined a village celebration of the taking of three white scalps. On her refusal to leave the dance, her scandalized husband "struck [the] disobedient wife a heavy blow in the head with the side of [a] battle-axe, which dropped her as if a ball had pierced her heart."[24] Contrary to expectation, the girl's father agreed that the act was justified, and even presented Jim with another daughter. During the night who should come cringing to his bedside but the repentant first wife, fortunately recovered from the brutal blow. "I thought myself now well supplied with wives, having *two* more than I cared to have; but I deemed it hardly worth while to complain, as I should soon leave the camp, wives and all," Beckwourth commented casually.

This is not quite the way Alonzo Delano heard the tale; in his versions (there were two),[25] the first wife did not recover from the assault: in other words, she was murdered. There are other variations in the story: Delano says the episode occurred while Jim was a chief of the Crow nation: "According to the custom of Indians who are friendly with each other, Jim had a wife among the Blackfeet as well as the Crows," thus revealing that the story came to him from someone who knew very little about those Indians. Delano believed there was only one white scalp, not three, and that instead of Jim's leaving the Blackfoot camp amid cordial farewells, he was escorted to a certain point and given a start of six miles before he would have to begin worrying about his own scalp.

Beckwourth's fantasies may have produced the adoring Blackfoot-wives, but scarcely a verified event of the fur trade of the twenties can be mentioned without finding some reference to it in the *Life and Adventures.* The naming of Cache Valley for the luckless victim of a cave-in; Sublette's and Harris's famous trip to St. Louis in mid-winter; the two Indian attacks on General Ashley's party as they made their way to the Missouri; the subsequent journey downriver with General Atkinson and Major O'Fallon (with a lengthy account of O'Fallon's clash with a Crow chief)—all these and many others Beckwourth remembered.[26]

James Bridger (From *Crofutt's Overland Tourist, 1879–80*)

General Ashley's diary has confirmed the fact that, most providentially, he encountered Étienne Provost's party in the Uinta basin, although, as Dale L. Morgan says, historians had previously laughed at Beckwourth's assertion to this effect.[27] The latter's version of the famous "fight in the willows" between the Blackfeet and Robert Campbell's party en route to the rendezvous of 1828 agrees with other records. The lurid detail of Jim's account probably brought excitement and blood-chilling fear to his early readers. Nevertheless, there is an air of veracity about this story that justifies accepting Beckwourth's claim that he and one other man ("Calhoun") "dashed through the ranks of the foe" to go for assistance. General Ashley, writing on the authority of William L. Sublette, merely says, "the Indians saw two men, mounted on fleet horses, pass through their lines, unhurt. . . ."[28]

Amusingly, Dale L. Morgan turns the tables on General Ashley for his summing up of losses in this battle. Jim Beckwourth recorded that their side lost four men killed and seven wounded. "From the enemy we took seventeen scalps, most of them near the willows; those that we killed on the road, we could not stop for. We were satisfied they had more than a hundred slain; but as they always carry off their dead, we could not ascertain the exact number. We also lost two packs of beavers, a few packs of meat, together with some valuable horses."[29]

General Ashley, in the letter referred to above, reports that one man was killed and that the party "lost five thousand dollars worth of beaver, forty horses and a small amount of merchandize." And, says Dale L. Morgan, "Since Ashley blamed all these murders and robberies on the British, he was not inclined to understate the losses, and his figures as a rule would do credit to Jim Beckwourth; in this instance he puts Beckwourth in the shade."[30]

Jim Beckwourth's deep-seated love of nature found an outlet in the mountains—the early years with Ashley and the Rocky Mountain Fur Company probably were the happiest in Beckwourth's life. He became a mountain man under the tutelage of such stalwarts as Jedediah Strong Smith[31] and James Clyman, both of whom had survived many harrowing experiences on previous Ashley expeditions. Such teachers as these could not be hindered by cowards or dullards; a man depended on his wits and his courage if he wished to remain alive in the fur trade.

Jim Beckwourth proved to be an apt pupil. That he was resourceful there can be no doubt, and his rash courage became legendary in his own lifetime.

Domestic Bliss Among the Crows

Perhaps Jim had been having poor luck with the beaver and saw an opportunity to do better with less effort and danger, or perhaps he was merely seeking new adventures. Whatever the reason, Beckwourth decided to be an Indian for a time. And out of this decision he managed to weave two wonderful tales for his memoirs.

The groundwork of the first was laid at the rendezvous and summer encampment of 1828. An old trapper, Caleb Greenwood, whose Crow relatives insisted on hearing lengthy tales of Jim's great bravery and limitless victories in battle, finally tired of his role as storyteller and "invented a fiction" designed to end the boredom. He revealed to the Crows that Jim was actually one of their own, having been captured years before by the Cheyennes and sold by them to the whites, with whom he had lived ever since. Much excitement and rejoicing greeted this astonishing news, followed by demands that Jim be turned over to the tribe forthwith. Jim and Old Greenwood privately had a hearty laugh at the simple Indian mind; nevertheless, Jim concluded that it might be advantageous to be welcomed by his own "relatives" in the trapping months ahead.

All this occurred before the breakup of the summer encampment of 1828. Now, deep in winter, the second part of the comedy was acted out. Beckwourth says that he and "Gabe" Bridger went out together to set traps, separating at the forks of a stream. The former blundered onto an Indian horse herd and was promptly captured by its guards, who marched him to their village. Our hero was not worried—he was fairly sure these Indians were Crows—and was he not one of them?

Bridger, who watched the capture from a hill dividing the forks of the stream, was not so complacent. He concluded that the Indians were conducting Jim "to camp, there to sacrifice me in the most approved manner their savage propensities could suggest, and then abandon themselves to a general rejoicing over the fall of a white man."[1] Gabe headed for his own camp post-haste, leaving his partner to his fate, according to Jim's tall tale.

Jim's unresisting departure, however, had a more prosaic explanation. He had signed a promissory note on January 6, 1829: "On a settlement of all acounts up to this date with Smith, Jackson & Sublette there appears a Balance due by me to them of Two Hundred and Seventy five dollars which I promise to pay in good merchantable Beaver Furr at Three Dollars per

Crow Lodge, after Catlin (From T. D. Bonner, *James P. Beckwourth*, 1892 edition)

47

pound for value received."[2] Probably, when he joined the Crows, he arrived well equipped to take up trapping as a free agent. Such, at least, was the conclusion of Dale Morgan, who deduced that Jim's departure to the Crows was prearranged and that Robert Campbell may have outfitted him to this amount.[3]

Dale Morgan's pragmatic explanation of Beckwourth's departure and Jim's own account may both contain elements of truth, but a further conjecture is possible. Prior to the telling of the Bridger tale, Beckwourth reports another event that took place just before his final separation from the Rocky Mountain Fur Company. It grew out of Jim's failure to bring off a good joke he had prepared for the evening campfire. Gabe and Jim were out searching for a lost trap when they came across what they thought was a badger, and both made a rush for him.

> On closer inspection, however, it proved to be my [lost] beaver, with trap, chain, and float pole. It was apparent that some buffalo, in crossing the river, had become entangled in the chain, and, as we conceived, had carried the trap on his shoulder, with the beaver pendent on one side and the pole on the other. We inferred that he had in some way got his head under the chain, between the trap and pole, and in his endeavors to extricate himself, had pushed his head through. The hump on his back would prevent it passing over his body, and away he would speed with his burden. . . . [We felt] much satisfaction at the solution of the mystery. When we arrived at camp we asked our companions to guess how and where we had found the trap. They all gave various guesses, but, failing to hit the truth, gave up the attempt.
>
> "Well, gentlemen," said I, "it was stolen."
>
> "Stolen!" exclaimed a dozen voices at once.
>
> "Yes, it was stolen by a buffalo."
>
> "Oh, come, now," said one of the party, "what is the use of coming here and telling such a lie?"
>
> I saw in a moment that he was angry and in earnest, and I

replied, "If you deny that a buffalo stole my trap, *you* tell the lie."

He rose and struck me a blow with his fist. It was my turn now, and the first pass I made brought my antagonist to the ground. On rising, he sprang for his gun; I assumed mine as quickly. The bystanders rushed between us, and, seizing our weapons, compelled us to discontinue our strife, which would have infallibly resulted in the death of one.[4]

This quarrel may have been of serious proportions. A greater tone of veracity than when he describes his insubordination to General Ashley is apparent: there is less braggadocio and aggression here. Also, it is easy to understand Jim's anger; in jovial mood, pleased at having done a bit of detective work and eager to share the fun, he had met with blunt rejection.

"I could have taken his expression in jest, for we were very free in our sallies upon one another; but in this particular instance I saw his intention was to insult me, and I allowed my passion to overcome my reflection," Beckwourth recalled.[5]

As a result of this encounter, Jim and Bridger set out with their traps, intending to absent themselves long enough for tempers to cool down. But one wonders if Bridger was not merely accompanying Beckwourth until he reached the known Crow camp. Perhaps Jim had had enough of insults and taking of orders and had determined to play his own game henceforth.

In relating the story of his Indian capture and Gabe's flight, Jim characteristically attributes the highest of feelings to Bridger and the other trappers (not failing, of course, to toss a few encomiums to himself):

[Bridger] was on a hill, crossing over to me as agreed upon, when he saw me in the hands of the Indians, being conducted to their village, which was also in sight. Seeing clearly that he could oppose no resistance to my captors, he made all speed to the camp, and communicated the painful news of my death.

. . . With the few men he had in camp it was hopeless to attempt a rescue; for, judging by the size of the village, there must be a community of several thousand Indians. All were plunged in gloom. All pronounced my funeral eulogy; all my daring encounters were spoken of to my praise. My fortunate escapes, my repeated victories were applauded in memory of me; the loss of their best hunter, of their kind and ever-obliging friend, was deeply deplored by all.

"Alas! had it not been for that lamentable quarrel," they exclaimed, "he would still have been among us. Poor Jim! peace to his ashes!"[6]

All very solemn and proper, if perhaps a little overdrawn. But then, if one has not sensed it already, a touch of fun creeps in; one can almost see the eyes twinkle and the shadow of a grin: "The faithful fellows little thought that, while they were lamenting my untimely fall, I was being hugged and kissed to death by a whole lodge of near and dear Crow relatives, and that I was being welcomed with a public reception fully equal in intensity, though not in extravagance, to that accorded to the victor of Waterloo on his triumphal entry into Paris."[7] Jim then launches into an expansive and mirthful account of his welcome by Big Bowl, his putative father, and by his new mother, "Mrs. Big Bowl." All his "sisters" were pretty; they lavished attention upon their long-lost brother, who willingly accepted their enraptured kisses.

Thus began the adventurer's sojourn with the Crow Indians. As he saw it, he was conferring a favor. "Even if I should deny my Crow origin, they would not believe me. How could I dash with an unwelcome and incredible explanation all [their] joy. . . ? I could not find it in my heart. . . ."[8]

Although he frequently deplored the fact that Crow women, in mourning, hacked off their fingers, lacerated their bodies, and daubed themselves with blood and dirt as well as paint, Beckwourth is gallant in his description of his wives and sisters. The latter were four in number, "very pretty, intelligent" young women. They dressed him in their finest robes, competing for the honor, and prepared him a bed "not as high as Haman's gallows certainly, but just as high as the lodge would admit. This was a token of their esteem and sisterly affection."[9] To Jim, *all* women were to some degree beautiful, but there were few commentators of that day who could look upon the Crow women with his uncritical eye. In the main, they were considered to be the least attractive of the Upper Missouri Indians.[10]

Offered his choice of "three pretty daughters" of Black Lodge, one of the tribe's greatest braves, the long-lost Crow selected Still-water. The girl was gentle and obedient, as well as affectionate, and she knew when to hold her tongue. "No domestic thunder-storms, no curtain-lectures ever disturbed the serenity of our connubial lodge," Jim complacently recalled. Nor did he have mother-in-law problems, since it was an inviolable rule with the Crows that the parents of the bride never spoke to her husband on any subject whatsoever.

Domestic bliss did not prevent Jim's seeking other "hymeneal" pleasures, as he liked to term them, in his own and others' lodges. The list of Indian wives is almost as long as that of his Indian names. With all this taking of wives, it is curious that he acknowledges but one child, Black Panther (also called "Little Jim"), born several years after Jim's marriage to the "little wife." This wife, Nom-ne-dit-chee, apparently held his genuine affection. According to Beckwourth, she offered herself so frequently and insistently that he finally accepted, though in the beginning, because of her youth, he placed her in the lodge of one of his "married sisters." At the time Jim already had seven wives, by his own count, and he was willing to wait a while before consummating a marriage with the "little innocent."

Jim Beckwourth himself was smitten—he experienced an inordinate admiration for Pine Leaf, an Indian maid whose unusual interest in war had brought her to Jim's attention. Jim admired Pine Leaf's mind almost as much as her body:

She possessed great intellectual powers. She was endowed with extraordinary muscular strength, with the activity of a cat and the speed of an antelope. Her features were pleasing, and her form symmetrical. She had lost a brother in [an] attack on our village. . . . She was at that time twelve years of age, and she solemnly vowed that she would never marry until she had killed a hundred of the enemy with her own hand. Whenever a war party started, Pine Leaf was the first to volunteer to accompany them. Her presence among them caused much amusement to the old veterans; but if she lacked physical strength, she always rode the fleetest horses, and none of the warriors could outstrip her . . . and when I engaged in the fiercest struggles, no one was more promptly at my side than the young heroine. She seemed incapable of fear; and when she arrived at womanhood, could fire a gun without flinching and use the Indian weapons with as great dexterity as the most accomplished warrior.[11]

In his amours, Jim met with only one serious rebuff—Pine Leaf would have him as husband only "when the pine-leaves turn yellow." It took him a few days to realize that pine leaves do *not* turn yellow, but he was undaunted. He continued to woo Pine Leaf for several years, but, having won his suit at last, he abandoned her as calmly as he did all the rest.

Although some have considered the story of Pine Leaf to be pure fantasy on Jim's part, or an invention of T. D. Bonner,[12] there is good reason to believe that such a woman existed. E. T. Denig has left a vivid biography of Woman Chief, in which he describes "the Heroine" as a Gros Ventre of the prairie, captured at the age of ten by the Crows.

She was taller and stronger than most women—her pursuits no doubt tending to develop strength of nerve and muscle. Long before she had ventured on the warpath she could rival any of the young men in all their amusements and occupations, was a capital shot with the rifle, and would spend most of her time in killing deer and bighorn, which she butchered and carried home on her back when hunting on foot. [In a Blackfoot attack on the Crow trading post] several men were killed and the rest took refuge within the fort saving most of their horses. . . . Neither Whites nor Crows could be found to venture out. But this woman, understanding their language, saddled her horse and went forth to meet them. . . . When within pistol shot, she called to them to stop, but they paid no attention to her words. One of the enemies then fired at her and the rest charged. She immediately shot down one with her gun, and shot arrows into two more without receiving a wound. . . . The main body . . . fired showers of balls and pursued her as near to the fort as they could with safety. . . . But she escaped unharmed and entered the gate amid the shouts and praises of the Whites and her own people.[13]

Denig continues with a recital of Woman Chief's remarkable victories in war and horse stealing; her accomplishments were such that the tribe no longer could rule her out of the council. As a result of her urging, perhaps, still more dangerous battles and raids were undertaken, in each of which this woman distinguished herself. The old men believed that she led a charmed life and paid her honor and respect seldom rendered to male, much less female, members of the tribe. Denig recalled that "the Indians seemed to be proud of her, sung forth her praise in songs composed by them after each of her brave deeds. When council was held and all the chiefs and warriors assembled, she took her place among the former, ranking third person in the band of 160 lodges. On stated occasions, when the ceremony of striking a post and publicly repeating daring acts was performed, she took precedence of many a brave man whose career had not been so fortunate."[14]

Writing in 1856, Denig asserts that he knew this woman personally, that she was killed by the Gros Ventre in 1854, and that for twenty years she set a valued example in matters of hunting and war. Thus Woman Chief fits into the Beckwourth story perfectly, with one exception. Denig has our heroine a female version of the *berdêche*, not interested in any man whether the pine leaves turned yellow or not.[15]

Robert H. Lowie's study of the Crows adds still another confirmation to the existence of Pine Leaf: "There are memories of a woman who went to war; indeed, Muskrat, one of my women informants, claimed to have struck a coup and scalped a Piegan, thus earning songs of praise."[16] Dr. Lowie, in assessing the literature on the Crow Indians, gives Beckwourth his due:

> Whether the mulatto Beckwourth was or was not a chief, he lived among the Crow for many years and while a *Munchhausen* in the recital of his own deeds, he reproduces with admirable correctness the martial atmosphere of Crow life in the 'twenties and 'thirties of the last century. He refers to such social usages as the parent-in-law taboo, the rivalry of clubs, the restraining power of the police. Rotten Belly is made to figure as head-chief and his divining with a shield is an interesting detail. . . . Every once in a while the genuineness of the record is forcibly demonstrated, as when a maiden promised to marry Beckwourth "when the pine leaves turn yellow," an expression still in vogue. The book is disappointing on Crow religion. While Beckwourth repeatedly notes the planting of sacred Tobacco and essays a description of the Sun Dance, he evidently does not know clearly what it is all about. Nevertheless, for the latter ceremony the recital of coups, the sham battle, and the part played by a virtuous woman are registered.[17]

Finding a virtuous woman in a Crow village was a matter of no small difficulty, necessary though her presence was to tribal ceremonies. Beckwourth relates that his "little wife" once confided that she intended "to go into the medicine lodge" to take part in the Sun Dance; he adds that he was astonished at her daring, unconsciously revealing that he did not expect even his child-bride to remain chaste. (An unchaste woman who attempted to take part in this ceremony was subject to ridicule or

54

beatings if exposed.) Three years later the "little wife" realized her aim most successfully, to Jim's great pride.

It is curious to find Denig commenting that "if such a thing as an honest woman can be found in this tribe it is one who has been raised under the husband's own care from a child, and taken for a wife at the age of 10 to 13 years."[18] So Jim may have been telling the truth about Nom-ne-dit-chee after all.

Some Crow rituals also required the participation of a virtuous man. Denig says: "Singular as it may appear, the moral character of the males is not superior to the female part of the community, and several weeks have often been employed in the seeking and approving of a man free of incest. At one time so great was their anxiety to proceed with their custom [the tobacco-planting ceremony] and so rare was the proper person that they were obliged to hire one of the Fur Company to fill the office."[19]

Crow Chief; Crow Woman, after Catlin (From T. D. Bonner, *James P. Beckwourth*, 1892 edition)

A Crow warrior would find it difficult to make a false claim of innocence, according to Beckwourth, because of the so-called "war-path secret." Jim's account of this ritual, though presenting a slightly ludicrous picture, is apparently sound:

We all assembled together and marched on. In the forenoon we killed a fine fat buffalo, and rested to take breakfast. The intestines were taken out, and a portion of them cleansed and roasted. A long one was then brought into our mess, which numbered ten warriors, who formed a circle, every man taking hold of the intestines with his thumb and finger. In this position, very solemnly regarded by all in the circle, certain questions were propounded to each in relation to certain conduct in the village, which is of a nature unfit to be entered into here. They are religiously committed to a full and categorical answer to each inquiry, no matter whom their confession may implicate. Every illicit action they have committed since they last went to war is here exposed, together with the name of the faithless accomplice, even to the very date of the occurrence. All this is divulged to the *medicine men* on the return of the party, and it is by them noted down in a manner that it is never erased while the guilty confessor lives. Every new warrior, at his initiation, is conjured by the most sacred oaths never to divulge the war-path secret to any woman, on pain of instant death.[20]

This is almost the only comment Beckwourth makes on the subject of promiscuity (other than his own) among the Crows, although they have been described as the most lascivious and carnal of men—and women.[21] Jim seems to have been much more concerned and irritated by the howling, weeping, self-mutilating mobs that greeted news of defeat or death in battle, and he would go to great lengths to avoid any situation that might result in such an uproar. When, at last, he decided to leave the Crows it was partly because he could no longer endure the savagery of these expressions of grief.

Nevertheless, Beckwourth had done his share over the years to produce such frenzy, and his accounts of some of the battles in which he participated have become classics in the annals of gruesome warfare.

Indian War Chief

Among the Crow Indians, a man could rise to chieftaincy if he could claim success at least once in the following four feats: the striking of an enemy, wounded or not; leading a successful raid; capturing a horse picketed within a hostile camp; snatching a bow or gun from an enemy in hand-to-hand combat.[1] That Jim Beckwourth could have remained with the Crows for very long without striving to gain the rank of chief is improbable. For, as Lowie says, a man who had achieved none of the necessary exploits was simply "a nobody."

> Value was set on other qualities, such as liberality, aptness at story telling, success as a doctor. But the property a man distributed was largely the booty he had gained in raids; and any accomplishments . . . were not substitutes for a man's record as a warrior.[2]

The role of "nobody" was one that Beckwourth never cared to play and therefore little time elapsed before he joined a Crow war party in attacking a band of Blackfoot Indians. In hand-to-hand combat, Jim despoiled his "victim of his gun, lance, war-club, bow and quiver of arrows," thus passing steps one and four on the road to distinction. Beckwourth was now "the great brave, the Antelope."[3]

Not long afterward, Beckwourth's new father urged him to lead a raid. At first reluctant, on the grounds that he was not eager to push himself forward, he at last took out a party of youthful braves. Their success in killing two enemy Indians and recovering stolen horses led to still more accolades. Other exploits, each remarkably successful, followed: they usually resulted in a new name for Beckwourth—Bull's Robe, Enemy of Horses, Red Fish, and The Bobtail Horse are only a few of the laudatory titles bestowed on the mighty warrior.

The Crow Indians were among the most warlike of the tribes in the plains or mountains. Though they boasted that no white man had lost his life at their hands, and trappers and traders generally felt secure in their company, they engaged any and all Indian tribes. This preoccupation with war was noted as early as 1805 by Tabeau, who observed that the Cheyennes "do not manage their affairs as well as the Mandanes and others of the upper Missouri and they lost the past year twenty-five or thirty persons in a single affair with the Corbeaux [Crows], who are considered, it is true, the best warriors of the nations of the North."[4]

James Clyman, who had ample opportunity to observe the Crows, was well aware of their overriding interests: "The whole employment of the males [is] hunting and war and at the time we ware there at least one third of the warriors ware out in war parties in different directions they being in a state of warfare with all the neighboring tribes."[5]

Given the conditions of chieftaincy and the incessant battles, it would seem that in this tribe, at least, there should have been more chiefs than Indians. Because of the high loss of life in battle, there was always room on the ladder, if not at the top. Indeed, the title of chief did not by any means indicate that a man so designated was either a commander-in-chief or even a five-star general.

Save for a few cases in which autocratic chiefs managed to eliminate their rivals through the use of poison, tribal governments tended to be relatively democratic. The concept of Indian "kings," as well as "princesses," was a white man's fiction. Decisions affecting tribal policies were made by experienced and mature men in council by talking things out until they arrived at a consensus—a sort of prototype of Johnsonian democracy.[6]

A similar political organization prevailed in most Indian tribes of the West. Francis Parkman noted it when he came across a village of "Ogillallah" and met a former acquaintance, the Frenchman Reynal. The Indians had been out on a buffalo hunt, and Reynal informed Parkman that

> the Whirlwind too had been unwilling to come so far, because, as Reynal said, he was afraid. Only half a dozen lodges had adhered to him, the main body of the village setting their chief's authority at naught, and taking the course most agreeable to their inclinations.
>
> "What chiefs are there in the village now?" I asked. [Reynal named seven.]
>
> By this time we were close to the village, and I observed that while the greater part of the lodges were very large and neat in their appearance, there was at one side a cluster of squalid, miserable huts. I . . . made some remark about their wretched appearance. . . .
>
> "My squaw's relations live in those lodges," said Reynal, very warmly; "and there isn't a better set in the whole village."
>
> "Are there any chiefs among them?"
>
> "Chiefs?" said Reynal; "yes! plenty!"[7]

Reynal could not produce any very impressive list, but it is evident that Parkman expected and Reynal asserted that there might be several chiefs in one family.

James Beckwourth's prestige with the Crows and other Indians rested upon his position of leadership—no trapper or trader could have allowed himself to be relegated to the menial role of hanger-on. Jim was there to make money from trapping and hunting: at a very early stage he represented the American Fur Company. The Crows needed guns and ammunition, red beads and cloth, and the Company wanted elk skins, beaver pelts, and buffalo robes.[8]

To balance the demands of Company and tribe, it was necessary to find and maintain a role of influence, and this Beckwourth apparently did, although he admitted later that war eventually won the day: the Crows provided fewer skins than other tribes, despite the fact that Kenneth McKenzie had, in 1832, built a trading post for them near the mouth of the Big Horn on the Yellowstone, with Samuel Tulloch in charge. Still later, the Company established Fort Van Buren, on the Tongue, for the greater convenience of all, but with the same result.[9]

During all this time, Jim Beckwourth had been building his reputation as a war chief. Many years later, Charles Larpenteur recalled that Beckwourth was "the great brave warrior among the Crows."[10] This assessment, while accepted by nearly everyone who knew him, is not necessarily conclusive. It would be difficult to prove that Jim *was* a chief, but in 1865, before a commission of Congress, he was questioned as to his understanding of the solemnity of an oath. He was then sworn and testified concerning the Sand Creek massacre. The last question put to him was whether he had, indeed, been a chief among the Crow Indians. Jim's answer was, "Yes." Unless one wishes to repudiate his entire testimony, his answer must be taken as the truth.[11]

Throughout the account of his life with the Crow Indians, Jim Beckwourth confuses dates and exaggerates the number of the enemy as well as the number of scalps taken or lost. He simply could not deal accurately—some would say, honestly—with figures. His salary from the American Fur Company (which went from $500 to $800 in three years);[12] his potential wealth from trapping; the number of horses stolen or retrieved—all were asserted to be far greater than they really were. Yet, in actual business dealings, there is ample evidence that he was honest; in only one instance has his integrity been officially challenged, and in that case by a man against whom Jim Beckwourth had brought suit in an effort to collect a debt.[13]

Similarly, Beckwourth exaggerates the Crow Indian population; he estimated that at the time he joined it, the tribe could raise an army of sixteen thousand. Denig says that there were formerly eight hundred lodges or families, but that by 1856 they were reduced to 460 lodges. Seven or eight persons lived in each lodge; therefore, the Crows numbered about 6,400 persons, including women and children, a far cry from 16,000 warriors. George Catlin, in the 1830s, also placed the number at "7,000 in the nation, and probably not more than eight hundred warriors or fighting men." Zenas Leonard, who spent some time with the Crows in the fall of 1833, observed that the Crow nation

contain from 7,000 to 8,000 souls, and are divided into two divisions of an equal number in each—there being too great a number to travel together, as they could not get game in many places to supply such a force. Each division is headed by a separate chief, whose duty it is to pilot them from one hunting ground to another, and to lead his followers to battle in time of war—one of them they call Grizzly Bear and the other, Long Haired Chief, which name he derives from the extreme length of his hair, which is no less than nine feet eleven inches long.[14]

The Crows engaged in one of their bloodiest encounters with the Blackfeet during Leonard's stay with them—the famous battle of the Blackfoot Fortress. Thanks to Leonard's account, it is perhaps the best documented of any of Jim Beckwourth's stories. Typically, Beckwourth recalled that one hundred and sixty scalps were taken, whereas Leonard makes the number sixty-nine.

The natural fort in which the Blackfeet had taken their stand was almost impregnable. Its exact location is not clear from either Beckwourth's or Leonard's books, but, in October, 1833, Robert Campbell, at Fort William near the mouth of the Yellowstone, heard that Chief Rotten Belly was on the Grey Bull and "Burn" on the Little Horn.[15] The latter was actually Chief Long

Hair; it is evident that Leonard and Beckwourth were with his band. Whether they moved camp frequently is not known, but Leonard says that the Crows traveled three or four days in search of buffalo. On the morning of November 21, they encountered the Blackfeet, who, it would seem, had come dangerously far into Crow country, but who at the moment had all the advantage. The fortress, says Leonard, "was situated on the brow of a hill, in a circle of rocks shaped similar to a horse-shoe, with a ledge of rocks from three to four feet high on either side, and about ten feet, on the part reaching the brink of the hill, with a very creditable piece of breastwork built in front, composed of logs, brush and stones."[16] Beckwourth described the fort as "a huge mass of granite, forming a natural wall in front of a graduated height, varying from twenty-five to six feet, the lowest part; it was solid and nearly perpendicular all around."[17]

Reinforcements were sent for, bringing the number of Crow warriors from five to seven hundred, according to Beckwourth, whose estimate in this instance tallies with Leonard's. Even with this added strength, the Blackfeet could not be driven from their stronghold. Desperate efforts on the part of the Crows consistently met defeat; there was a concerted urge to retreat. Chief Long Hair himself despaired of victory, and it was then that Beckwourth delivered his renowned harangue to the Crow braves:

No, hold! Warriors, listen! If these old men can not fight, let them retire with the women and children. We can kill every one of these Black Feet: then let us do it. If we attempt to run from here, we shall be shot in the back, and lose more warriors than to fight and kill them all. If we get killed, our friends who love us here will mourn our loss, while those in the spirit land will sing and rejoice to welcome us there, if we ascend to them dying like braves. The Great Spirit has sent these enemies here for us to slay; if we do not slay them, he will be angry with us, and will never suffer us to conquer our enemies again. He will drive off all our buffaloes, and will wither the grass on the prairies. No, warriors! we will fight as long as one of them survives. Come, follow me, and I will show you how the braves of the great white chief fight their enemies![18]

Leonard heard this speech—he says it was made by a Negro— and summarized it for his readers:

[The Negro] advanced a few steps toward the Crows and ascended a rock from which he addressed the Crow warriors in the most earnest and impressive manner. He told them that they had been here making a great noise, as if they could kill the enemy by it—that they had talked long and loud about going into the fort, and that the white man would say the Indian had a crooked tongue, when talking about his war exploits. He told them that their hearts were small, and that they were cowardly—that they acted more like squaws than men, and were not fit to defend their hunting ground. . . . The old negro continued in this strain until they became greatly animated & told them that if the red man was afraid to go amongst his enemy, he would show them that a black man was not, and he leaped from the rock on which he had been standing, and, looking neither to the right nor to the left made for the fort as fast as he could run. The Indians, guessing his purpose, and inspired by his words and fearless example, followed close to his heels, and were in the fort dealing destruction to the right and left nearly as soon as the old man.[19]

Leonard and Beckwourth both say that *all* the Blackfoot warriors were killed and that the Crows lost between thirty and forty dead. Beckwourth's remarks on the battle present a picture grim and gory enough:

The carnage for some minutes was fearful. . . . The clash of battle-axes, and the yells of the opposing combatants were truly appalling. . . . The interior of this huge rock was concave, and the blood all ran to the center, where it formed a pool,

James P. Beckwourth in hunter's costume (From T. D. Bonner, *James P. Beckwourth*, 1856 edition)

Robert Campbell, who trapped with Beckwourth during the Ashley expedition of 1825 (Courtesy Missouri Historical Society)

La Barge Creek, in the vicinity of Beckwourth's first encounter
with hostile western Indians (Photograph by Elinor Wilson)

A portrait of Jim Beckwourth from Twitchell's *The Leading Facts of New Mexican History*

Fur Boat on the Missouri, from an 1873 engraving

Pine Leaf (From T. D. Bonner, *James P. Beckwourth*, 1856 edition)

"Crow Indians," painted by Charles Bodmer (Courtesy Joslyn
Art Museum, Omaha)

Old Fort Union (Courtesy Western Department, Denver Public Library)

Colonel Henry B. Carrington. In 1866 he employed James P. Beckwourth as scout and trapper (Courtesy National Archives)

which emitted a sickening smell as the warm vapor ascended to our nostrils. . . . Victims who were making away with their bowels ripped open were instantly felled with the battle-axe and stilled in death.[20]

In this instance, however, the "Bloody Arm" found a rival; his observations are nowhere near as shocking as those of Zenas Leonard: "Many of the Blackfeet who were scattered over the battleground had fallen by broken limbs or wounded in some way, & were yet writhing in agony, unable to injure anyone or help themselves in any way. All such were collected together, and then tormented in a manner too shocking to relate."[21] Nevertheless, Leonard proceeds to describe these ghastly tortures in detail.

Beckwourth was well aware of the revulsion such accounts could inspire:

I trust that the reader does not suppose that I waded through these scenes of carnage and desolation without some serious reflections on the matter. Disgusted at the repeated acts of cruelty I witnessed, I often resolved to leave these wild children of the forest and return to civilized life; but before I could act upon my decision, another scene of strife would occur, and the Enemy of Horses was always the first sought for by the tribe.[22]

Among other white witnesses to the gory battle just described was "Mildrum" (Robert Meldrum). In his usual generous manner, Jim describes Meldrum: "There was in our camp a young Kentuckian named Robert Mildrum, naturally a brave fellow, though he seldom went out in war parties; but when the village was assaulted, he always fought like a tiger. He was a good trapper and skillful blacksmith, and had been out in the employ of the American Fur Company."[23] Meldrum displayed no similar generosity toward Jim.

[Meldrum] knew Beckwith well. Says he was a humbug.

The whole narrative was humbug. He was a white man from Virginia and his mother a negress. He was therefore a mulatto. He had Crow wives but was not a chief. He was adopted into a good family. His wife was not the daughter of a chief, a pretty woman, but of low stock. His influence was but little except while he was interpreter for the company. He never distinguished himself in fights. Meldrum was with him in three fights. He was not a coward, but was awkward. James P. Beckwith says he killed the enemy, but Meldrum thinks he never did.[24]

Something more than a debunker's zeal is apparent here; perhaps the answer can be found in the journals of Lieutenant James H. Bradley:

[Robert Meldrum] was born in Scotland about the year 1802, but removed with his parents to Kentucky at an early age. There he learned blacksmithing, but found his way into Bonneville's service and accompanied him into the wilderness in his fur trading expedition in 1832. Upon quitting his service, enamoured of the savage life he had tasted for three years, he remained upon the plains making his home among the Crow Indians. Adopting their dress, glueing long hair to his own to make it conform to the savage fashion, having his squaw and lodge, and living in all respects the life of an Indian, he was quickly enabled by a superior intelligence and courage to acquire great influence with his savage associates and soon became regarded as a chief. He was a man of many adventures and was accustomed to complain bitterly that Beckwourth in the autobiography published by Harper Brothers, had arrogated to himself many of his own experiences. A representative of this firm endeavored subsequently to win from Meldrum a narrative of his life, promising ample reparation for any misappropriation of his experiences in Beckwourth's autobiography, but he proudly rejected all overtures, and a fascinating record of strange adventures is lost to the world.[25]

In the 1880s an obscure newspaper account of an 1840 trapping party carried a seeming confirmation of Meldrum's jealousy and dislike of Jim Beckwourth:

Joining the Crow Indians, [Beckwourth] distinguished himself as a warrior in their battles with the Blackfeet and other tribes with which they were at war, until his prowess and sagacity won for him *the rank of war chief and a high place in the council house of the tribe.* . . . He never would have left them, he told me, if an intense longing to visit his old home in St. Louis, and some relations he had there, had not taken possession of him to the exclusion of every other consideration. . . .

Bill Williams, who claimed to "know all about it," gave another reason for Beckwourth's abandonment of the Crows. According to his story, it was caused by a rival in the person of one Meldrum, a white man, whose long residence and assimilation with the tribe had given him influence sufficient to bring about him all the malcontents and some who, ostensibly the friends and supporters of Beckwourth were not averse to the removal of a formidable obstacle to the accomplishment of their ambitious hope.

Jim discovered the conspiracy when too late—he saw that his deposition was certain in any case, and if he remained, his enemies would dispatch him to the "happy hunting grounds" and so dispose of him and his claims of supremacy together.[26]

Meldrum was, to say the least, no friend of Jim Beckwourth, but these accounts indicate that the latter's influence was that of a leader and chief, and his position one to inspire rivalry and hatred from a lesser man. Beckwourth always took pride in the fine spectacle the Crows presented and boasted that he did not debauch them with liquor. Kenneth McKenzie once declared that "the Crows were the finest Indians of his acquaintance."[27] Yet, when Captain William F. Raynolds, of the U.S. Corps of Topographical Engineers, came across Robert Meldrum in 1859, he was still living with the Crows. By this time, they were filthy

67

and degraded and Meldrum was not able to prevent their incessant stealing and prowling about the white camp. The Crows
had always been noted for their thefts, but their physical well-
being seems to have deteriorated from its former high state.[28]

Another who could scarcely be called a friend was in the
mountains during Jim's heyday. Sir William Drummond Stewart,
a Scottish nobleman and the most colorful Englishman to invade
the Far West, returned again and again to his beloved Rockies.
When, finally, he could no longer arrange a safari, he took to
his home in Scotland every possible memento, including Indians
and buffalo, of the happiest period of his life.[29]

It was Jim Beckwourth's lot to be present in the fall of 1833
when Thomas Fitzpatrick, by now a famous mountain man, led
a party of twenty-five or thirty trappers to the valley of the Big
Horn River. Accompanying the group as paying guests were
Sir William, Dr. Benjamin Harrison (son of William Henry
Harrison, later ninth president of the United States), and several
other adventurers. Fitzpatrick left his distinguished Scottish
companion in charge, while he himself went to call on the Crow
chief. During his absence a large group of hostile, surly young
Crows invaded the camp, intent on removing everything of
material value that they could lay their hands on. They succeeded: guns, goods, horses, and peltries were stolen, and, in
addition, Captain Stewart lost his fine watch.[30] Some restitution
was later made, but this event was to prove a severe blow to
Thomas Fitzpatrick and Robert Campbell of the Rocky Mountain Fur Company, competitors of the American Fur Company.
In his bitterness, Fitzpatrick accused the Company of having
instigated the robbery; it is certainly true that some beaver skins,
stamped R.M.F.C., and stolen on that occasion, ended up in the
hands of Samuel Tulloch at Fort Cass.[31]

Probably because Jim himself is so voluble in denying complicity, tradition accuses him of having inspired the robbery of
Fitzpatrick. (If a contemporary document exists in which Jim

Beckwourth is actually named in this connection it has not been found.) Thomas Fitzpatrick wrote two letters about this episode, one to General Ashley and one to Milton Sublette. In the former, Fitzpatrick says that before he had time for "ceremony or form of any kind they robed me and my men of every thing we possessed save some horses and a few traps and all this accordingly to the order of the American Fur Co as they told me the agent of there people who was there present did not pretend to deny it. . . ."[32]

Several references to this event occur in Kenneth McKenzie's correspondence. A well-known letter from McKenzie to David Mitchell at Fort McKenzie states that Beckwourth and Winter passed the fall with the Crows: "While Mr. Winter was with the Crows Mr. Fitzpatrick of the R.M.F.C. (my friend Captain Stewart was with them) . . . encamped near the village. He had not been long there before a large party paid him a visit and pillaged everything he had. . . ."[33] Winter may have been responsible, but Beckwourth says that, on running to the lodge where Winter slept, he found that the latter had been prevented from leaving it to intervene on behalf of the trappers.

Still later, McKenzie wrote to Tulloch, discussing various plans for defeating the opposition in the fur trade—and he was willing to go to almost any lengths. McKenzie's letter concludes thus:

Mr. Campbell charges A.F.C. as instigators of Crows to pillage Mr. Fitzpatrick he read me a letter from him on the subject. I scouted the idea and laughed at his ungenerous imputations; it is now worth enquiring who instigated the Crows to pillage the trappers I equipped from this place or who have been equipped by you? but disappointed men must look out for some back to bear the burden which to them is irksome, though by shifting the saddle they seldom place it on the right horse.[34]

Nobody was admitting a thing about this affair and probably

the whole truth will never be known, but that Beckwourth was conversant with a great deal of what actually occurred is obvious. As he had in the past with Ashley, Jim witnessed many of the most dramatic episodes of the later fur-trading days when Kenneth McKenzie was "King of the Missouri." Jim's story of the deaths of Edward Rose, Hugh Glass and one Menard, and the subsequent brutal burning of two Arikara Indians in retaliation, coincides very closely with that of John F. A. Sanford, U.S. Indian Agent on the headwaters of the Upper Missouri. Sanford wrote:

> The Aricaras have abandoned the Missouri River since last fall, and where they are at present, I am unable to say; I could not learn from either their friends or enemies; but it is presumed that they are some place in the Blackhills or on the Great Platte. During the last winter a war party belonging to that nation came on the Yellowstone below the Big Horn, where they fell in with three men belonging to the A. Fur Co. who they treacherously killed. Two of these men had been despatched from Fort Cass (a New Fort mouth of Big Horn) in the morning with the express to go on to Fort Union (mouth of Yellowstone) The third was a *free* man a veteran trapper, who was accompanying the others as far as a camp of White Hunters some short distance below the Fort. They scalped them and left part of the scalps of each tied to poles on the grounds of the murder. A large party of Crows went in pursuit of them the same evening or next day but could not overtake them. The names of the men killed are Rose, Menard & Glass. . . . Another party of Arickaras came into a camp of hunters this Spring, eat with them, etc; at a concerted signal they all rose, gave the Yell & succeeded in running off all the horses belonging to the hunters; who however succeeded in making three of their young men prisoners. One of these three they sent after the party to tell them, if the horses were not returned immediately they would put to death their prisoners. The party laughed at them, supposing they would not dare to put

their threat in execution. The horses were not given up, & they killed those [prisoners] they had in possession—Good!! Is it not time that the Government should put in execution some of their numerous and repeated threats against this band of Robbers and Murderers?[35]

Jim's version is this:

It was now early spring, and I started for the fort [Cass]. . . . On my arrival, I was informed that a Mr. Johnson Gardner had bought quite a large lot of goods, which he had taken to his camp eighteen miles down the river. The morning after my arrival, three men were dispatched from the fort to acquaint him that I had come. Early in the morning one of my followers went out to fetch up the horses, when he found them all missing, and the trail on which they had been taken away. The alarm was instantly given, and I ran to the top of the hill to make a general survey. I saw two objects on the ice, which appeared to me to be men; and this excited my apprehensions that they were two of the men dispatched from the fort, as they lay in the direction which they had taken. I collected my warriors instantly for the pursuit, placing all our women and children in the fort. I ordered some of the white men down on the ice to bring in the supposed bodies. Alas! my suspicions proved too true! all three men had been butchered, and when we rode up their bodies were scarcely cold . . . on we swept in pursuit of revenge. We traveled about thirty miles (each man leading his war-horse), and our saddle horses were beginning to tire, and we saw nothing of the enemy. Darkness would close over us, we feared, before we could overtake them. We then mounted our war-horses, which were as swift as the wind, and, leaving the saddle-horses behind, on we went faster than ever. Darkness was already upon us, when we came in sight of a large fire in the distance.

[At this point, Beckwourth describes the entry of his party into the camp of Johnson Gardner, who told him that the Indians had stolen his horses; to balance the account, he had

taken two prisoners and had almost taken a third, but] Garro
stood off at a safe distance and demanded the two Indians.
"You cannot have them until you bring me my horses," said
Gardner. "Then we will have the tops of your heads," threatened the old rascal. . . . They rode off taking every horse
Gardner possessed. [Beckwourth then describes the gruesome
fate of the prisoners.][36]

This story is a springboard to the narration of other thrilling
exploits in which Beckwourth casts himself as leader; he speaks
of his pride in "my warriors," and the number of scalps and
ponies taken grows apace.

But while the "Medicine Calf" was busily passing the tests of
chieftainship, he was also creating a force that would be his
undoing: the American Fur Company wanted peltries, not scalp-
locks, and it was beginning to take a dim view of such unprofit-
able activities as intertribal warfare.

VII

Farewell to Ap-sa-ro-kee

Having been in the mountains for more than ten years, Beckwourth was ready for something new. His yearning for exotic
experience was never quite satisfied, but now he had begun to
reflect on the past and to ponder the future. As Jim put it, he had
joined the Crow Indians just "to gratify a youthful thirst for adventure; I had traversed the fastnesses of the far Rocky Mountains in summer heats and winter frosts; I had encountered
savage beasts and wild men. . . . And what had I to show for so
much wasted energy, and such a catalogue of ruthless deeds. . . ?[1]

The Company's decision not to rehire him may have inspired
this philosophic frame of mind. Had he really wished to remain
with the Crows, however, he could certainly have trapped as a
free trader; instead, he seems to have felt a sincere, if temporary,
desire to return to a settled, conventional existence.

Beckwourth does not say why the Company did not re-engage
him, but as early as 1834 Kenneth McKenzie was expressing
some irritation over his and Winter's failure to remain in the
Crow village in order to protect the firm's interests. The com-
plaint went to Samuel Tulloch at Fort Cass:

> I thought Mr. Winter and J Beckwith went out to winter
> with the Crows what reason do they give for acting contrary
> to your orders, & in these times of strong opposition it is
> somewhat extraordinary that Mr. Winter should come away &
> leave by his own admission 30 beaver in [?] Crow Camp. They
> should not have left the Crows while one beaver remained &
> even when they had traded all for the day more might have
> come in the days following. I consider your instructions should
> have been as implicitly obeyed as if they had come direct from

73

me & it is a grievous reflection to think that two or three men and a few pack horses should get an advantage which I have been at so much expense to secure, moreover it was of paramount importance that when my opponents were in the village my people should be there also to see what was doing and be ready to answer & satisfy the Indians on all points & statements made, as no doubt many would be tending to the disadvantage of A. F. Co. & endeavoring to possess the Crows favorably toward the new Co. My object & resolve was & is to secure the Crows to the A. F. C. They shall be supplied with such articles as they want and approve, on reasonable terms, & I would make almost any sacrifice even to sell goods at cost rather than let my opponents get a skin. Further what object could W. and J B have in returning to Fort Cass there were no Indians there, or prospect thereof & by remaining with them, they would have encouraged them to make robes during the winter & hunt well in the Spring as you were well prepared to supply all their wants when they came in to trade.[2]

Despite this, in an earlier paragraph of the same letter, McKenzie spoke well of Jim:

As I have said before I want no more of J. Beckwith than is justly due from him to Am. Fur C. if the a/c I sent by you was erroneous it was just as I rec'd it from Little Mo, no part of the debt was contracted here. I believe the surplus arises from some transactions at the Aricara post, if he has no knowledge thereof or says it is not just I will at once strike it off the book as I know him to be honest: I think you did well to engage him altho' his Salary is high.[3]

Another allusion to this erroneous charge occurred in a subsequent letter. McKenzie deducted $206.37 from Jim's debt and credited him with "salary horses etc" at $650 as of September 1, 1833, leaving Jim still some $200 in debt to the Company.

McKenzie then got back to matters nearest his heart:

If W. and B. had conformed to your instructions last fall

even had they not traded another skin it would have been for the Co interest, as their presence alone would have compelled the opposition to pay dear for what they got; your arrangements were good, if disregarded it was no fault of yours.[4]

Jim attributes much of the Company's dissatisfaction to his failure to control his war-hungry Crow Indians. He was aware that

these incessant wars were very prejudicial to the Company's interest, but it was impossible for me to remedy the evil. Other tribes were continually attacking the Crows, killing their braves, and stealing their horses, and, of course, they were bound to make reprisals. In justice to the Crows I must say, that other tribes were generally the aggressors, until the policy was forced upon me of endeavoring to "conquer a peace." I thought, if I could make the Crow nation a terror to all their neighbors, that their antagonists would be reduced to petition for peace, and then turn their battle-axes into beaver-traps, and their lances into hunting-knives.[5]

Oblique references to this situation turn up in other letters to Tulloch. McKenzie recounts an attack on some Piegans camped at Fort Union by several hundred Assiniboines and the ultimate necessity of ordering the inhabitants of the fort to fire upon the attackers. "Thus you see you do not monopolize all the war," added McKenzie.[6] Again, he remarked, "I know your influence with your Indians & have full confidence you will control them if in power of white men to do it."[7]

Beckwourth recalled that he, also, received a letter from McKenzie: "A deputation of fifty As-ne-boines came to the post, leaving a letter from Mr. M'Kenzie at the lower fort addressed to me, requesting me to constrain the As-ne-boines into a treaty of peace with the Crows, in order that their incessant wars might be brought to a close, and the interests of the company less interfered with."[8]

Unfortunately, the prospects that Tulloch had held out to McKenzie for a successful hunt in the spring of 1834 did not materialize. In a letter to Pierre Chouteau, Jr., McKenzie reported that the Crow returns "fell short 200 Packs of what I wrote you in the winter I expected would be made then, this arises from my having been wrongly informed on the subject by the Clerk at that post."[9]

Several put-upon Indian tribes, as well as the Company, complained that the Crows were the aggressors in battle. On one occasion, when Jim brought his followers in for trade at Fort Cass, he found a letter from Jacob Halsey, then in charge of Fort Union:

> The letter was couched in rather strong terms, and was evidently written when he was under the influence of temper. The Company had their trading posts among every tribe with which the Crows were at war, and for many months past there had been a great falling off in trade. The Indians had brought in but little peltry, and the universal complaint among all was that it took all their time to defend themselves against the Crows . . . their trappers dare not go out to trap for fear of the Crows; their hunters dare not, and could not, kill buffalo for fear of the Crows. . . .[10]

It appears that Jim had succeeded very well indeed in turning his Indians into a terror and Halsey was tired of it. "For ——'s sake, do keep your d——d Indians at home, so that the other tribes may have a chance to work a little, and the Company may drive a more profitable business," was his final irritable plea, according to Jim.[11]

A letter from J. Archdale Hamilton, though not addressed to Beckwourth, substantiates his statements. There began to be talk of abandoning not only Fort Cass, but also perhaps the entire Crow trade. In his testy, irritable way, Hamilton communicated with Tulloch:

I observe with concern that your prospects of Trade are so unfavorable, your expenditure of the most costly articles appears to me unusually large for so very small a return. . . . It is quite out of my power to send the men you require to rebuild your Fort and it is therefore my desire that you will make arrangements to come down here in the Spring with your whole establishment, as early as you think desirable to leave. . . .[12]

In reply to a letter from Tulloch, Hamilton commented on the scarcity of beaver this season and the falling off of prices in New York. He also had something to say about Jim Beckwourth: "I believe that under you, Beckwith as also some others would render good services to the Company and yet perhaps under other authority their exertions might be less zealously directed."[13]

Samuel Tulloch evidently protested the order to abandon Fort Cass, and wrote once again to ask for assistance in rebuilding the post. Daniel Lamont angrily replied:

I am not conscious of having said one word in my last letter which could have led you to infer that the Crow Trade would be abandoned and I now authorize you to say to the chiefs that they shall certainly have a trader next season upon the principle avowed by Mr. McKenzie that he would give them a fair trial and they will therefore have still an opportunity of redeeming their promises, but as we came into this country to make money it would be sheer madness to continue to Trade with the Crows at this year's prices, the prices of this season or last season.[14]

Jim asserts that he took occasion to lecture his followers whenever some event "furnished me with an opportunity of enlarging to the Crows upon the superior delights of peace." A trace of irony must have crept into his voice, for he was obliged to admit almost in the same breath that he was unsuccessful: "An old warrior despises the sight of a trap; hunting buffalo, even, does not afford him excitement enough. Nothing but war or a horse-

77

raid is a business worth attending to, and the chief who seeks to control this predilection too far loses popularity."[15]

Whatever the cause, the days of youthful high adventure were coming to a close for Jim Beckwourth. On July 15, 1836, Charles Larpenteur recorded that two horse thieves and renegades, who had been previously punished by whipping, were sentenced to banishment to the States. "A few days afterward James Beckworth a yellow fellow the interpreter for the Crow Indians started for St. Louis these two gentlemen were sent down with him."[16] Beckwourth and his charges stopped off at Fort Clark on July 26, and François Chardon noted their arrival. Two days later they were again under way. "Beckworth & Co. started for St. Louis—sent P. Garreau with them as far as the Little Mo . . . with letters to Mr. Papin—the river rising—shower of rain in the afternoon. . . ," Chardon recorded.[17]

The canoe trip down the river had its own excitement. Jim's account of being captured by the Aricara Indians and Antoine "Garro"[18] and of then being rescued by Garro, senior, seems utterly without foundation, but one learns to be careful about rejecting these stories completely.

Once arrived in St. Louis, Beckwourth was lost. No haven was to be found with Jennings, who had long since left the area and had died in Virginia the previous year. The formerly primitive settlement had changed. St. Louis had grown from a village of muddy unpaved streets and scattered farms to a bustling center of trade. New buildings and warehouses lined the streets close to the river and, farther out, magnificent homes had been built to accommodate the families of men grown rich in business and industry. A new theater was being planned—"the first real theatre west of the Mississippi."[19]

Jim found himself in a brawl at the "St. Louis Theatre." Although told in the context of 1836, this event must have occurred after July 3, 1837, the date of the theater's opening. The story seems to have considerable veracity, although the cause of the fight is doubtful.

Friends had cautioned me that there were large sums of money offered for my life [for supposed complicity in the Crow robbery of Fitzpatrick], and that several men had even undertaken to earn the rewards. . . . Shortly after . . . I went to the St. Louis Theatre. Between the pieces I had stepped to the saloon to obtain some refreshments, and I saw Fitzpatrick enter, with four other not very respectable citizens. They advanced directly toward me. Fitzpatrick then pointed me out to them, saying, "There's the Crow."[20]

Immediately knives were drawn and Jim was at bay ("momentarily hesitating whether to give the Crow war-hoop or not") when Sheriff Buzby laid hands on him and ordered him to be quiet. "Although boiling with rage, I respected the officer's presence, and the assassins marched off to the body of the theatre. I followed them to the door, but the sheriff becoming angry, and threatening me with the calaboose, I straightway left the theatre."[21]

The leader of his assailants was one Forsyth, who "had long been the terror of St. Louis, having badly maimed many men"; it is just possible that this was Thomas Forsyth, Jr., son of the highly respected Thomas Forsyth. The younger Forsyth "was a rover and died away from home."[22] One element of Jim's story can be accepted wholeheartedly—there *was* a "Sheriff" Daniel Busby in St. Louis at that time, although his official title was Constable.[23]

In April, 1837, Jim made one last visit to the Crows before finally accepting the Company's decision not to rehire him. In doing so, he laid himself open to a charge so malicious it is almost without parallel in the history of the fur trade: Beckwourth brought smallpox to the Indians.

Only Francis Parkman has described Jim Beckwourth as cruel, treacherous, and inhumane. But Jim was friendly, outgoing, eager for fun, and proud of his strength and good health. Furthermore, he had learned over the years respect for Indian enemies as well as Indian friends—he expressed no hatred for any tribe, with the possible exception of the Pawnees. That he would deliberately introduce into an Indian tribe a dreadful plague that would decimate that people is beyond belief. Yet that is exactly what he has been accused of doing by several writers. This story became a firmly established part of the Beckwourth legend with the publication of Frances Fuller Victor's *River of the West*, a collection of reminiscences by the famous mountain man, Joe Meek:

> The Blackfeet found the camp of Bridger too strong for them. They were severely beaten and compelled to retire to their village, leaving Bridger free to move on. The following day the camp reached the village of Little Robe, the Chief of the Peagans, who held a talk with Bridger, complaining that his nation were all perishing from the small pox which had been given to them by the whites. Bridger was able to explain to Little Robe his error; inasmuch as although the disease might have originated among the whites, it was communicated to the Blackfeet by Jim Beckwith, a negro and principal chief of their enemies the Crows. This unscrupulous wretch had caused two infected articles to be taken from a Mackinaw boat, up from St. Louis, and disposed of them to the Blackfeet—whence the horrible scourge under which they were suffering.[24]

Osborne Russell described this same encounter as taking place on July 6, 1838, not far from the headwaters of the Madison Fork of the Missouri. He does not mention Beckwourth. Still another account repeats the story of Bridger's meeting with Little Robe, with no comment on Bridger's having used Jim's name. However, Stanley Vestal keeps the tale alive and properly embellished: "But Bridger knew how the small pox had come up the Missouri, and explained that though the disease may have originated among the white men in the settlements, it had been brought to the Blackfeet by Jim Beckwourth, a Negro. . . . 'Blame the Negro, blame the Crows, not the whites!' "[25]

To blame any one man for the spread of a plague is as foolish as it is evil, but if Jim's known enemies were told that he was responsible for a horror that they could neither escape nor understand, the mountain men were guilty, at least, of character assassination and, at worst, of exposing him to certain death should he encounter the Blackfeet. In any case, there is something less than honorable in this relation: if Bridger blamed Jim, he was lying; if Meek manufactured the tale, then he and Mrs. Victor maligned both Bridger and Beckwourth.

However, once told, the story spread rapidly and was snatched up for use in reminiscences such as those of General Bernard Pratte, Jr., and of the Reverend Samuel Allis, a missionary with the Pawnee Indians. General Pratte recalled in his old age that Jim had been a passenger on his boat and had caught the smallpox from sleeping on some infected clothing which had been put aboard by a disgruntled former employee. However, the general treated Jim by giving him a dose of ipecac; happily, the patient recovered. The cure may have been worse than the ailment—an Indian mother, for whose child the general proposed the same treatment, declined, saying, "Let him go. . . . It is better that he should die a natural death."[26] Christian charity did not prevent the Reverend Allis from reporting that he "got the varioloid from a Jim Beckwith, who resides with the Blackfeet Indians. This Beckwith was a negro. He gave the small pox to several on the boat, three of whom died on their way up the river. Several of the Indian tribes above caught the small pox. Beckwith and some 20,000 died of it."[27]

This scrambled account needs no analysis, but it is interesting to note that, although Allis says he departed St. Louis on April

6, records show that Jim Beckwourth was charged $3 for "7 ys of calico" in that city on April 17, 1837.[28]

Jim remarked that his journey took fifty-three days "as the traveling was bad. Our last resting place was Fort Clarke. Thence we struck directly across through a hostile Indian country. . . ." Thus Beckwourth avoided Fort Union, where Charles Larpenteur noted in his journal that the smallpox was introduced by Jacob Halsey, who was suffering from it on arrival at the fort on June 24.[29]

Larpenteur was a young man at the time he wrote his journal. He was even then quick to denigrate the morals of others; as he grew older his cynicism deepened. The language of his published autobiography has led many writers, including Chittenden, to criticize severely his attitude toward the tragic events of 1837.[30] In fairness to Larpenteur, however, it must be stated that he expressed horror at the scenes of misery around him and complained bitterly that nobody had listened to his advice to immediately send away the Indians at Fort Union.

Instead, says Larpenteur,

Doctor Thomas Medical Book was brought down from the library and the treatment of small Pox vacination noculation was read over and over and was informed that by noculating that the Small Pox would be much lighter and great deal less danger haprehended that by preparing the system well before the operation that one case of six hundred might prove fatal Perhaps and very likely if Doctor Johnson [sic] himself had prepared opperated and attended to the noculated cases he would have had succeeded but the future will prove otherwise.[31]

The bewildered men at Fort Union proceeded to follow Dr. Thomas's advice and inoculated all the women at the post with material taken from Jacob Halsey. It will never be known just how many died, but the results were dreadful. Lacking delicacy, and having little sensitivity to the English language, Larpenteur could describe the death of "my squaw" in words that are appalling today. This poor woman, according to him, was attacked by maggots two days before her death. But, with a cry of anguish, Larpenteur recorded: "There's noculation for you[!]"[32]

Chittenden says the disease reached the Blackfeet through the negligence of the American Fur Company's officers in allowing one of the tribe to board the *St. Peters* and return to his people before it was known if he had been infected.[33]

Whatever its origin, the frightful pestilence swept across the western prairies, into the valleys and mountains, and left in its wake thousands dead and other thousands living in abject fear and misery. Inevitably, this plague affected the fur trade; it may have contributed to the American Fur Company's decision not to make a "satisfactory" agreement with Jim Beckwourth in 1837. It is evident, however, that the Company did not abandon him outright: the firm carried him on its books throughout 1836, paying him the balance of his salary, $341.75,[34] in July "for services ending this summer," and advancing him $40 each in October and November, and $50 in December. Jim repaid this debt in June, 1838, not forgetting to include the $3 for calico.[35]

VIII

Renown in the Everglades

The fall of 1837 found Jim Beckwourth still adrift; whatever had been the purpose of his brief visit to the Crows in the spring, it had ended in disappointment. Jim was forced into realistic self-appraisal and a straight-forward admission of rejection. "I was disappointed in my expectation of entering into a satisfactory engagement to the agent of the company, so I kept on at St. Louis," he recalled. Later, though admitting that he could see no virtue in continuing his Indian life, he added:

> It certainly grieved me to leave a people who reposed so much trust in me, and with whom I had been associated so long; and, indeed, could I have made an engagement . . . as I had hoped to do, I should have redeemed my promise to the Crows, and possibly have finished my days with them. But, being mistaken in my calculations, I was led on to scenes wilder and still more various, yet dignified with the name of greater utility, because associated with the interests of civilization.[1]

The Seminole Indians, whom Jim was about to encounter, had split from the Creeks, who had fled the Carolinas to what is now Georgia, before the Revolutionary War. The Seminole name means literally "wild wanderers," or "runaways."[2] The fugitives found a haven in Florida, then under Spanish rule, and lived comparatively unmolested lives until southern planters began to press for the return of their slaves, many of whom had taken refuge with the Seminoles and with whom they sometimes intermarried. The Indians also held some Negroes as slaves and considered them their lawful property.

A long series of treaties made and broken, years of battle and persecution, and unlawful kidnaping of supposed slaves culminated in the arrest of the young Seminole chief Osceola, whose part-Negro wife had reportedly been carried off in chains.[3]
After his release, Osceola successfully plotted the murder of General Wiley Thompson at Fort King, also killing another man. The war was on. Major Francis Dade was ordered to march to Fort King; en route, the column fell into an ambush. Of 110 men, only two are said to have survived.[4] Skirmishes and isolated battles ensued, and still more treaties were made and broken. With an increasing sense of futility, the United States Army struggled to defeat these Indians or to effect their emigration, and seemed incapable of achieving either aim.
Beckwourth says he was lured into the Florida adventure by several forces. Not only was the fur trade declining, but there was also a general collapse of the economy and jobs were hard to find. William L. Sublette had some advice to offer on the latter subject. Jim, speaking of General Edmund P. Gaines's recruitment of men for the Seminole campaign, recalled: "Sublet recommended me to engage. Florida, he said, was a delightful country, and I should find a wide difference between the cold regions of the Rocky Mountains and the genial and salubrious South."[5] Also, perhaps Jim could bring along some congenial companions, for "there were plenty of unemployed men in the city ready to engage in any enterprise." The chief inducement, however, was the opportunity for "renown," and that Jim could not resist.
Beckwourth's account of his going to Florida to participate briefly in the Seminole Wars, which lasted from 1835 to 1842, rings true. In general, he had the names and ranks of officers correct; he mentions the enemy leaders "Sam Jones" and "Alligator,"[6] and he is quite accurate in describing the battle of Okeechobee. Still, one could do no more than grant that internal evidence in Jim's account pointed toward its authenticity. Ber-

nard De Voto's comments reveal the difficulties posed by the lack of documentation: "Jim's venture among the Seminoles is probably true. Its chronology is precise, for one thing, and the demigod lapses into a wholly credible scout. Two such organizations as Jim mentions were recruited in St. Louis and one of them participated in the battle of Okeechobee. . . . He was probably not an officer in the scouts, but only an enlisted man."[7]

As it happens, he was neither. He was a civilian employee of the army, under the command of Major Joshua B. Brant, quartermaster at Fort Brooke, Florida.[8] It is partly Jim's own fault that the records have proved so elusive, for Bonner understood him to say "Major (sometimes "Colonel") *Bryant*," and only by careful culling of the text can one finally determine who, indeed, was the quartermaster.

Major Brant's reports do more than confirm Beckwourth's presence in Florida; they also verify his statements that he was higher ranking and better paid than the majority. With the exception of calling himself "Captain," there is no false pride in Jim's description of the work he did in Florida. The company was raised for muleteer service and Jim makes no bones about it. He speaks, for example, of "two or three weeks at Fort Brooke, during which time we were engaged in breaking-in mules." The men were wagon drivers and baggage custodians, but they were also fighters. Jim's experience with the Crows no doubt made him a natural choice for the carrying of dispatches, if he did not, in fact, volunteer for the job.

Jim was not a member of the Missouri Volunteers, nor yet of the group known as Morgan's Spies. His activities inevitably touched upon theirs, however, and many of the events he describes are corroborated by records of the first-named group.

The pay for the Missouri Volunteers was $8 a month for enlisted men, and forty (later reduced to twenty) cents a day for the subsistence of their horses. In contrast to this, the quartermaster's record for January, 1838, shows that James "Beckwith" was employed at $50 a month as "Express rider and sub. cond." Out of a list of forty-two civilians, only eight received as much or more than he, the usual wage being $25. Similarly, in February, March, and April, Jim was paid $50 as "Master Teamster; Sub-Conductor, Muleteers; and Ass't Wagon Master," respectively. (In January, the wagon master was paid $100.)[9]

The involvement of the Missouri troops in the Florida Seminole War grew out of Senator Thomas H. Benton's displeasure over the steady drain of men and money to carry on the campaign. By 1837 $12 million had already been spent, with no apparent results. Senator Benton concluded that the expertise of western frontiersmen, with their knowledge of tracking and Indian-style warfare, was just the ingredient needed for victory. The senator took the floor so often to argue his point that President Martin Van Buren finally gave in and Congress then authorized a call for a volunteer cavalry regiment from the western state, much to the disgust of the regular army. At Benton's suggestion, Secretary of War Joel Poinsett wrote to Richard Gentry, of Columbia, Missouri, directing him to raise six hundred volunteers and to have them ready for duty by November, 1837. Gentry's commission as Colonel of Volunteers created political controversy and a storm of public argument; despite this, he proceeded with his recruitment in central and western Missouri. Boone, Callaway, Howard, Chariton, Ray, Jackson, and Marion counties supplied the troops.[10]

It was not long before Gentry had his quota. Few of these men, however, had enough money to buy equipment for themselves or their horses. They appealed to Gentry, who generously offered to endorse their notes: "Poor Gentry! Little did he realize that he would be dead and buried . . . and that the notes would be presented as claims against his estate, leaving nothing for his wife and nine children."[11]

The citizenry of Columbia gathered to do full honor to the Volunteers on October 15, 1837. A Miss Wales made local history by giving the first public address ever delivered by a woman in Columbia, and the ladies of the community presented a silk flag they had made, upon which was printed a laudatory pledge of support. These troopers took five days to reach St. Louis and were then taken to Jefferson Barracks to await the arrival of Senator Benton, who was to address them. It was here that they were also joined by General Gaines and the men that Jim Beckwourth had rounded up in St. Louis as baggage masters, muleteers, carpenters, and blacksmiths.

Senator Benton spoke to the regiment on the morning of October 25 and the troopers boarded steamboats for New Orleans. That evening a dinner was held on one of the boats, with both officers and men attending. A letter to the *Missouri Republican* describes the refusal of one of the soldiers to drink the health of "that damned fellow Benton!" The other "boys" promptly threw the dissident off the steamboat—bag, baggage, and horse.[12] The dinner was in honor of General Gaines, but somehow another impression seems to have been left with Jim Beckwourth. He remembered that while he was waiting in New Orleans several old acquaintances gave him an elegant parting dinner. Perhaps there were *two* dinner parties.

At New Orleans, the troops under Gentry's command transferred to sailing vessels. The passage to Tampa Bay was successfully accomplished in five days, without incident. The horses, however, and the men responsible for them were placed on smaller vessels. Having no experience of the sea and anticipating no difficulties, the muleteers simply drove the horses aboard and stowed them in the holds without seeing that each was firmly secured. When the small craft were overtaken by severe storms, the animals were crushed and maimed; many died of starvation.

If one doubts Jim's story of his tribulations aboard one of these ships, he need only read Colonel Gentry's letter to his son-in-law John Bryant:

. . . you cannot imagine the mortification I have had to undergo since my arrival; the horses were embarked at as early a day after our departure as was expected, but the whole did not arrive until last night, none accomplishing the trip under three weeks,[13] during which time many were thrown overboard, having died from the effects of the storm; more have subsequently been condemned as unfit for service, from injuries occurred during the transportation, leaving me at present not exceeding 150 horses, scattered thruout the different companies of the Regiment. . . . The Regiment being thus awkwardly situated, one half mounted and the other half afoot, and doubts entertained as to the uniformity of the pay, dissatisfaction naturally began to raise its head; to quiet which, Colonel [Zachary P.] Taylor, the Commandant of the Army, gave instructions to "discharge all that portion of the Regiment that has lost their horses on the passage from New Orleans to this place, and are unwilling to make a campaign on foot."[14]

Thus began what turned out to be a mounting quarrel between the regular army and the Volunteers that was never quite settled. The Volunteers complained that Colonel Taylor and his staff treated the Missouri officers and men with the utmost contempt and they eagerly sought their pay and discharges.[15] However, they were to endure further humiliations. After having been told that they would be paid "in coin," they were offered only twenty cents a day for their horses, this to be paid in "shinplasters," scrip worth nowhere near its face value. This was discounted at New Orleans and yet again at St. Louis. There could have been little left by the time they all "got home broke and many in debt, travel-worn and disillusioned."[16]

The troops remaining with Colonel Gentry had their complaints also. Colonel Taylor, in planning his Okeechobee battle of December 25, refused Gentry's advice and all but accused him of cowardice because he advocated a flanking action rather than a frontal attack, in which the men would be greatly impeded by the mud and mire of the swamp. The Missouri Volunteers and Morgan's Spies found themselves in the front rank with the regulars (6th, 4th, and 1st Infantry Regiments) backing them up—and sometimes shooting into their ranks. Some of the Volunteers broke and ran for the rear, but others supported their colonel, fighting bravely enough until he and some of their comrades fell wounded. Beckwourth told Bonner that

On the morning of Christmas-day [1837] our camp was beleaguered by a large force of Indians, and Colonel Taylor ordered an advance upon them. The spot was thickly overgrown with trees, and numbers of our assailants were concealed among the branches; as our line advanced, therefore, many were singled out by the enemy, and we lost fearfully in killed and wounded. . . . The country lost several valuable lives through this slight brush with the Indians.

The gallant Colonel Gentry . . . was shot through the head; Colonel Thompson, and several other officers, were also among the slain. The enemy had made an excellent choice of ground, and could see our troops while remaining concealed themselves.[17]

According to another version, the battle of Okeechobee was planned by Coa-coo-chee (Wild Cat) who had recently escaped from the musty dungeon where he and Osceola had been confined after their capture under the truce of the white flag, while negotiating with the American officers. Coa-coo-chee, as if challenging the American army with retaliation and revenge for the indignity of such a violation of recognized warfare, now combined his forces for one great battle. . . .

The Indians had fled to the dark haunts of Florida's weird morasses. With his people already encamped in this vicinity, Coa-coo-chee naturally selected the battle ground for its advantage of position, within easy reach of his warriors and by strategy and decoys succeeded in leading the American army to the chosen site. Contrary to the usual tactics of fighting in

Coa-coo-chee, leader of the Seminoles in the Battle of O-kee-cho-bee, 1837 (From Minnie Moore-Wilson, *The Seminoles of Florida*)

small bands and at widely scattered points, the Seminoles staked their all in this supreme battle, apparently not awed by the overwhelming odds of four to one.[18]

Colonel Gentry, while not shot through the head, had been mortally wounded and died about midnight of Christmas Day, after having first asked Colonel Taylor to deal fairly with the Missouri Volunteers and making the direct accusation that Taylor had not sustained him. Taylor promised to do the men "full justice," and in the same breath ventured the belief that "you were rather imprudent."[19]

The Missourians resented the failure of the regulars to support them and there were more than hints that Colonel Taylor had maintained a safe distance until the battle was over. "It is not at all clear as to where Colonel Taylor kept himself during the engagement; he says nothing about it in his report, and no member of the Volunteers ever saw him until the fight was over that evening."[20] Beckwourth also made a subtle observation on this subject:

It was reported that Colonel Taylor was uncontrollably angry during the battle, and that his aids and other officers had to hold him by main force to prevent him from rushing among the enemy, and meeting certain death. I do not know what truth there was in this, for I saw nothing of it, nor, indeed, did I see the colonel during the whole of the four hours' fighting.[21]

In his report, Colonel Taylor had this to say:

On reaching the border of the hammock, the Volunteers and Spies received a heavy fire from the enemy, which was returned by them for a short time, when their gallant commander, Colonel Gentry, fell mortally wounded. They mostly broke, and instead of forming in the rear of the Regulars, as had been directed, they returned across the swamp to their baggage and horses, nor could they again be brought into action as a body, altho efforts were made repeatedly by my staff to induce them to do so.

Colonel Taylor did add, however, that "they acted as well or even better, than troops of that description usually do. . . ."[22]

Senator Benton angrily flew to the defense of the Missourians. He addressed the Senate, and soon had a conciliatory letter from Secretary of War Poinsett. Benton also hastened to offer what help he could to the bereaved family of Colonel Gentry. He wrote the following letter to the colonel's son:

Dear Sir, Yours of the 22nd is just received, and long before you receive this, you will see that I had, from the mere face of Colonel Taylors report and without having heard a word from any one of the volunteers, been convinced that great injustice had been done that brave and patriotic body of men, and had taken steps to vindicate them. The remarks which I made in the Senate, and the answer of the Secretary at [sic] War, will have been seen by you, and both will go to repair the wrong which has been done to the Missourians; but I could have been much more effective if I had your letter. It is probable that Colonel Taylor may send some reply to my remarks; if he does so I shall embrace the opportunity to do full justice to you all; and I can assure you that the President feels the highest regard for all the volunteers, and will gladly take any opportunity to show his sense of their merits. . . .

Your mother will have received the Post Office appointment long before this time; her pension also will soon be passed through the [?]. I have a Bill in the Senate to pay for the lost horses, and I know it to be the determination of the President and Sec. at War, to have you all paid in solid money for all your services and losses. . . .[23]

But the Missourians were not so easily appeased as some had seemed to hope. A long-drawn-out investigation finally resulted in the passage of resolutions in 1839 lauding the Volunteers and denouncing Colonel Taylor's report. Testimony given during these hearings would seem to indicate that the colonel had, indeed, sacrificed his volunteers to an unwise plan of battle.

Following the engagement at Lake Okeechobee, Jim was selected to carry the victory dispatches to Tampa Bay. He traveled alone, resting a short time at forts along the way. "I shouted 'Victory! victory!' which brought out officers and men, impatient to hear the news. I could not see that O-ke-cho-be was much of a victory: indeed, I shrewdly suspected that the enemy had the advantage; but it was called a victory by the soldiers, and they were the best qualified to decide."[24]

After the departure of the volunteer troops, the war settled down to a routine that Jim found unendurable. "Now we had another long interval of inactivity, and I began to grow tired of Florida, with its inaccessible hummocks. It seemed to me to be a country dear even at the price of the powder to blow the Indians out of it, and certainly a poor field to work in for *renown*."[25]

It was inevitable that Jim Beckwourth should have grown disillusioned with Florida, and one can only admire his courage in traveling alone in this Indian- and serpent-infested territory. The Kissimmee Swamp was, perhaps, typical of much of the land Beckwourth traversed:

About ten miles from Kissimmee, west by south, is a cypress swamp made by the junction of the Davenport, Reedy and Bonnett Creeks. It is an aquatic jungle, full of fallen trees, brush, vines and tangled undergrowth, and darkened by the dense shadows of the tall cypress trees. The surface is covered by water, which, from appearance, may be any depth, from six inches to six feet; this infested with alligators and mocassins would have been an unsurmountable barrier to the white troops.

[On exploration, it] proved to be a complete chain of small hommocks or islands running through from one side of the swamp to the other; the topography of the marsh being such that a skirmish could take place on one side of the jungle and an hour later, by means of a secret route through the swamp, the Indians could be ready for an attack on the other side, while for the troops to reach the same point, by following the only road known to them, it would have required nearly a day's marching.

Lying between Fort Brooke (Tampa) and Fort King (Ocala) within a distance of thirty miles from the scene of the Dade massacre, about forty miles from Fort Mellon, the present site of Sanford, the camp could have been reached in a few hours by Indian runners after spying the movements of the troops at any of the forts. The old government road, over which the soldiers passed in going from Fort Brooke to Fort Mellon, passes so close to the old Indian camping ground that all travel could have been watched by the keen-eyed warriors.[26]

Except for carrying an occasional dispatch, there was little for his company to do, Jim complained, and he wanted excitement. "I was indifferent of what nature, even if it was no better than borrowing horses of the Black Feet. The Seminoles had no horses worth stealing, or I should certainly have exercised my talents for the benefit of the United States."[27]

Beckwourth decided to be on his way again and in early summer, he was back in St. Louis, looking for a job.

95

The Santa Fe Trail

The American Fur Company had successfully won for its own exploitation a major share of the fur trade on the upper Missouri and well into the valleys of the Platte tributaries. Farther south, Charles and William Bent, with their partner Céran St. Vrain, had almost a monopoly on trade along the Arkansas, down past the Spanish Peaks, over Raton Pass, and deep into Mexico. But there were still opportunities for the small trader—or, at least, so some of them believed. Thus, Jim Beckwourth found himself idle in St. Louis for only five days. Andrew Sublette[1] and Louis Vasquez were trying their luck with the Indians of the southern plains and they needed men with courage and know-how to conduct the trading.

Andrew Sublette never achieved the success of his elder brother William. The younger man apparently had to seek financial backing from William, and after the failure of the firm of Vasquez and Sublette assumed, for a while, a position of virtual dependence on his brother.[2] That Andrew was in debt—perhaps not as drastically as Jim Beckwourth says—is clear. He eventually went to California in the express led by Lieutenant Edward Fitzgerald Beale in 1848 and is said to have gone to the Sonora mines in the summer of 1849.

Jim Beckwourth remembered that Sublette was known as "Left Hand" by the Indians, but Bayard Taylor gives him a more romantic name: "From his bravery and daring [he] has obtained among the Indians the name of Kee-ta-tah-ve-sak, or "One-who-walks-in-fire." He was destined to die a death feared by all mountain men: in 1853 he was mauled and fatally injured by a bear.[3]

As an old friend of Beckwourth, Louis Vasquez was probably glad to have his services. How eagerly Jim snatched at the chance to join the party can only be conjectured, but he was longing to put the dullness of Florida and the demands of city life behind him. Now he could count on a little "excitement"—he would be dealing with Cheyennes, Arapahoes, and Sioux, all traditional enemies of the Crows.

The party was under way early in July, Jim recalled. "I bade my friends adieu; and, stepping on board a steamboat bound up the Missouri, we were soon breasting its broad and turbid current. We spent the Fourth on board, amid much noise, revelry and drunken patriotism."[4]

After leaving Independence, the group followed the well-worn Santa Fe Trail. Then Jim and Vasquez struck out ahead of the wagons. In doing so, they were in constant danger of Indian attack, but it was Beckwourth's practice, throughout the ten years he spent in the southwest, to travel either alone or in a small party. He discounted the dangers:

> Many times wonder has been expressed how I could always travel the road in safety while other men were attacked and killed. The only way in which I could account for the marvel was that I knew how to act the "wolf," while the others did not. . . . The Indians knew perfectly well what my business was. They knew I was conveying orders back and forward from the great white chief to his war chiefs in New Mexico. . . . Sometimes I would tell them that the great chief at Washington was going to send on a great host of warriors to rub them all out. They would laugh heartily at the supposition, for they conceived that all the American forces combined would hardly be a circumstance before them. I promised to apprise them when the white warriors were to advance. . . . I had to say something to keep on good terms with them.[5]

He may have been safe from Indians, but the merciless summer sun of the plains found a victim in Beckwourth: he suffered a

97

sunstroke while traversing the ridge between the Arkansas and the Platte rivers. Jim described his plight in typically vivid language:

> We were at that time twenty miles from water: I was burning with thirst, the heat was intolerable, and hostile Indians were before us. After incredible suffering we reached the river bank, and crossed the stream to an island, where I lay me down to die. All our medicines were in the wagons, and two days journey in our rear. My fatigue and suffering had thrown me into a fever; I became delirious, and grew rapidly worse. I requested my companion to return to the wagons and procure me some medicine; but he refused to leave me, lest I might die in his absence.[6]

Louis Vasquez finally agreed to return for help, first making sure that ample water was available to the sick man. Jim's recovery had already begun before help reached him, but he was still so ill that it was necessary for him to travel on wheels for a while.

In 1835 Vasquez had established a fort on the Platte River, about a mile from the present town of Platteville, Colorado, and about six miles distant from the rival Fort St. Vrain, built in 1837. Fort Vasquez was of medium size, a little over one hundred feet square, but adequate for the protection of goods and men. Sublette and Vasquez stocked it well, erected suitable buildings within the walls, and took in forage from the generous country-side—a hay barn was soon filled, Beckwourth remembered.[7] As soon as these arrangements were completed, Sublette announced that he was making Beckwourth agent-in-charge. That he should have done so is not incredible. Jim was known to be honest, a hard worker, tough, and fearless to the point of rashness. He was perfectly capable of handling Indians, either in trade or in war, and he knew ways to win their confidence and turn the advantage away from his competitors. Years later Louis Vasquez again displayed his confidence in Beckwourth by employing him in his store in Denver—at a salary three times that paid to James Bridger in the same period. After a brief show of modesty Jim accepted the responsibility and promptly set out to locate his subposts in the territory. His own was placed "at the mouth of Crow Creek," but as he was, in effect, a traveling salesman, Jim left a man in charge there.

Beckwourth's knowledge of Indian ways saved him many a weary mile of travel; he tosses off bits of this information quite casually in his autobiography:

> We had not, as yet, found any customers; but, as we were in the Cheyenne country, I knew some of that nation could not be very far off. I sent three different messengers in search of them to invite them to trade, but they all returned without having discovered the whereabouts of the Indians. Tired of these failures, I took a man with me, and started in the direction of the Laramie mountain. While ascending the mount, I cast my eyes in the direction of a valley, and discovered buffalo running in small groups, which was sufficient evidence that they had been chased recently by Indians. We went no farther, but encamped there, and at nightfall we saw fires. The next morning a dense smoke hung like a cloud over the village of the Cheyennes; we ate a hasty meal, and started to pay them a visit.[8]

On this occasion Beckwourth encountered William Bent, ("an interpreter," according to Jim) who was engaged in trading at this same Cheyenne village. Although Bent, probably the wealthiest and most influential landholder in the Southwest at that time, was to be a future employer, Beckwourth did not stand in awe of him. Jim speaks of "Bent," but in referring to Vasquez it is always "Mr. Vasquez." Apparently Louis Vasquez had inspired his lasting respect, as he had that of such mountain men as Robert Campbell, Thomas Fitzpatrick, the Sublettes, and many others.[9]

The new trader understood perfectly well how intense com-

99

petition for Cheyenne robes was going to be. He deliberately began, through a Crow interpreter, a lengthy display of braggadocio, defiantly counting coup on the astonished Indians and playing on their pride, as well as on their respect for the brave deeds of enemy warriors:

I have killed a great Crow Chief, and am obliged to run away, or be killed by them. I have come to the Cheyennes, who are the bravest people in the mountains, as I do not wish to be killed by any of the inferior tribes. I have come here to be killed by the Cheyennes, cut up, and thrown out for their dogs to eat, so that they may say that they have killed a great Crow Chief.[10]

Bent's observation seems apt: "You are certainly bereft of your senses," he remarked, "the Indians will make sausage meat of you."

But braggadocio worked. That, and two ten-gallon kegs of whisky. Up to now, he had always opposed the sale of liquor to Indians, Beckwourth reminded Bonner,

and, during my chieftainship of the Crows, not one drop had ever been brought into the village; but now I was restrained by no such moral obligation. I was a mere trader, hazarding my life among the savages to make money for my employers. The sale of liquor is one of the most profitable branches of a trader's business, and, since the appetite for the vile potion had already been created, my personal influence in the matter was very slight. I was no lawgiver . . . if I had refused to sell it to the Indians, plenty more traders would have furnished it to them . . . and my conscientious scruples . . . would deprive my embarrassed employer of a very considerable source of profit.[11]

Beckwourth recalled that Sublette and Vasquez had a successful fall and winter trade, making enough money to clear Sublette's debts and leaving enough to outfit the next season's trade. That winter, however, was to prove a disappointment; in 1840 the firm sold out.[12]

But for Beckwourth the years with Vasquez and Sublette had been rich in another way. They left him with a fund of Indian stories for his reminiscences and they apparently cemented a long-term friendship with the Cheyennes—a friendship that ended only with the so-called "Chivington massacre" nearly thirty years later.

Bent, St. Vrain and Company had triumphed once again; it was not long until Jim was on their payroll, dealing with the same customers as before. Isolated instances of liquor-inspired quarrels and threats of death were, with one exception, easily handled. The close call occurred while he was stationed at the Laramie Fork of the North Platte. When the furious Cheyennes attempted his life, Jim "fled to a post in the Arrap-a-ho country, in charge of Mr. Alex. Wharfield, now a colonel in the army; he resigned the post to me, and took my place at Bent's post."[13] From there, Beckwourth ranged the Arapaho country for a while; when the fall hunt ended, he returned to Bent's Fort and assisted the other employees in loading wagons for St. Louis.

But that was enough. Jim had begun to weary of the monotony of his life. "I was within five days' journey of New Mexico, and I determined upon going to take a look at the northern portion of this unbounded territory."[14] With one other man, Charles Towne, he made the rugged journey over the passes and down into Taos. There Jim formed a partnership with an old acquaintance ("Lee").[15] They returned to the Cheyennes to trade on their own account, with plenty of liquor and a fine stock of "fancy articles." Again it was necessary to deal with dangers inherent in the noisy, drunken gatherings that trading always produced. Jim Beckwourth thought he was equal to the challenge.

I deposited my goods at Old Bark's lodge, who felt highly honored with the trust. The villagers collected round, and a dispute arose among them whether the whisky should be broached or not. Porcupine Bear objected, and Bobtailed Horse, his brother-in-law, strongly advocated my opening the kegs. This led to a warm altercation between the two warriors, until the disputed question was to be decided by the arbitrament of battle. They both left the lodge to prepare for the combat, and returned in a few minutes fully armed and equipped.[16]

Beckwourth must have known Porcupine Bear, but he has evidently misplaced him in time. The latter, in 1837, had become an "outlaw," ostracized for the killing of Little Creek. Beckwourth traded with two outlaw camps in the Cheyenne-Arapaho area; probably he met this warrior in one of them. The outcast may have returned to his tribe by the time of Beckwourth's visit, but his counsel would have been ignored—an outlaw could never regain his former high status in the tribe.[17] However, Beckwourth assigns to Porcupine Bear a powerful and moving speech in which he decries the use of alcohol in trading. For the sake of regaining their former strength and skill, for peace and plenty in the lodge, for courage and pride, he implored his tribesmen to abstain:

> Our fires begin to burn dim, and will soon go out entirely.
> . . . I have spoken all I have to say, and if my brother wishes
> to kill me for it, I am ready to die. I will go and sit with my
> fathers in the spirit land, where I shall soon point down to the
> last expiring fire of the Cheyennes, and when they inquire
> the cause of this decline of their people, I will tell them with
> a straight tongue that it was the fire-water of the trader that
> put it out.[18]

The appeal failed. Old Bark permitted the trading to begin. "We will all drink this once," he said, "but we will not act like fools. . . ." According to his invariable custom, Jim dealt first with the women, each of whom was usually allowed by her mate to keep a robe or two to trade for food or other necessities, possibly even for finery. All knew that if the men traded first, few wives would have anything left with which to barter.

As a result of this venture, Lee and Beckwourth were able to set themselves up as merchants in Taos. "Here we established a store . . . for the Indian trade, where I resided for some time, living very fast and happily, according to the manner of the inhabitants. Among other doings, I got married to Senorita Louise Sandeville [Luisa Sandoval]."[19]

In October, 1842, Beckwourth took his wife north to the Arkansas and there he built a trading post. Although sometimes he is credited with being the founder of Pueblo, it will be seen that Beckwourth does not claim the honor for himself alone.

We reached the Arkansas about the first of October, 1842, where I erected a trading post, and opened a successful business. [A "trading post" could be a mere shelter on a river bank; it was not necessarily a fort.] In a very short time I was joined by from fifteen to twenty free trappers, with their families. We all united our labors, and constructed an adobe fort sixty yards square. By the following spring we had grown into quite a little settlement and *we gave it the name of Pueblo.* Many of the company devoted themselves to agriculture, and raised very good crops the first season, such as wheat, corn, oats, potatoes, and abundance of almost all kinds of vegetables.[20]

A rough, tough crew gathered at Pueblo and many a brawl must have taken place as the "Taos lightning" made the rounds. Jim Beckwourth got into his share of trouble: tradition has it that he quarreled with Old Bill Williams, who ended by calling Jim "a low-down half-breed nigger Frenchman." Those were fighting words and Beckwourth came at Williams with a knife. According to the story, Williams knocked his assailant unconscious.[21]

There is no reason to disbelieve the tale, except that Bill Williams was much older than Jim[22] and far more dissipated; it would take a powerful blow to bring down an enraged Beckwourth. Whatever the circumstances, the affair was in keeping with the reputation of El Pueblo: David Lavender has said that this was "a collecting spot for the scum of the mountains." Nevertheless, several of the early Pueblo settlers and visitors moved on eventually to California and became responsible businessmen and civic leaders.[23]

The Pueblans were not popular in Bent country, for Charles and William Bent saw the newcomers as competitors of their own great trading firm. Though this company had always used liquor as an inducement to trade, Charles Bent wrote to D. D. Mitchell, Superintendent of Indian Affairs (he had been in the employ of the American Fur Company when Jim was with the Crow nation). "There are several renegate [sic] Americans, who have built houses on the Arkansas river. . . . This [Pueblo] is also a harbor for all Mexican traders. . . . The only mode to put a stop to the liquor trade from Mexico is to establish a military post."[24] Other such attempts came to nothing and Pueblo was not abandoned until the Ute massacre of 1854.[25]

Sporadic conflicts between Mexico and Texas meanwhile had somewhat lessened the welcome that citizens of the United States could expect below the border. Jim was forced to look elsewhere, now that he was out of the good graces of the Bents as well as the Mexicans. He decided upon California. Taking fifteen men and loading his goods on horses that he obtained by trading whisky, Jim was soon on his way. Three Mexicans who accompanied his party straggled behind and paid for it with their lives, the Utes being particularly hostile toward their Mexican neighbors. The others arrived in Pueblo de (los) Angeles in January, 1844, and there Beckwourth indulged his "new passion for trade."

Out of more than "two hundred foreigners shown by the records to have visited California in 1844. . . ," says Hubert H. Bancroft, "one hundred may be regarded as pioneer residents.

... .["]26 Beckwourth's name is fourth on the appended list. There were other familiar names as well. Thomas Fallon, for one, had worked for the Bents until a brawl on July 4, 1843, ended in his killing another man; he then found it convenient to join Frémont's expedition of that year. Daingerfield Fauntleroy, whose ancestors were peers of the Beckwiths of Virginia, must have seemed as much out of place with the rugged mountain men as his name is different from plain Jim Waters or Caleb Greenwood, who were also listed. Alexis Godey, who set out to be a permanent resident of California in 1849, was a "pioneer resident" in 1844, along with Louis Robidoux, who had been a Santa Fe trader at least as early as 1827.[27] Doubtless Beckwourth had known nearly every man listed at one time or another.

With his usual talent for being at the scene of excitement and action, Beckwourth found himself embroiled in the 1845 revolution of the Californians against Mexican control. According to Bancroft, he "was one of the mountaineers serving against Micheltorena, at the battle of Cahuenga in '45 . . . of which he gives an absurdly false account. Before the troubles of '46 he left California with a large drove of stolen horses to continue his career in New Mexico."[28]

In relating his experience in the attempt to expel Governor Micheltorena, Beckwourth (or Bonner) encounters the usual difficulty with names. Micheltorena becomes "Torrejon," and Rowland, one of the leaders in recruiting the insurgents, according to Bancroft, is called "Roland" by Jim. Juan Alvarado is not even mentioned. The fact that Beckwourth had only a superficial understanding of the etiology and seriousness of the civil diseases that beset California is of little importance. He was producing a popular adventure tale, not a history. Even so, he seems to have grasped the "comic opera" atmosphere that prevailed; it was a perfect setting for James P. Beckwourth, actor. On this make-believe level, Jim directs "his" men up hill and down dale; *he* persuades the mountain men to desert the governor's ranks and come over to the rebels; *he* reconnoiters the enemy position, waiting until it should be in proper range (it never was) before attacking. But on the highlights and essential facts of the battle of Cahuenga, Beckwourth is often substantiated by Bancroft; the former's account is important mainly for the picture it gives of United States citizens casually interfering in the affairs of another nation, as though, in fact, they were on their own soil.

The air of California was heavy not only with resentment toward Mexico, the mother country, but also with apprehension over this increasing arrogance of the "foreigners," who were beginning to act as though *that* title belonged to the Californians. Then came news of the war between the United States and Mexico. It was a time to take up sides, and for Jim Beckwourth there was only one choice. He went home to Pueblo.

But not entirely unaccompanied. He, with

> five trusty Americans, collected eighteen hundred stray horses we found roaming on the Californian ranches, and started with our utmost speed from Pueblo de Angeles. This was a fair capture and our morals justified it, for it was war-time. We knew we should be pursued, and we lost no time in making our way toward home. . . . We again found the advantage that I have often spoken of before of having a drove of horses before us, for, as the animals we bestrode gave out, we could shift to a fresh one, while our pursuers were confined to one steed.[29]

Home was not quite the home it had been: Jim's wife had remarried. Beckwourth accused the new husband, John Brown, Sr., of having deceived her with a forged document expressing Jim's wish to be free. "She manifested extreme regret at having suffered herself to be imposed upon so readily, and, as a remedy for the evil, offered herself back again; but I declined," said Beckwourth coldly, "preferring to enjoy once more the sweets of single blessedness."[30]

In common with many mountain men, Jim Beckwourth was

apparently incapable of forming any deep, satisfying attachment based on affection for one woman. His heart was as errant as his feet, and his needs were as basic as hunger. It hurt him not at all to leave Luisa Sandoval, the mother of his infant daughter.

Having no perception or concern about the needs of his wives, Jim's observations about them ("very pretty, intelligent young women") are shallow. His interest in their lives was nonexistent. They were wives. They cooked, scraped hides, sewed, did their beadwork, bore children, cooked, sewed, and went to bed again. With the possible exception of the "Little Wife," he expresses no warmth, and in her case affection was tinged with amusement. Yet the number of his wives alone would indicate that he was not despised by women.

Inevitably, Jim Beckwourth and the other mountain men around Santa Fe and Taos were caught up in the swift-moving events of 1846. The "bloodless conquest" of Santa Fe provided Jim with a job he liked: he carried dispatches for the army and acted as guide and interpreter. Equally as surely, he got into trouble: someone accused him of conniving with the Indians to steal army horses and otherwise betray his trust. A respected defender—the local newspaper—came to his assistance:

> Injustice. We learn from the St. Louis papers that reports injurious to the good name of Jim Beckwourth, well known in the States as a mountain man, have obtained publicity and currency there; and we take this occasion to say they are believed here to be entirely unfounded. He has had no connexion whatever with the hostile Indians, and at all times was a good citizen, acting as Col. Willock's guide when he marched against them. A communication has been handed in from him concerning it, but is too lengthy for publication, and contains personal reflections which make it objectionable, as we exclude all such.[31]

In Santa Fe, Jim and his partner operated the hotel so graphically described by Lewis Garrard. Although he is not named, it has been deduced that the "partner" in this enterprise was Jim Waters. He had gone to California with Beckwourth and, on their return, had traded with John Brown at the latter's store on the Greenhorn, late in 1846. Waters' name did not appear again in Brown's account books until the spring of 1848. He may, therefore, have been living in Santa Fe in the interim.[32]

Beckwourth's hotel saw the comings and goings of army officers and men, of traders suddenly freed from the onerous red tape of dealing with Mexican officials, of Mexicans who may or may not have known of the rebellious plot that resulted in the dreadful slaughter of Charles Bent and Circuit Attorney James White Leal; of Narciso Beaubien and Charles Bent's young brother-in-law Pablo Jaramillo; of Prefect Cornelio Vigil and Sheriff Steve Lee, at San Fernandez de Taos.[33]

It was to Jim's hotel that Charles Towne (who himself would soon die at the hands of the Apaches) raced, after that night of horrors, to bring the news of the massacre and to seek help.[34] Probably the mountain men, friends and employees of William and Charles Bent, gathered there, eager for revenge. Jim Beckwourth left the hotel to look after itself and went along with his comrades:

> All the ox-drivers, mule-drivers, merchants, clerks, and commissariat-men were formed into rank and file, and placed in a condition for holding the city. Then, placing himself at the head of his army, four hundred strong, General [Sterling] Price marched toward Taos. On arriving at Canjarra [Cañada], a small town about twenty miles from Santa Fe, we found the enemy, numbering two thousand Mexicans and Indians, were prepared to give us battle. The enemy's lines were first perceived by our advance guard, which instantly fell back upon the main body. Our line was formed and an advance made upon the enemy, the mountaineer company, under Captain Saverine [St. Vrain], being placed in charge of the baggage. As soon as the battle was begun, however, we left the baggage

and ammunition wagons to take care of themselves, and made a descent upon the foe. He fled precipitately before the charge of our lines, and we encamped upon the field of battle. The next day we advanced to Lamboda [Embudo], where the enemy made another stand, and again fled on our approach.[35]

Ralph Emerson Twitchell, the early historian of New Mexico, gives a similar version:

The insurgents were assembled in force near the present village of Santa Cruz, twenty-five miles north of Santa Fe, under Generals Ortiz and Montoya, with a view to making an assault upon the Capital. Colonel Price met them at Cañada, the enemy numbering about two thousand men. The American force consisted of four hundred and eighty men and four pieces of artillery, mountain howitzers. . . . A sharp fire from the howitzers was directed against the enemy, but with little effect, whereupon Colonel Price ordered Captain Angney to charge the hill, which was gallantly done, being supported by Captain St. Vrain with a company of citizen soldiers. . . . The enemy was hotly pursued by Price and was again encountered at Embudo. . . . A charge was ordered and was made by three companies under Captain Burgwin and Captain St. Vrain and Lieutenant White, resulting in the total route [sic] of the insurgents.[36]

Jim Beckwourth, of course, witnessed the defeat of the Indian and Mexican rebels at Taos and saw the hangings that brought final retribution for the murders committed on the night of January 19, 1847.

Jim stayed on in the southwest another year or so, carrying dispatches and roaming about on various jobs for the commissary or the quartermaster. His trips between Fort Leavenworth and Santa Fe brought newspaper attention:

J. Beckwourth, an old campaigner, who was entrusted with the express for the U.S., which left this place on the 21st, arrived at Fort Leavenworth Dec. 13th. The Indians ran him back from the crossing of Red River, to the place Major

Edmonson fought them, and from that place he went to Turkey Mountain, from which place he took a direct route to Ft. Leavenworth, without road, trail or anything else. He had to turn in to Fort Mann, to get fresh animals, his being broken down trying to escape the Indians—at Pawnee Fork, he saw a large party of Pawnees, from which he ran to the big bend of the Arkansas, where he saw another party, when he retreated and dug holes, expecting to be forced to fight, but they failed to discover him, at night he started and came to Cow Creek, having a very cold night to travel. Thinking that he had escaped all danger, he laid down and turned his mules out, and at day break, as usual, he was up, and saw an Indian approaching who turned out to be a Kaw, from which place he had no further difficulty.

He left Fort Leavenworth Jan. 2 with two others. The winter in the States had been very favorable, and everything prosperous. The day before he left the Fort, news came that Russia and France were about to engage in a war, but we cannot learn all the causes for such a blow up. From Fort Leavenworth to Fort Mann, he had no difficulty. Two companies of Gilpin's battalion are quartered at this place, numbering about one hundred and fifty men. There he learned that Pawnees and Comanches were on the Arkansas, and that he might expect to meet enemies. The artillery company of this battalion was to leave the next day for Bent's Fort, and he staid one day to have an escort and protection. The next day he left and camped at the place designated, but they failed to reach it and camped about three miles behind. Between sundown and dark they fired the cannon five times in rapid succession, and he waited to hear if they had a battle, but not hearing from them, he started and travelled all that night and all the succeeding day, —about sunset he saw a party of eleven men, about three miles off, charging on him, and he travelled on five or six hundred yards to find a suitable place for defence, but having nothing but the open prairie, he tied all his mules to one, and the young man with him being inexperienced on the plains, he took his rifle and made him hold the animals. He advanced about twenty-five yards, and enquired who they were, when they neither spoke nor made signs, and continued to advance. He then fired and shot one, and took up the other gun and shot another. They then retreated and he reloaded, when they charged and he fired again and continued to shoot. In all he shot seven times, and thinks he killed two and wounded three. They then left and he travelled on, not wishing to be detained longer. The Indians were Pawnees. From this he met with no hostile Indians until he reached the Vermeho, where he fell in with a party of Bent and St. Vrain's men, and the Indians (Apachees) pursued them to the Moro.

Here he left the road and took to the mountains, crossing direct from the Moro to this place, where he arrived on Thursday last. He met Fisher, who carried an express between Fr. Mann and Pawnee Fork, Mr. Aubry he met at the Hundred and Ten on the 4th of Jan., having been thirteen days out from this place. Mr. Beckwourth suffered much from sickness until he reached Bent's Fort. There was but little snow on the prairie, and the grass was burnt from Pawnee Fork to Council Grove. Gilpin's battalion were all at Bent's Fort, excepting those stationed at Man's Fort.[37]

A Fort Leavenworth correspondent filed the following:

Messrs. Editors — An express arrived at this place last night from Chihuhua [sic]. It was brought from Santa Fe by James Beckwourth, an old mountain man, Charles McIntosh, a half-breed Cherokee and Henry Hamilton on the 26th of June and were seventeen days making the trip. There is no Santa Fe news of any interest.

Soon after leaving Bent's Fort, they arrived at a village of the Cheyenne Indians containing about 1000 lodges. A large number of the Arapahoes, Kiowas, Apaches and other Indians had joined the Cheyennes. They learned from these Indians, that the Pawnees had assembled in large numbers on the Smoky Hill Fork, about a days' travel from the Cheyenne village. Their object in assembling in these large bodies is unknown. It is supposed that the Pawnees had been driven from the Platte River by Col. Powell's troops.

Kit Carson, with eight men and thirteen mules, was to have left Taos the day after Beckwourth, and was intending to have joined him. Though Beckwourth delayed some time, hoping that Carson would overtake him, nothing has been seen or heard of him. It is feared that he may have been cut off by the Pawnees. . . .

Beckwourth and McIntosh start tomorrow for Santa Fe. . . .[38]

Beckwourth, when talking to Bonner, recalled the incident of having missed Kit Carson, but he misdated it, his memory telling him that it occurred in 1846. He also remembered "my brave and faithful friend, M'Intosh," and mentioned that he was known to the other Plains Indians as a Cherokee, but the significance of his comment is not clear.

Beckwourth told Bonner that his shortest trip from Santa Fe to Fort Leavenworth was eighteen days, not seventeen; in any case, if he left Leavenworth on July 30 he arrived home in ample time to settle his affairs and to make preparations for going to California. Late in the month of August, 1848, he was on the Old Spanish Trail, headed for new adventures.

"Most Terrible Tragedy"

Diarists are notorious for omitting the names of their associates in exciting events: General Ashley himself has caused many a baffled groan by his failure to name the men who took part in his adventures. Who, for example, *did* pull the general's boat from Green River just as "she was about making her exit and me with her for I cannot swim"? With barely a nod of gratitude, Ashley says "two of the most active men" saved his life.[1]

Yet, now and again, the casual mention of an employee or comrade can settle some irksome question for the biographer. Thus, Orville Pratt has helped to place Jim Beckwourth in Santa Fe in late summer of 1848. Pratt was going to California on a mission for the War Department and he required an escort.[2] Among the sixteen or more men he engaged was one "Beckwith," named as a member of Pratt's own mess. The latter also kept a list of men who were indebted to him: this time, Jim is "James P. Beckwourth Dr to one pair blankets $14.00."[3] (All accounts, including Jim's, were marked "settled.")

Pratt's party set out on August 27, 1848. Jim, of course, recalled that *he* was the bearer of dispatches and, therefore, casts himself as the leader of the group. He does not even mention Orville Pratt; in the style of the diarists, he ignores the other members of his "escort of fifteen men." Jim promptly gets his charges as far as "Abbeger," a Bonnerism for Abiquiú, a little village northwest of Santa Fe. Immediately, there was trouble: a large party of Apaches was on a drunken spree. "We camped inside the corral," said Beckwourth, "that being as safe a place as we could select." But Jim had to play his role: he sallied forth to settle the matter.

I visited every place in town where [liquor] was kept, and informed every seller that, if another drop was sold to the Indians, I would hang the man that did it without a minute's delay; and I would have been as good as my word, for they were all Mexicans, and I had felt no great liking for them since the awful tragedy at Taos.[4]

Pratt, having been delayed, arrived on August 29 and found "my men who had been sent from Santa Fe as far as Ab. to graze and wait for us to come up, on their retreat! The Apaches had threatened to attack them—500 in number & the Al cade of Ab. had advised them to go out of town."[5] At first glance, it seems that Beckwourth has spun another yarn—until one remembers that he was in Pratt's mess and probably came in with him. Further, Pratt recorded that they did go into the village and there was no more trouble with the Indians. "The Spaniards evidently were the worst of the crowd," according to Pratt.[6] Having the added strength of Pratt's group to back him up, it is entirely possible that Jim did just what he said he did.

Other trifling incidents in Jim's story—the loss of a gun to the Utes, for example—are confirmed by Pratt's diary. In the case of the rifle, Beckwourth may have appropriated another's role, for on September 3 Pratt said, "A Euta Indian . . . got a gun from Wilson one of my men to go & get some game for our supper, did not come into camp; and it is suspected that he has given us the slip[.]"[7] Jim says *he* lent a gun "belonging to one of my men" to an Indian who went in search of game. Eight days after this incident, Pratt recorded the theft of another rifle; if Jim's was stolen, however, it did not suit his purposes to admit it. Beckwourth's brief assessment of the causes for Indian hostility toward the party agrees very well with Pratt's, as does his description of the behavior and numbers of the various tribes.

Pratt's journey was difficult. The group was frequently lost (was Jim the guide?), and the men and their animals occasionally went without water and food. They arrived in Los Angeles on October 25, 1848, almost two months after leaving Santa Fe. Orville Pratt rode north to Monterey, and apparently Beckwourth went with him. There, their paths inevitably separated, Pratt's to lead him to a distinguished career in law[8] and Jim's to take him into one of the more macabre of his adventures.

After rambling about the environs of Monterey for a brief time, Jim "engaged in the service of the commissariat at Monterey, to carry dispatches to Captain Denny's ranch, where I was met by another carrier." No detail of Jim's reminiscences had caused more confusion than Bonner's recording the name of "Denny's" ranch. There was a "Denny's" northeast of Monterey,[9] on the way to the Stanislaus mines, but if Jim's route took him to San Miguel, as he says, he obviously could not use that direction. A manuscript in the Bancroft Library calls the ranch "Cenny's," but no such name appears in any directory consulted.[10]

As it turns out, Beckwourth was referring to Captain William Dana's ranch in Nipomo, a few miles north of what is now Santa Maria.[11] Contrary to the usual rules of pronunciation, the first "a" in "Dana" is short, thus increasing the similarity in sound to "Denny." It may be that Bonner was familiar with the northern waystop to the mines and assumed that Beckwourth was speaking of it. Once the identity of the ranch is known, an astonishing array of evidence confirms Jim's story that on his route from Dana's *rancho* he stumbled across one of the most atrocious crimes of that unruly period in California's history.

> On my road lay the mission of San Miguel, owned by a Mr. Reed, an Englishman;[12] and, as his family was a very interesting one, I generally made his home my resting place. On one of my visits, arriving about dusk, I entered the house as usual, but was surprised to see no one stirring. I walked about a little to attract attention, and no one coming to me, I stepped into the kitchen to look for some of the inmates. On the floor I saw some one lying down, asleep, as I supposed.

I attempted to rouse him with my foot, but he did not stir. This seemed strange, and my apprehensions became excited; for the Indians were very numerous about, and I was afraid some mischief had been done. I returned to my horse for my pistols, then, lighting a candle, I commenced a search. In going along a passage, I stumbled over the body of a woman; I entered a room, and found another, a murdered Indian woman, who had been a domestic. I was about to enter another room, but I was arrested by some sudden thought which urged me to search no farther. It was an opportune admonition, for that very room contained the murderers of the family, who had heard my steps and were sitting at that moment with their pistols pointed at the door, ready to shoot the first person that entered. This they confessed subsequently.[13]

Jim went for help and returned with a posse of some fifteen men. "On again entering the house, we found eleven bodies all thrown together in one pile for the purpose of consuming them; for, on searching further, we found the murderers had set fire to the dwelling, but according to that Providence which exposes such wicked deeds, the fire had died out."[14]

Bonner concludes Jim's story with the assertion that the execution of the criminals "ended the lives of two Americans, two Englishmen, and ten Irishmen." There was no reason for Beckwourth to have exaggerated in this way—he had drama enough at hand. Knowing Bonner's ear, one can conclude that Jim had said, "and an Irishman."

Jim could have heard the lurid tale of the Reed murders around the miners' camps or picked it up from newspaper accounts. But there are far too many references to his part in this tragic discovery to doubt that he was, indeed, the *correo* who brought the first news of it.

William Reed was a partner of Petronilo Rios, whose *hacienda* lay some nine miles south of Mission San Miguel, at El Paso de Robles. Mrs. Reed was a niece of Señora Rios. The two men had bought the mission in 1846; for many years after Reed's death, it was considered the sole property of Rios.[15] In 1877 the widow of Petronilo Rios dictated to Thomas Savage her recollections of the massacre:

In the year of 1849 [1848], in the month of December, Mr. William Reed, an Englishman married to Maria Antonia Vallejo, a native of Monterey, was living in the old mission of San Miguel. These people had in their company a brother of hers, named José Ramon, and a little boy of their marriage of two or three years. She was within moments of having another child, for which reason a midwife, named Josefa Olivera, was present. With her was a daughter of the age of fifteen or sixteen years, and a young grandson. Also present was an Indian of about sixty years of age, and with him a grandson four or five years of age. This family, as has been said, lived peacefully in the mission, giving generous hospitality to all those who passed by—and they were many, because of the news of the gold having been recently discovered. For those going north it was absolutely necessary to use this road. This mission had been given to Petronilo Rios and to Mr. Reed by the last Mexican governor, Pio Pico.

One afternoon in the month of December, there arrived three or four [Irishmen?] in the company of an Indian from Mission San Diego, to ask for lodging. The Reeds admitted them and supplied their needs as though they were trusted members of the family. These men remained there as lodgers for some five days. When they left, they asked to change a few coins of gold that they were carrying. Mr. Reed sent his brother-in-law to bring a canvas bag in which were all mixed together gold and silver nuggets that he had acquired with his own work. He changed the coins, and the men took the road late in the afternoon, but they did not continue beyond the neighborhood of Rancho San Marcos, perhaps half a league distant. From there they returned in the middle of the night to the house of the Mission. They sat in conversation with Mr. Reed in a room in which there was a fireplace. The family was in other rooms in the house but the women had not gone to bed—they were found in their daytime clothing. It was already very late when the fire went out. One of the men went to the corridor to cut some wood, taking with him a hatchet.

It is not known when they first struck Mr. Reed, but he was wearing his sombrero and it was cut through at the back of his head; a pool of blood formed where he fell dead. Then they went to the other rooms and began killing their victims there, a trail of blood and a bloody handprint on the wall showing their passage. The two children were killed in their sleep.

After all this, they put all the bodies together, piled one on top of the other in the nearest room. They then went to the kitchen and killed the Negro cook, leaving his body on the floor, and then proceeded to the room where the Indian shepherd slept with his grandson. Their bodies were both left there.

Having committed all these atrocities, these men went to collect the horses that belonged to Mr. Reed, and some that he was keeping for travelers. They got together all the money and the jewelry of the family and even extended their disgraceful behavior to selecting certain clothing. When they had finished, they took to the road, later camping on the river at El Paso de Robles. There they built a fire and it is known that they had breakfast, because they left some cans that were found by the Indians at Paso Robles; they also found a new knife and one little box that contained some gold earrings that had belonged to Maria Antonia.[16]

Señora Rios could not remember whether the frightful news was brought to her by Señor Price, Señor Branch, or the *dispatch carrier*. But, she said, "It is believed that the news was carried all along the Camino by the *correo*; what is certain is that they all left to pursue the assassins, who were captured near Santa Barbara."[17]

Following the capture of four of the murderers, and the subsequent death of one by drowning, a brief trial was held and the three men were executed. Some of these murderers may have been deserters from the *Warren*, then in the harbor at Monterey. One may have been the notorious Peter Raymond, or Remer, of the New York Volunteers. For several weeks prior to the Reed slayings, rewards had been posted for this man's apprehension for the murder of Von Pfister.[18]

The Reed atrocity was long remembered in California and accounts of it turn up in several reminiscences and histories.[19] The most interesting is that of General William T. Sherman, at that time a lieutenant, who clarifies Jim Beckwourth's situation and confirms his presence in Monterey in 1848.

As soon as General S. W. Kearney had established his headquarters in Monterey (March, 1847), he ordered the quartermaster, Captain Folsom, at Yerba Buena (now San Francisco) to establish a semi-monthly mail from San Francisco to San Diego, a distance of 500 miles. Captain Folsom divided the route into four parts—San Francisco to Monterey, Monterey to "Dana's" (Nepomo), Dana's to Los Angeles, and Los Angeles to San Diego. This was the first regular mail route ever established on the Pacific Coast. General Kearney, in May, 1847, returned to what we then called the United States, leaving Colonel R. B. Mason, First Dragoons, in his place, and me as his Adjutant General. All reports, messages, etc., came to me, and I had a small adobe house, with a negro boy, "Jim," who was supposed to take care of me. The mail rider from Monterey to Dana's was an old trapper, Jim Beckworth, a counterpart of Jim Bridger, except that Beckworth was a cross between a voyageur of Canada and a Crow Indian, and was, in my estimate, one of the best chroniclers of events on the plains that I have ever encountered, though his reputation for veracity was not good.

General Sherman says that sometime in the fall of 1848, Jim came in with his saddlebags of mail and breathlessly exclaimed:

"Leftenant, they killed them all, not even sparing the baby." A short time later . . . with an earnestness not to be mistaken,

he reiterated: "Leftenant, I tell you that Reed at San Miguel is
killed, all his family and servants, not excepting the baby." He
then told me, with a vividness not exceeded by Dickens, how
he had received his mail at Dana's, had ridden on to San Louis
Obispo, and so on to San Miguel. . . .

With minor variations, General Sherman repeated Jim's story,
and added, "The whole scene was so horrid that Jim Beckworth,
though he had spent his whole life with Indians and hunters,
confessed that he was *scared*, that he regained his horse down in
the orchard, and did not stop until he reached me, ninety miles
away at Monterey."

Jim told his story to Colonel Mason, who then ordered Sherman to send Lieutenant Ord, with a detachment of soldiers, to
ascertain the facts and to pursue the murderers "to the death."
No other account mentions the presence of troops at the execution, but General Sherman was quite definite about it:

> As before stated, Lieutenant Ord, afterwards Brigadier-
> General E. O. C. Ord, of the regular army, overtook them at
> Angostura Pass, below Santa Barbara, and delivered them to
> the Alcalde, Lewis Dent, brother of Mrs. General Grant.
> They . . . were sentenced to be shot. They *were* shot, Lieu-
> tenant Ord present but not assisting; and no men ever better
> deserved death than these three.[20]

The *California Star and Californian* carried a story that seems
to imply that Jim *wrote* to someone about his experiences at
San Miguel:

> Atrocious Murder. Ten Persons Killed at the Mission of San
> Miguel. Through the kindness of a friend, we have been fur-
> nished with extracts from a private letter from Monterey,
> containing the account of a most fiendish murder. . . . The
> particulars are as follows: Reed had just returned from the
> Stanislaus Mines and had considerable gold. This tempted
> the murderers to this deed, and they carried off from the house

nothing but gold and valuable property. Calicos, mantas, etc., were left strewn about the mission. The man tells that he saw all the dead bodies piled up, to the number of ten, as though intended to be burned; but it is supposed the murderers did not finish this task before they heard some horsemen approaching, when they ran away. They are followed, and this man says he feels sure they have been taken at the Rancho of Alamo's some twenty miles this side of St. Inez. Reed was shot below the ear by a large ball, and all the rest were killed by axes.

This mail man rode up to the mission while the bodies were yet warm, and whilst the blood was oozing from their wounds. He first gave notice of the murder and collected the rancheros and put them on the track, and he would have continued he [sic] pursue, had he not met the bearer of this express and turned to Monterey.

His tale is too minute to admit of doubt, and you may safely assert that Reed of San Miguel, and his entire family, servants and all, were murdered by five white men, believed to be discharged volunteers. . . .[21]

Surely "this mail man" was none other than James P. Beckwourth, who, when he could find no one to talk to, was a great one for writing letters.

The Forty-niner

The lure of the California gold fields was too much; it was only to be expected that Jim Beckwourth should join the tawdry throng on its hopeful way. But he continued to serve as dispatch carrier for some three months after the Reed murders, occasionally altering his route to permit a visit to San Francisco.[1] He took note there of the lawlessness, debauchery (the "rankest excesses"), and the murders that finally resulted in the organization of citizen groups intent upon reprisal and from which the Vigilance Committees eventually grew.

In 1851 Jim was uncritical of the Committees and, ironically, approved their high-handed methods of dealing with criminals, including horse thieves and cattle rustlers. Yet there have always been rumors, never substantiated, that he fled California because the reconstituted Vigilance groups of 1856 were taking a hard look at his part in such activities.

At the end of February Jim could no longer resist: his trading instincts emerged once again, and when "the steamship *California* touched at Monterey, she being the first steam-vessel that had visited there from the States," he stepped aboard.[2]

Jim and a friend debarked at Stockton; carrying a small stock of clothing for sale, they made their way across the country. Probably they followed a well-worn trail over the low rolling hills to William Knight's ferry on the Stanislaus; then up the gentle valley to Jimtown, founded by Colonel George James, a San Francisco attorney.[3] The going became a little rougher, but to an old mountaineer these hills could present few problems. The two followed Woods Creek a few miles northeast until they reached Sonora, tucked into a narrow canyon of the Sierra foothills. Tents and a few stone huts dotted the slopes. Perhaps the residents had already found it necessary to begin shoring up the hillside terraces; today, miles of stonework still assist the narrow winding streets in "the way they should go."

Jim had found an ideal setting for his purposes of the moment. John S. Robb ("Solitaire") who visited the new bonanza while Beckwourth was there, saw it thus:

> "*Sonorania*" [is] about midway between the farthest discovered southern placer and Stockton, and is surrounded by the richest diggings in the mines. The roads from above and below, and north and south, pass through it; it has its principal hotel, its bull-ring for Sunday amusements, its French eating houses, and stores containing not only articles for general use, but luxuries of the most costly character. At night a string of a dozen *monte* tables, all in a row, are in operation on the main street, under awnings in front of the stores; these are not sufficient to supply the anxious candidates; a dozen *serappas*, therefore, may be seen spread upon the ground in the main thoroughfare, and surrounded by the eager votaries of chance. . . . Some of the merchants are already contemplating the erection of substantial buildings on the site occupied by their trading tents.[4]

Their initial success at trading led Jim to send his partner back to Stockton for more goods, while he stayed behind to mind the store and "attend to other affairs." The latter probably included dealing a little monte, or at least sitting in on a game. In any case, Jim says he was soon able to erect a suitable building for his new venture. Shortly, however, the businessman was overcome by the wanderer, "for inactivity fatigued me to death." Jim sold out whatever interest he may have had in the store and headed for Sacramento. It was left to another chronicler of the period to give us the best picture of the Beckwourth of gold-rush days—still cocky, still yarning, already rehearsing the material for his *Life and Adventures.*

In late summer, John M. Letts had set himself up as store-keeper at Mormon Bar, about forty-five miles up American River from Sacramento, and hence met numerous "strange adventurers . . . who have as great an aversion to law and civilization as they have to the manacles of a prison."[5] Letts's store was open but a few days when one of these curiosities hove into sight.

> About nine in the morning, I saw, approaching the store, a strange looking being, mounted on a gray horse, a *poncho* thrown over his shoulder, over which was slung a huge rifle, skins wrapped around his legs, a pair of Mexican spurs on, and a slouched hat which partially obscured his copper complexion. As he rode up, Tracy recognized him as an old mountaineer, whom he had seen in Santa Fe. After the recognition, Tracy says, "Jim, whose horse is that?" Jim—"how do I know whose horse it is?" Tracy—"where did you get him?" Jim—*"I stole him from an Indian, of course."*[6]

Jim announced that he was dead broke and hungry, and his hosts treated him to breakfast. He responded by giving the story of his life, a tale willingly received:

> It was a most exciting romance, interspersed with thrilling adventures and "hair-breadth 'scapes." I was convinced that his story, in the main, was true, not because he *swore* to it all, but because Tracy was acquainted with the most important facts. He was a mixture of the negro, Indian, and Anglo-Saxon blood, and born in New Mexico.[7]

Letts mentions Jim's early training, as he calls it, in the art of horse and mule stealing, and repeats some of Jim's highflown claims of his value to the army by the exercise of this talent. Jim related that he had been a chief of the Crow Indians and that he still had a wife and child among them. Tracy and Letts must have listened eagerly to his instruction in reading Indian sign language and in some of the finer points of woodcraft, for Letts recorded it at length. Then back to more personal matters:

Jim's legs had the appearance of being bound with cords under the skin, in consequence of the general rupture of the blood vessels. He says he was taken prisoner by the Indians, and in making his escape was chased ninety miles, without stopping for food or rest. The condition of his limbs then compelled him to stop, and secrete himself, where, in consequence of his lameness, he was obliged to remain for three weeks subsisting on roots. Jim, with his other accomplishments, was considered one of the best "*monte*" dealers in Mexico. On visiting the frontier towns, he would spend his time in gambling. Sometimes he would win several thousand dollars in one night, and the next day he would have every man drunk in town; what he could not spend in drink, he would give to the poor, or to his friends. Money was an incumbrance to which he would not submit. After remaining two or three days he mounted his horse and started up the river, designing, as I supposed, not to return.[8]

But Letts had not seen the last of his grateful guest. Some three weeks later, Jim and Old Gray came flying up to the door at a wild gallop, causing Letts to wonder which one would arrive first. On entering, Jim threw a handkerchief, filled with gold and silver, on the counter and exclaimed, "Well, I vow, Captain, I've made a raise." The silver he pressed upon Letts, assuring him that he himself had not the least use for it.

He had been up the river twenty miles, had fallen in with a Mormon who had some money, and who proposed that Jim should deal "monte" and share the profits; in a few nights they had won $13,000; the half of this was more money than he cared to have on him at any one time, and was on his way to Sacramento to spend it. He felt in high spirits and as there were two gamblers along in the evening, who wished to open a "monte bank," he wished me to allow them to do so, which I did; they had a capital of a few hundred dollars, and Jim was to try his luck at betting, which, by-the-way, he understood *as well* as the other branch of the game. He watched the run of the cards for some time, then wished to cut them; soon he made a small bet—it won; he made a larger bet, and won it also; after making a few successful bets, he *"tapped the bank,"* and won it; at about midnight he mounted Old Gray for Sacramento, with as much money as he could conveniently carry.[9]

The next morning a traveler reported to Letts that he had come upon Jim sleeping under a tree, his money pouch forming a cushion under his head; he had traveled about five miles on his way to town. Reports filtered back to Mormon Bar that Jim had taken Sacramento City *in toto* as his guest and had provided entertainment suitable to the occasion.

He had all the inhabitants drunk who were disposed that way . . . and one week after his advent, he had *invested* his last dollar. He had engaged to pilot the mail through to Santa Fe, for the government, and the time arrived while he was *entertaining* the city. Of course, he could not leave just then, and when the officer in charge ordered him to start, he declared in the *strongest* language, that he considered himself full as good as some men, and better than others. The result was that he was put in irons. One day of such confinement would be sufficient to bring him to his senses, and make him long for his mountain air. I have no doubt that, ere this, he has seen the mail safely deposited at Santa Fe, and is, perhaps, again extensively engaged in the mule trade.[10]

This last report seems to be hearsay, but there is some evidence that Jim returned to Santa Fe at least once after his departure with Orville Pratt.

Beckwourth may have encountered old friends while on his Sacramento spree: John Brown, Sr., James W. Waters, V. J. Herring, and Alexis Godey, and others had arrived at Sutter's Fort on September 15.[11] One wonders if Jim saw Luisa Sandoval (Brown) who, with her children, including Jim's daughter, had accompanied her husband.

The year was wearing on, and Jim was footloose again. Not

caring enough for money to brave the icy streams or to labor over a "rocker," he wandered until he found an old comrade, "Chapineau," on Murderer's Bar, a couple of miles south of Auburn. Charbonneau was "house-keeping," and Jim moved in, to stay until the rains came.[12] Here James Haley White came across "Beckweth" once again. White says that he had gone to school with "Choboneau" in St. Louis. "The last time I saw this person was in the year 1849 in passing on a road from Sacramento to Cold Springs to Placeville [sic] Cal. I stopped at a house for a night and it was kept by Jim Beckweth and John Baptiste Chaboneau [sic]."[13] Jim, according to White, had been "accused by General Kearney of aiding the Mexicans and disloyality [sic] to his country during the Mexican war, and a sum was offered for his head; but he gave sufficient evidence to satisfy the government that he was innocent of the charges, and complained to me . . . of such unjust accusations by his countrymen."[14]

From Murderer's Bar (now El Dorado), Jim made his way to Greenwood Valley, where John Greenwood, son of Old Caleb, had settled in '48 as a trader.[15] This exquisite spot, heavily forested with pine and dense shrubbery, offered an ideal shelter, but unfortunately Jim suffered an attack of inflammatory rheumatism and he "had a nice time of it that winter." Nevertheless, he was able to help out the residents by killing a grizzly bear. The later memory of that event reminded Jim of still other bear stories for his book. One of these had to do with a man called (by Bonner) "Keyere." This man was spare of build and never weighed more than one hundred pounds. He was able, even so, to knock down a grizzly with his fist. The bear was too quick; it again grasped Keyere, who, in his desperation, seized the animal by the tongue and, holding it thus, plunged a knife into its heart. The story was repeated from camp to camp as a good joke, but Jim avers that the evidence bore out the tale. What is more, Beckwourth himself took no credit for any part of the exploit.[16]

With the arrival of spring, Jim prospected a little along the American River, apparently, for there is some evidence that he went to Michigan Bluff.[17] As usual, Jim Beckwourth attracted attention even in that remote outpost, for someone contributed this confused report:

> Some distance above Michigan Bluff, between Big Secret and Van Clief cañons is a smaller stream than either of the two named, but having the same general course, as the waters flowing down it find their way into the North Fork of the Middle Fork, and is known as Antoine Cañon. It was first discovered to contain gold by a half-breed Indian who came into California in company with Jim Beckwourth from the Crow Indian country. Antoine (or Antwine, as always pronounced) in the spring of 1850, was one of the Bronson party that came to Bird's Valley and the mouth of El Dorado Cañon, near Michigan Bluff, but not liking the outlook there had returned to Pilot Hill. . . . The Indians about Pilot Hill that spring, being quite numerous, were saucy as well, and inclined to be troublesome. While coming to this country, Beckwourth and Antoine, though of Indian blood themselves, had been attacked by the Shoshones, and badly used, having lost their animals and everything else but their lives, which they barely saved by their superior art and endurance as plainsmen.[18]

But Beckwourth's preferred route lay north. He and a companion (Antoine?) went to American Valley, thence to Pit River country, prospecting and, perforce, hunting as in the old days. Nothing much came of it and the only outstanding event, in Jim's view, was that he saw a pass, "far away to the southward that seemed lower than any other." He kept silent about it, but resolved that at some future date he would do a little exploring.

> After a short stay in the American Valley, I again started out with a prospecting party of twelve men. We killed a bullock before starting and dried the meat, in order to have provisions

Louis Vasquez (Courtesy State Historical Society of Colorado)

Old Fort Vasquez (Courtesy State Historical Society of Colorado)

Ruins of Old Church at Taos, site of retaliatory action by soldiers
and mountain men following murder of Governor Charles Bent
(Photograph by Elinor Wilson)

Captain Edward L. Berthoud, under whom Beckwourth served as an army guide in 1862 (Courtesy State Historical Society of Colorado)

Major General Stephen Watts Kearny, during the Mexican War. James P. Beckwourth served him as dispatch carrier (From a mezzotint engraving in the Library of Congress, taken from an original daguerreotype engraved for *Graham's Magazine* by J. B. Welch. Courtesy U.C.L.A. Photographic Department)

Lieutenant George L. Shoup (later Colonel) for whom Jim Beckwourth acted as guide and interpreter at the Battle of Sand Creek (Courtesy Denver Public Library)

Colonel John M. Chivington, commander of the Battle of Sand Creek, where he used Jim Beckwourth as a guide (Courtesy of Library, State Historical Society of Colorado)

"Sand Creek Battle," painting by Robert Lindneux (Courtesy State Historical Society of Colorado)

Morman Bar (From John M. Letts's *California Illustrated*)

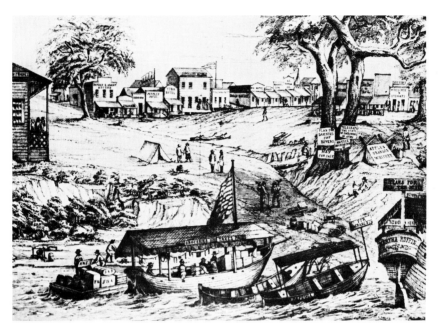

Marysville Plaza, Alta California (Courtesy Marysville City Library)

Adobe Fort at Pueblo (Courtesy State Historical Society of Colorado)

to last us during the trip. We proceeded in an easterly direction, and all busied themselves in searching for gold; but my errand was of a different character: I had come to discover what I suspected to be a pass.

It was the latter end of April when we entered upon an extensive valley at the northwest extremity of the Sierra Range. The valley was already robed in freshest verdure, contrasting most delightfully with the huge snowclad masses of rock we had just left. Flowers of every variety and hue spread their variegated charms before us; magpies were chattering, and gorgeously-plumaged birds were caroling in the delights of unmolested solitude. Swarms of wild geese and ducks were swimming on the surface of the cool crystal stream, which was the central fork of the Rio de las Plumas, or sailed the air in clouds over our heads. Deer and antelope filled the plains, and their boldness was conclusive that the hunter's rifle was to them unknown. Nowhere visible were any traces of the white man's approach, and it is probable that our steps were the first that ever marked the spot. . . . This, I at once saw, would afford the best wagon-road into the American Valley. . . .[19]

Three of the most trustworthy men in his party were taken into his confidence and Jim says that they engaged to assist him in the opening of the road.

It has been said that Jim could not have discovered the pass in 1850. The argument has been that he could not have gone to Pit River that winter, returned to American Valley, and arrived at Beckwourth Valley at the end of April. Furthermore, it has been stated that there were no bullocks in American Valley for Jim to slaughter in 1850 (although there were some in 1851) and that the Turner brothers, proprietors of the American Ranch, did not settle there until late summer of 1850.[20]

The counterargument is that 1850 was well into spring—there would still be storms, but the coldest months were over. The road from American Valley to Beckwourth's Pass was comparatively easy; the deepest canyons and highest ridges lay far behind, to

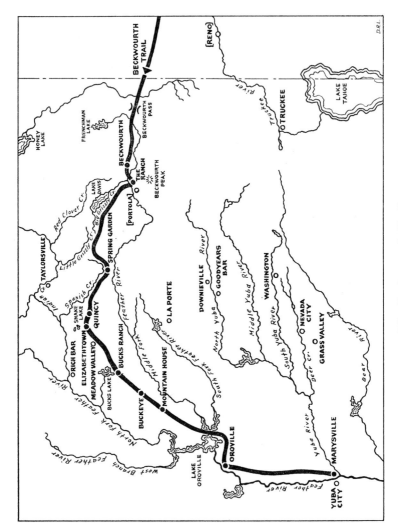

The Beckwourth Trail

the west and north. As to the "bullock," Beckwourth does not say that he killed it at American *Ranch* (now Quincy). It is perfectly possible that he told Bonner that the party killed a "bull elk," an animal not unknown in those regions. Jim does not mention "Mr. Turner" until speaking of his own return to American Valley, and there is no way of knowing how long he and his road builders remained in their own valley to the east.

Finally, in midwinter of the year 1851, young John Steele and one companion, John Donnelley, made a trek into this country in an unsuccessful attempt to locate eighteen of their company who had set out the previous year. The two men departed from Poorman's Creek, a tributary of Nelson Creek, on January 27, intending to go to the North Fork of the Feather River.[21] With little comprehension of what they were facing, they took provisions for two weeks and came close to starving; they encountered Indians, severe storms, and wolves. Their journey led them northwest, across the Middle Fork of the Feather and then west below American Ranch until they came to the "Big Meadows" (Meadow Valley). On February 5, Steele recorded a typical experience:

> While the light lasted we could mark our way and slide from tree to tree, and sometimes by rocks and branches of trees, swing ourselves down the ledges, but clouds overcast the sky, the light faded, and darkness became intense before we reached the river. At times, as we lingered on the brink of some precipice or tried to rest or plan for the next move, it seemed as though we could neither retain our position nor go on with safety.[22]

Although the conditions of travel were extremely difficult, there can be no doubt that many men had challenged this rugged country during the previous year. On February 10, believing that they had reached the valley of the North Fork, Steele recorded that "our exertions were redoubled and before night *we had crossed the immigrant road* and were near the upper boundary

131

of the plain."[23] Later, Steele says, "Since approaching the immigrant road we had found places where camps had been established and trees chopped . . . but there was no evidence that any white man had visited these places since the snow fell."[24]

At first glance, it appears that the two men may have come across Peter Lassen's Cut-off, carved out of the wilderness in 1848. But, since Steele and Donnelley did not cross the North Fork (they probably reached its East Branch) that would have been impossible, for Peter Lassen led *his* followers down the (even today) tortuous Deer Creek canyon, many miles to the north of the Feather.[25]

Evidently, Beckwourth & Co. had been laying out their road in 1850 and with the descent of winter had been forced to retreat to the camps below. Since Steele speaks so casually of the "immigrant road," he may have known of it before he started on his journey. Perhaps it was already a matter of discussion among the miners.

Jim Meets the "Squire"

Beckwourth and his associates had evidently worked on their road in the summer and fall of 1850, but where the erstwhile forty-niner wintered in 1850–51 is somewhat of a mystery. There is an indication that he went back to Santa Fe during that period. A letter written by Jacob Hall, of McCoy, Waldo & Company and addressed to Manuel Alvarez, in Santa Fe, is one clue:

> You say in a letter written in August last [1851] that Beck-with acknowledged to you that he owed us $35.00 and was ready to pay it. Would not that be evidence enough to prove his suit a piece of villainy? I have written to Garey and Pellins and asked them to send a commission here to take the deposition of Young, Martin, Van Epps, and a man by the name of Joseph Kitham, *who lived with Beckwith last winter.* I have depositions of these men here in our case against Beckwith in this court. They prove that the contract between me and Beckwith was that he only was to get pay for the cattle that were alive and in good traveling order in the Spring. Beck-with's own witnesses prove that they all died but one. I expect to be in Santa Fe next season and if I can get Van and Young and Martin's evidence before the grand jury, Mr. Beckwith will have to stand a trial for perjury or I am much mistaken.[1]

More conclusive is a receipt from McCoy, Waldo & Co., of Santa Fe dated January 1, 1851.[2] The company acknowledged payment from Beckwith of $159.09 for forty-one pounds of to-bacco at $1.75 per pound; thirty-one pounds of starch at twenty-five cents; two handsaw files which came to fifty cents. The balance was credited to "Act. St. Vrain & McCarty." That Beck-wourth was planning to take such necessities as tobacco and files back to California would not be surprising, but thirty-one pounds of starch would seem a strange commodity to transport on such a journey.

Beckwourth must have busied himself with the development of the new emigrant trail during the spring of 1851, however, for early in June he was actively seeking help in getting it open and in use. He went to Marysville and talked to the publisher of the local newspaper. That gentleman responded with enthusiasm and a nod toward the civic cashbox.

> The New Emigrant Route—Mr. James P. Beckwith, the discoverer and projector of this new and important route, called upon us yesterday morning, and states that he now has several men at work cutting a wagon road, by which the emigration can save 150 miles in coming to this city; and, crossing the Truckee but once, having good grass and water all the way. The ascent is gradual, and the road joins the Feather River road at Grass Valley.[3] Mr. Beckwith wishes to obtain subscriptions for this enterprise, to be paid when he has brought the trains here. Books are left at Wilman's, McDonald & Co's for that purpose. This route is by far the most important to the emigration and valuable to our city, taking into consideration the distances involved and the advantages of the road; and we call upon all our citizens to assist Mr. Beckwith in his undertaking.[4]

The *Marysville Herald* continued to watch Beckwourth's progress, noting the new route on June 12, 1851, and again on July 10 of the same year. Jim had not been idle elsewhere. He dropped in to see the mayor of the city, "Mr. Miles,"[5] and found him an enthusiastic partisan. The mayor thought the speculation would yield some six to ten thousand dollars profit, and he guaranteed expenses until the road should be made usable. "Mr. Turner," of the American Ranch, had previously been sold on the idea; he made up a subscription list and headed it with a pledge of two hundred dollars, according to Jim, who also related that the town of Bidwell Bar "was seized with a perfect mania for the opening of the route." Beckwith & Company, happily unaware of future disappointment, were now in business.[6]

Sometime in late July or early August, the first wagon train began its slow, hazardous passage through sagebrush and sand near the pass itself and then up and down the rugged mountains, fording streams but avoiding canyons and keeping to the ridges as much as possible. There were Indians aplenty along the way; illness and fatigue plagued the travelers. Still, at least one of the newcomers kept long, happy memories of her experience. Ina Coolbrith has left a delightful picture of her first acquaintance with James P. Beckwourth:

> Ours was the first of the covered wagons to break the trail through Beckwourth Pass into California. We were guided by the famous scout, Jim Beckwourth, who was an historical figure, and to my mind one of the most beautiful creatures that ever lived. He was rather dark and wore his hair in two long braids, twisted with colored cord that gave him a picturesque appearance. He wore a leather coat and moccasins and rode a horse without a saddle.
>
> When we made that long journey toward the west over the deserts and mountains, our wagon was driven over ground without a single mark of a wagon wheel until it was broken by ours. And when Jim Beckwourth said he would like to have my mother's little girls ride into California on his horse in front of him, I was the happiest little girl in the world.
>
> After two or three days of heavy riding, we came at last in sight of California and there on the boundary Jim Beckwourth stopped, and pointing forward, said, "Here is California, little girls, here is your kingdom."[7]

This report of the first use of the road again leads to a realization that Jim Beckwourth *must* have discovered the route in 1850. He made his first public appeal for funds in Marysville on June 2, 1851, as noted. He then returned on horseback to the pass, a distance of some two hundred miles, taking perhaps ten or more days. He proceeded on to the Humboldt, where he was ill for a time, being forced to remain with an emigrant train while the ladies ("God bless them!") nursed him back to health. July and August thus were spent in bringing in the wagons. It appears that at least the western portion of the trail must have been cleared in the spring of 1850, for it could not have been possible to break a wagon road for the entire distance in the one-month period available between the end of April and the first part of June of 1851.

It has been said that Ina Coolbrith's party arrived in Marysville on August 30, 1851.[8] (She recalled that the wagon train arrived in Marysville in September, 1852, but this was an obvious error of memory or transcription.) Such an event was proper cause for a celebration. It promptly took place, with perhaps too much intensity, for, according to Beckwourth's story, ". . . that same night [the city] was laid in ashes."[9]

Yet on September 1, 1851, at a meeting of the Marysville City Council, "Alderman Garst presented a memorial of J. P. Beckwith & Co., praying remuneration for expenses incurred in making and discovering a new emigrant path to this city." In the manner of city councils, ever and always, the memorial "was referred to Committee on Petitions."[10]

Readers of the *Life and Adventures* have assumed that the first train's arrival coincided with the August 31 fire, which caused extensive damage to Marysville. But the minutes of the council meeting say nothing of Jim's presence; the memorial was presented for him by Alderman Garst. Probably, Jim came in later—in September, as Ina Coolbrith said—and on the night of September 10, 1851, the town suffered another conflagration.[11] First train; second fire. And now the town council had a good reason to forget Jim's request; nothing more is heard of it until May 9, 1853. "No action," the minutes noted at that time.[12]

There was no time for Beckwourth to get back to the pass and bring in another train in the fall of 1851. But that was good: he was about to meet a man who would make his dream of "renown" a far more solid reality than even he could have hoped. A more unlikely amanuensis could scarcely be imagined, but when he got around to it, he did his work well. His name was Thomas D. Bonner.

By the end of October, Jim was up on the North Fork of Rio de las Plumas in the vicinity of Rich Bar. And, fortunately, another chronicler was also there—in this case a woman with a sharp eye for current events and not less so for interesting "personalities." Her pen was facile and her good humor boundless. She put all of these gifts into letters to her sister, signing herself "Dame Shirley."[13] She was not unaware of Jim Beckwourth.

Ned is not the only distinguished person residing on this Bar. There is a man camping here, who was one of Frémont's guides during his travels through California.[14] He is fifty years of age, perhaps, and speaks several languages to perfection. As he has been a wanderer for many years, and for a long time was the principal chief of the Crow Indians, his adventures are extremely interesting. He chills the blood of the green young miner, who, unacquainted with the arts of war and subjugation, congregate around him by the coldblooded manner in which he relates the Indian fights that he has been engaged in.

There is quite a band of this wild people herding a few miles below us; and soon after my arrival it was confidently affirmed and believed by many, that they were about to make a murderous attack upon the miners. This man who can make himself understood in almost any language, and has a great deal of influence over all Indians, went to see them, and told them that such an attempt would result in their own certain destruction. They said, "that they had never thought of such a thing, that the Americans were like the grass in the valleys, and the Indians fewer than the flowers of the Sierra Nevada."[15]

Dame Shirley had observations to make on several oddities at Indian Bar. She devoted more attention to T. D. Bonner, perhaps, than to any other: "But the great man—officially considered —of the entire river, is the 'Squire,' as he is jestingly called."[16]

It seems that Bonner had had his eye on the office of "Justice of the Peace," a position known everywhere in the gold country as being nicely lucrative, if one wished to make it so.[17] And, with the help of a few political shenanigans, Bonner had managed to get himself elected to that post. Dame Shirley's description of him is the best we have:

> Imagine a middle-sized man, quite stout, with a head disproportionately large, crowned with one of those immense foreheads eked out with a slight baldness (wonder if according to the flattering popular superstition, he has *thought* his hair off) which enchant phrenologists, but which one *never* sees brooding above the soulful orbs of the great ones of the earth; a smooth, fat face, grey eyes and prominent chin, the *tout ensemble* characterized by an expression of the utmost meekness and gentleness, which expression contrasts rather funnily with a satanic goatee, and you have our good "Squire."[18]

Then, launching into an intelligent and witty discussion of leadership qualities (she felt that Bonner lacked them), Dame Shirley concluded that "we must 'take the goods the Gods provide. . . .'" And, she added, "the 'Squire' may, after all, succeed. . . . In the meantime, we all sincerely pray that he may be successful in his laudable undertaking, for justice in the hands of a mob, however respectable, is at best a fearful thing."[19]

Dame Shirley's sanguine hopes were not to be realized. Tales of Bonner's misuse of his judicial authority became traditionary in the gold-mining country: "Another rule of his court was to allow no witness to testify until he had exhibited his poll-tax receipt; and at one time, on Rich bar, middle fork, he made Aaron Winters and several others weigh out three dollars in dust, and pay it to him for their poll tax, before he would permit them to go on the stand to give testimony."[20] Bonner, on one occasion, attempted to force a defendant to place bond for the costs of a suit and five hundred dollars damages, *before* the suit had been heard and the court's decision rendered. This was going just a little too far, and the enraged citizens made their feelings known. Bonner took the hint:

It was now supper-time, and the worthy justice adjourned court until the next morning; but before the hour arrived he was seen ascending the mountain, his legs dangling on either side of a patient pack-mule. He had a seat of justice in Onion valley, many feet higher in the air than the river, which he called his higher court, where he sat to hear appeals from his decisions in the lower courts. Here he continued the case without the presence of the defendant, and gave judgment, being unable to either enforce the judgment or collect the desired costs. At another time, he undertook to hold court at Rocky bar, but was compelled to hastily adjourn proceedings to his higher court in Onion valley.[21]

Jim Beckwourth, inevitably, got together with the "Squire." They must have talked at length, but the time was not yet. Though Bonner's brain may have seethed with ideas, more than two years would elapse before the two men got down to the serious business of writing a book.

T. D. Bonner was an enigmatic character. He was evidently a "con" man of some proportions, but he had a background of respectability and, because of his drinking, one of tragedy. His involvement with New England Temperance Society affairs began at least as early as 1842, when he published "The Temperance Harp . . . a Collection of Songs . . . suitable for Total Abstinence Societies . . . Composed and Selected by T. D. Bonner."[22] At that time he was living in Northampton, Massachusetts. Two years later, Bonner had set himself up as a newspaper publisher in Pittsfield, Massachusetts:

THE

TEMPERANCE HARP;

A COLLECTION OF

SONGS,

SUITABLE FOR

WASHINGTONIAN

AND OTHER

TOTAL ABSTINENCE SOCIETIES

In the United States,

AND RESPECTFULLY DEDICATED TO THEM.

———

COMPOSED AND SELECTED BY
T. D. BONNER,
NORTHAMPTON, MASS.

———

With rum-sellers, be fully bent,
To trade with them no more;
But send them where the swine were sent,
Or some barbarian shore.

———

NORTHAMPTON:
PRINTED FOR THE PROPRIETOR.
1842.

The Temperance Harp (Courtesy American Antiquarian Society)

In 1844, T. D. Bonner, a violent temperance reformer, established the *Cataract*, as an organ of his peculiar views regarding that interest. It was grossly personal and scurrilous, and its office was at one time mobbed; the only instance of that kind in the history of Berkshire. After two years, it passed into the hands of Quigley, Kingsley, and Artell who continued it eighteen months, and then sold the subscription list to an Albany publisher.[23]

A still earlier county history took note of shocked community reaction to Bonner's highly colored prose: "The Cataract, a temperance paper . . . was imprudent in the expression of its views, and stands alone in the Berkshires in the honor of having its office mobbed."[24] The champion of sobriety did not limit himself to the printed word—he fought Demon Rum in somewhat more direct ways as well:

T. D. Bonner, who in 1844 established a weekly paper on North Street, Pittsfield, called the "Cataract," which he ran for two years, was without a doubt the most violent "ink-slinger" the county ever knew. His office was finally mobbed by those opposed to his manner of temperance agitation, and his press and types thrown into Silver Lake where it is asserted they are still buried in the mud. He not only fought with a terribly vindictive pen, but he acted as a detective as well, and caught and secured the legal punishment of men who were disobeying the law by bringing liquor into the county from abroad, and secretly keeping dealers in supplies. On one occasion he went up to North Adams in disguise and pretended to be digging roots for medicinal purposes in the Kingsley swamp, just to the south of the then village. It was on this visit that he caught one Ingraham who had driven in with a four-horse load of the ardent from Troy.[25]

Bonner reissued his collection of temperance songs in 1845 under the title "The New England and New York Cataract Songster";[26] still another edition appeared in 1847 as "The Mountain Minstrel, containing a collection of Temperance Songs, Hymns and Glees suitable for all Total Abstinence Societies— Original and Selected—by T. D. Bonner, Agent of the New Hampshire State Temperance Society."[27] This edition was printed at Concord, New Hampshire, by George S. Bonner, whose relationship to Thomas is not known, although he is thought to have been a brother.

The masthead of the *New England Cataract* carries the motto, "Protect the Fallen—and Punish the Tempter." It is this mood that permeates nearly all of Bonner's pronouncements in his paper. His intense, self-justifying essays had, of course, a deeply personal motivation. It is not to his credit that, in addition to ruining the happiness of a young wife, he was willing to exploit his past sins in the classic manner of reformed drunkards. No private *mea culpa* sustained him—rather, he penned verses for public consumption and reprinted such obituary tributes to his family as the following, written by "Miss Porter":

Lines in Memory of Mrs. Delia R.
wife of Thomas D. Bonner who died at
Chester, Mass. Aug. 18, 1839
Aged 33, years.

Fain would I sing thee, but how sad the lay
Which tells, that thou hast pass'd from earth away;
Joy to the mourner, that a pledge was given
Of earthly toils, exchanged for rest in Heaven,—
Joy that thy lowly bed, the infant shares,
And never lived, to need a Mothers prayers,—
A welcome guest he came, but not to stay,
Behold together sleeps their coffin'd clay.
Delia we trust thou'rt gone to worlds of light,
Where sorrow comes not, with its with'ring blight.
Domestic life, had stored no joys for you,
And death, had often pierced your heart anew;
Your children all, were gathered to the tomb,
You now have joined them in that peaceful home;
Angels, have welcomed thee to joys above,
Your harp is tuned to sing Redeeming love.—

We miss thee Delia, but we fain would say,
'Twas God who gave and God who took away.[28]

Bonner says that this "original poetry" was reprinted at the "particular reques[t] of several who have listened to the sorrowful story of our long captivity from our own lips. God have mercy, and save the drunkards wife."[29]

Despite their dismal resemblance to the works of one Emmeline Grangerford ("Oh, Art Thou Gone Yes Thou Art Gone Alas"),[30] the above lines are of value in that they provide almost the only information available on Bonner's early life. That he talked incessantly about his alcoholism is apparent from other sources; it is perhaps only faintly amusing that he should have met someone who could out-talk him. Fortunately, Jim was exulting, not bemoaning, the events of his career; his *joie de vivre* overwhelms anything morbid Bonner may have attempted to inject into the Beckwourth story.

"The Mountain Minstrel" contains T. D. Bonner's "Farewell to the People of Berkshire County," on resigning the editorial charge of the *New England Cataract*:

> Farewell! friends, but not forever
> 'Till the voice of God shall call,
> The last adieu, I'll bid thee never,
> 'Till call'd by death who conquers all.[31]

No explanation is given for Bonner's leaving New England, but another contribution to the collection again hints very strongly at the reason for his espousal of the temperance cause:

> To T. D. Bonner
> by O. Whittlesey, Esq.

He stood beside the counter,
But I saw his cheek was pale,
As the midnight tempest roared without,
In a storm of sleet and hail,

143

And listlessly he gazed upon
The dark throng gathered there,
And thought of that young, blooming bride
He'd driven to despair.

There is considerably more of the same—Bonner is pictured as reaching for "the cup," but suddenly determining to abstain, "resolved to do or die." And then:

He stood beside the church-yard,
For all he lov'd was there
And kneeling on a new made grave,
He breathed a solemn prayer,
And mournfully he call'd upon
The name he lov'd so well;
She heeds him not, but calmly sleeps
For angels with her dwell.[32]

"Miss Porter's" tribute to Delia Bonner states that Bonner and his wife had lost *all* their children prior to the death of Delia in 1839. If so, Bonner must have married again, for the records show that a child, T. D. Bonner, Jr., died in May, 1845.[33] No marriage record has been found, but this child died at the height of Bonner's temperance fervor and it can be assumed that he had married a fellow-worker in the cause. O. Whittlesey has implied that this wife took her own life in despair, but this is difficult to credit, in view of the fact that Bonner continued his temperance work until 1847. Once in California, however, Bonner apparently joined that unhappy number "who fall back and lose the track. . . ." He shortly gained a reputation as one who could hold his own with any toper he might encounter.

Bonner was not unknown to the Forty-niners. Kimball Webster recalled meeting him on the Sacramento River at the ranch of Charles H. Burch,[34]

where we found a boat ready to leave for Sacramento City

THE

NEW-ENGLAND AND NEW-YORK

CATARACT SONGSTER:

A COLLECTION OF

SONGS, HYMNS AND GLEES,

SUITABLE FOR ALL

Total Abstinence Societies.

Original and Selected.

By T. D. BONNER.

Editor of the New-England Cataract.

PITTSFIELD, MASS.

1845.

New England and New York Cataract Songster (Courtesy American Antiquarian Society)

early the next morning, and we concluded to engage a passage for that place. However, upon application, we learned that the seats were all engaged. The boat was owned by Mr. Burch and was only a whale-boat which would seat about twenty persons.

Thomas D. Bonner was captain. Captain Bonner was formerly president of the New Hampshire Temperance Society, but has resided in Massachusetts. Sometime previous to his embarkation for California he was said to be quite a poet and composed many of the songs used at the Temperance meetings, etc. He was formerly, according to his own account of his previous life, a real street drunkard—a mere sot. He called himself a reformed drunkard now.[35]

By 1852, Bonner had moved upriver from the Sacramento. He was elected justice of the peace in the Plumas section of Butte County and, although there were other justices in the county, he was undoubtedly the most colorful. Further, he "seems to have been the only one who made any effort of consequence to discharge the duties of his office."[36] This comment is not entirely complimentary, however:

Justice in his hands was not merely a blind goddess, with balances and sword, standing by her altar, ready to hear the plaints of the afflicted. Far from it. She was rather a lynx-eyed detective; or more properly, a knight-errant, going from place to place seeking for an opportunity to apply the balances and use the sword.

Let it be remarked that it was one of the inflexible rules of Bonner's court that the fees must be paid. That was what he held court for, he said, and unless the costs of court were promptly liquidated, there was no joy in life for the worthy justice. It was customary for him to decide against the party whom he thought was the best able to pay the costs. Good business principles would not permit him to do otherwise.[37]

Bonner seems to have had no fixed place of residence—he has been called "The Peregrinating Justice"—and it was not until the fall of 1854 that he settled in with Beckwourth at the latter's "hotel" near the pass.

Meanwhile, James P. Beckwourth, Trail-blazer, would not be lonely.

XIII

"My Pleasant Valley"

In the spring of 1852, Beckwourth made his decision: he went
to his "pleasant valley" and established himself as hotelkeeper
and trader. In that magnificent setting he could enjoy the rugged
freedom and independence so necessary to his well-being, and
he could earn a livelihood as well.

The usual difficulties with figures arose when Jim tried to
estimate the number of overlanders that might be expected to
enter California in 1852; he thought the total would be 75,000,
and that the large majority would come by way of Beckwourth
Pass.[1] The pass drew a good number of emigrants, but scarcely
that many. In 1855, some 10,151 settlers used it, as against
24,000 who chose Noble's Pass, which lay to the north, in Honey
Lake Valley.[2]

> My house is considered the emigrant's landing-place, [said
> Jim] as it is the first ranch he arrives at in the golden state, and
> is the only house between this point and Salt Lake. Here is a
> valley two hundred and forty miles in circumference, contain-
> ing some of the choicest land in the world. Its yield of hay is
> incalculable; the red and white clovers spring up spontane-
> ously and the grass that covers its smooth surface is of the
> most nutritious nature. When the weary, toil-worn emigrant
> reaches this valley, he feels himself secure; he can lay himself
> down and taste refreshing repose, undisturbed by the fear of
> Indians. His cattle can graze around him in pasture up to their
> eyes, without running any danger of being driven off by the
> Arabs of the forest, and springs flow before them as pure as
> any that refreshes this verdant earth.[3]

The ravages of the plains and the high Rockies on the weary

settlers moved Beckwourth to speculate on the contrast between
their present condition and their situation when they set out. He
envisioned the new equipment, the sturdy wagons, the fine cattle,
and all the preparations so hopefully made. The father and
mother dream of returning home with a cartload of wealth and
the girls look toward marriage to "a fine young gentleman who
is a solid pile of gold." But Jim could not forbear setting down
the facts:

> At the close of day, perhaps amid a pelting rain, these same
> parties heave wearily into sight. . . . Their wagon appears like
> a relic of the Revolution after doing hard service for the com-
> missariat: its cover burned into holes, and torn into tatters; its
> strong axles replaced with rough pieces of trees hewn by the
> wayside; the tires bound on with ropes; the iron linch-pins
> gone, and chips of hickory substituted, and rags wound round
> the hubs to hold them together, which they keep continually
> wetted to prevent falling to pieces. . . .
>
> The old folks are peevish and quarrelsome, the young men
> are so headstrong, and the small children so full of wants, and
> precisely at a time when every thing has given out, and they
> have nothing to satisfy them with. But the poor girls have
> suffered the most. Their glossy, luxuriant locks . . . are now
> frizzled and discolored by the sun; their elegant riding habit is
> replaced with an improvised Bloomer, and their neat little feet
> are exposed in sad disarray; their fingers are white no longer,
> and in place of rings we see sundry bits of rag wound round, to
> keep the dirt from entering their sore cuts. The young men
> of gold, who looked so attractive in the distance, are now too
> often found to be worthless and of no intrinsic value; their
> time employed in haunting gaming tables or dram-shops, and
> their habits corrupted by unthrift and dissipation.[4]

Despite this gloomy picture, some who stopped at Jim's ranch
remembered happy moments there. Granville Stuart's family
came early—in 1852—and he has a good word to say for Jim's
hospitality:

We crossed the Sierra Nevada Mountains by way of Beck-wourth's Pass, so named because old Jim Beckwourth was living there and claimed to have discovered the pass. We found him living in the valley leading to the Pass. His nature was a hospitable and generous one, and he supplied the pressing necessities of starving emigrants, often without money—they agreeing to pay him later, which I regret to say, a number of them failed to do. This so impoverished him that he was compelled to give up his place and resume a wandering life. From there he went to Napa, then back to Montana, and resumed his old life among the Crow Indians.[5]

Elisha Brooks hints that Jim went bear hunting occasionally: "We grazed our cattle in Beckwith's meadows and feasted on the meat of the grizzly bear with hospitable Jim Beckwith, the famous scout and Indian fighter."[6]

Jim Beckwourth had his own memories of those early days at the pass, and perhaps they conjured up the old guilt he felt long ago, while, hidden from his famished comrades, he had devoured the teal duck.

Numbers have put up at my ranch without a morsel of food, and without a dollar in the world to procure any. They never were refused what they asked for at my house; and, during the short space I have spent in the Valley, I have furnished provisions and other necessaries . . . to a very serious amount. Some have since paid me, but the bills of many remain unsettled. Still . . . I can not find it in my heart to refuse relief to such necessities and, if my pocket suffers a little, I have my recompense in a feeling of internal satisfaction.[7]

In 1853, along came a woman whose cheerful good will vied with that of Dame Shirley. Her name was Harriet Ward, and she knew how to keep a journal: she recorded names, weather, distances, privations and pleasures. She was as grateful as Jim Beckwourth for the delightful land in which she found herself: "Sunday, Oct. 1st. Morning bright and beautiful as any Sabbath

morn which has ever dawned upon this lovely world of ours. . . .
We descended to Beckwith Valley. . . . Grass and water good,
fuel scarce."[8] On October 3, the train encamped at Beckwourth's
ranch. While there, Mrs. Ward enjoyed Jim's tales:

> At evening Mr. Beckwith, the proprietor of this valley and
> ranch, passed an hour with us. He gave us some account of his
> wild, wandering way traversing unexplored regions and sur-
> veying roads across the mountain passes. He says he was once
> lost upon his own road and came very near perishing, whereas,
> had there been no road, he could have crossed the mountains
> without difficulty or danger. He claims to belong to the F.F.V.'s
> and is descended from an English Baron of the name Beck-
> with.[9]

Here is evidence that Jim Beckwourth knew his father's background rather thoroughly. He was in company that he knew
would not jeer at him for this statement, whereas the old mountain men would never have believed him nor let him live down
their (supposed) knowledge of his bastardy.

There was music at Beckwourth's ranch while the Wards were
there: their teenaged daughter Frances (called "Frank" or
"Frankie" in the journal) had brought along her guitar. Just
before arriving at Jim's, Mrs. Ward recorded that they spent the
evening "playing and singing in this lone wilderness which perhaps never before echoed to the sound of the guitar." And while
at the trading post, "We passed an hour or two very pleasantly
indeed at our pine tree home, beside a blazing fire. Frank played
and sang for [a friend]."[10]

Two days later, other wagons having gone on ahead, the party
was quite alone except for "Mr. Beckwith, whose house we have
made our encampment, and whose Indian stories are very
interesting indeed, he having been many years Chief of the
Crows. His life and adventures are to be published and will, I
presume, be read with much interest. He presented Father his

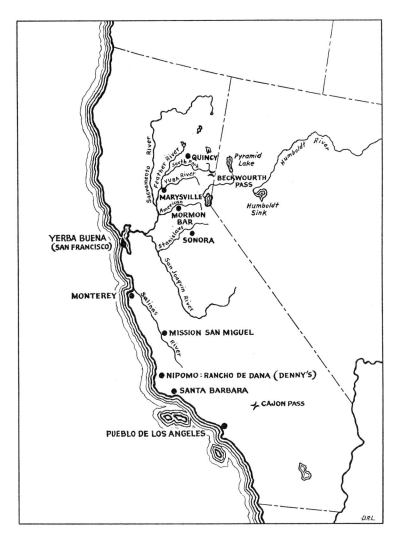

Area of Beckwourth's Adventures in California, 1848–58

picture, which I hope you may some day see."[11] By the ninth of October, there were new neighbors; the previous evening, Indians had stolen six of their horses: "Tomorrow Mr. Beckwith, with a party of twenty men, is going in pursuit of them."[12]

Harriet Ward's party left on the day of this entry, and that is the last we hear from her of Jim Beckwourth, but it is evident that he had gained her respect.

In October, 1854, Bonner arrived at Beckwourth's ranch. A long, cold winter faced the two men—there would be many days when they could put their feet up on the stove and do a little chinning. But first, they would be businesslike: they went down to Quincy to seal the pact:

Know all men by these presents that I, Jas. P. Beckwourth of the County of Plumas and State of California of the first part and Thos. D. Bonner of the County and State aforesaid of the Second Part shall write the autobiography of the Party of the first part and the said Party of the Second Part shall also incur all the expenses of writing and producing the said work in pamphlet form, printed and ready for market the first edition of said work to comprise from twenty-five to fifty thousand copies in the profits of which the said parties agree to share equal and they further agree to share equal in the profits that may arise from all subsequent Editions of Said Work and furthermore they agree that neither Party shall dispose of the Copy right of Said Work, without the consent of the other so to do and in case of the decease of Either Party, then by the consent of his legal representatives, furthermore the said party of the first part agrees with the said party of the second Part to furnish said Second Party with the Scenes and adventures of the life of said Party of the first part. In testimony whereof we have hereunto set our hands and seals this 25th day of October AD 1854   Witness R. I. Barnett

[signed] JAS. P. BECKWOURTH
THOS. D. BONNER

Oct. 25th AD. 1854 then filed and recorded the above article of agreement Jon Harbison Recorder By R. J. Barnett, Deputy.[13]

So far as is known, this is the first time this contract has appeared in print. It precedes by nine days the "Davis" contract, previously published.[14] The ambitious hope of bringing out such a book in pamphlet form indicates that Bonner and Beckwourth originally visualized a much shorter work. Bonner's connection with his (presumed) brother-publisher may have led him to think that he could arrange, through him, for the publication of "twenty-five to fifty thousand" copies. The later contract, in which one Joseph Davis agreed to advance two hundred dollars and share in future expenses, may have grown out of Bonner's realization that he had a "tome" on his hands.

T. D. Bonner must have worked most diligently at his task, for in June, 1855, he was living in Lynn, Massachusetts and was negotiating with Harper & Brothers for the publication of his work. At the risk of maligning Bonner's character, it must be pointed out that he represented himself as the sole proprietor of the book, apparently ignoring his contracts with Beckwourth and Davis.

Memorandum of an agreement made this Twenty-first day of June, 1855, between Thomas D. Bonner, of Lynn, Mass., and Harper & Brothers, Publishers, of New York.

Thos. D. Bonner being the Author and proprietor of the manuscript of a work which is the Autobiography of James P. Beckwourth, a celebrated mountaineer for thirty years in the Rocky Mountains, hereby grants to Harper & Brothers the exclusive right to publish the work during the term of copyright.

Harper & Brothers agree to stereotype, illustrate, print and publish said work in suitable style,—and in consideration of the right herein granted, are to pay to said Thomas D. Bonner, semi-annually, by note at four months, ten per cent on their

153

trade list price for each and every copy sold over and above the first twenty-five hundred.

It is further agreed between Thomas D. Bonner and Harper & Brothers, that the said Ms., with its subjects for illustration are to be carefully revised and prepared for publication by Mr. T. B. Thorpe, at the sole expense and cost of said Thomas D. Bonner. [signed] THOMAS D. BONNER.[15]

Harper & Brothers, it would seem, knew how to drive a hard bargain. Under these conditions, Bonner could not have hoped to make much money—the book was to sell for $1.25—but, even so, he evidently intended to keep what little was forthcoming for himself.

Harper's New Monthly Magazine gave the book a lengthy review in 1856, lauding it as a welcome gratification of the

intense desire of the imaginative and enlightened mind to know something of human nature in its wild estate. . . . We have at last something really genuine about the privations of the mountaineer; something to be relied upon relating to the inner life of the savage; the vail [sic] has been lifted, and although somewhat rudely done, the scene is before us in its deformity and its beauty. . . .[16]

Thomas D. Bonner apparently remained in Lynn, but little is known of his last years and the date of his death has not been established.[17] One last note of degradation concludes the sorry tale of a losing battle against alcoholism. In December, 1861, Bonner sued one Patrick Dow for "publicly, falsely and maliciously accusing the plaintiff of shop-breaking and theft, by words spoken substantially as follows: 'Bonner went into Flagg's shop with false keys and stole money out of the drawer. I saw Jeffrey arrest him, hand cuff him and carry him off. Bonner went into my shop with false keys and stole rum, and I can prove it.' "[18]

Occupation of the outraged plaintiff: night watchman.

With the publication of the *Life and Adventures*, the high

An Autobiography of Jas. J. Beckwourth

Memorandum of an agreement made this Twenty-first day of June, 1855, between Thomas D. Bonner, of Lynn, Mass., and Harper & Brother, Publishers, of New York.

Thos. D. Bonner being the Author and proprietor of the manuscript of a work, which is the Autobiography of James P. Beckwourth, a celebrated mountaineer for thirty years in the Rocky Mountains, thereby grants to Harper & Brothers the Exclusive right to publish the work during the term of Copyright.

Harper & Brothers agree to Stereotype, illustrate, print and publish said work in suitable style, and in consideration of the right therein granted, are to pay to said Thomas D. Bonner, semi-annually, by note at four months; ten per cent on their trade list price for each and every copy sold, over and above the first twenty-five hundreds.

It is further agreed between Thomas D. Bonner and Harper & Brother, that the said Ms., with the subjects for illustration are to be carefully revised and prepared for publication by Mr. T. B. Thorpe, at the sole expense and cost of said Thomas D. Bonner.

     Signed   Thomas D. Bonner

Contract between T. D. Bonner and Harper & Brothers, 1855
(Courtesy of Harper and Row, Publishers, Inc.)

point of Beckwourth's career had been reached: *renown* was his at last. Oddly enough, once achieved, fame seemed not to affect Jim Beckwourth in the least. He had still ten years to live, and he lived them as he always had—scouting, trading, hunting, and avoiding as much as possible the restraints imposed by civilization and burgeoning cities.

No evidence indicates that Jim ever saw any profits from the publication of his autobiography. Indeed, instead of becoming suddenly prosperous, he turned once again to the Marysville City Council, seeking compensation for his services in putting through the Beckwourth trail.

On January 19, 1856, a Committee of the Council, in response

to the petition of James P. Beckwith, asking that the city of Marysville would refund to him, a certain amount of money for work [?] said to have been performed in bringing a road, known as 'Beckwith's route' through the Sierra Nevada Mountains into Plumas County and thence to Marysville [reported that] they are unable to procure any evidence or facts in the case, as the parties, to whom application was made by the petitioner, are not residing in the city at this time and what promises they may have made, if any, we cannot ascertain.

That Marysville has received considerable benefit from the opening of this route, no one will doubt, but at the same time, we do not think the present Council has [any?] authority to act in the case, as it would more properly belong to the Council of 1851, and to whom the petitioner, should have applied for his [?], at the time when the road was said to have been completed. Your committee would therefore report adversely to the prayer of the Petitioner.[19]

In talking it over with Bonner, Beckwourth had earlier said,

nor do I see clearly how I am to help myself, for everyone knows I can not roll a mountain into the pass and shut it up. But there is one thing certain . . . when I go out hunting in the mountains a road for every body to pass through, and

156

expending my time and capital upon an object from which I shall derive no benefit, it will be because I have nothing better to do.[20]

Beckwourth's *Life and Adventures* closes with a word "for the Red Man," and justifies (in the latter's terms) the hostility encountered by white men as they pushed their relentless way westward.

The United States troops are often turned indiscriminately upon his race; the innocent generally suffer and those who have raised the storm cannot understand of what crime they can be guilty.
But if the government is determined to make war upon the Western tribes, let it be done intelligently, and so effectually that mercy will temper justice. To attempt to chastise Indians with United States troops is simply ridiculous; the expense of such campaigns is only surpassed by their inefficiency. The Indians live on horseback and they can steal and drive off the government horses faster than it can bring them together. The Indians . . . can travel faster, even with the incumbrance of their lodges, women, and children. . . . An army must tire out in such a chase before summer is gone, while the Indians will constantly harass it with their sharp-shooters, and, should several powerful tribes unite—not an unusual occurrence— many thousand men would make no impression.[21]

The words were prophetic, as the next twenty-five or thirty years would testify. Yet, the alternative suggested by Jim—that of deliberate starvation through the slaughter of the buffalo— was, and continued to be, repugnant to the avowed ideals of the conquerors of the Indian.

In his summing up, Beckwourth singles out the Pawnees for special castigation: "The Pawnees are probably the most degraded, in point of morals, of all the Western tribes; they are held in such contempt by the other tribes that none will make treaties with them. . . . Those who engage in warfare with the

Western Indians will remember that they take no prisoners except women and children."[22]

The Skidi division of Pawnees practiced human sacrifice; perhaps Jim had been revolted by the knowledge. Otherwise, his experiences with them seem to have been no more harrowing than those with any other Indians.[23] Still, a contemporary account seems to corroborate his statements: "With our camp were three Pawnees, who had joined us that day, and [a passing war party] were exceedingly anxious to get hold of them, and we were compelled to interfere to prevent their being killed. The Pawnees are at war with all other Indian nations and are held by them in very low estimation."[24]

T. D. Bonner had the last word in the *Life and Adventures*: he composed a poem to "Pine Leaf, the Indian Heroine." Flowing along in full Temperance-Society style, it goes on and on for twelve relentless stanzas of eight lines each, and does little to enhance the book. But, in their mellow, inebriated state Beckwourth and Bonner probably thought it was beautiful.

After the publication of the book Beckwourth remained at his trading post. Visitors came and went; emigrants left their horses to recruit at the ranch, sometimes also trading cattle and mules. There was work to be done: gardens must be planted, meat and other foods prepared for storage; corrals must be built and wagons be repaired for later sale or trade.

According to one visitor, Beckwourth had attracted a little community about his hotel:

> The colony occupied about twenty block houses in the largest of which we found Beckwourth seated in the doorway smoking. He received us rather coolly, but was evidently pleased to see us, and on learning that we had come a long distance out of our way to see him he insisted that we accept of his hospitality while we remained in the valley. He was then about sixty years old and looking somewhat worn and broken,

but his large muscular frame seemed still sound and capable of great endurance.

His long hair and dark swarthy complexion gave him the appearance of an Indian, and I had supposed that he had Indian blood, but he assured us that he was of French and English extraction. We stayed with him from ten in the morning until six in the evening, taking dinner with him. . . . Just before we left, he took us over his plantation, as he called the cultivated portion of his domain, and showed us some fields of fine vegetables, a herd of about two hundred sheep, a hundred ponies and immense flocks of domestic fowls.[25]

It perhaps will never be known why Jim left his pleasant valley in the Sierras. It may be that age and the painful condition of his legs made "wintering" in the high country too difficult. No evidence has been found to justify such statements as this: "The trouble was he improved [the ranch] by methods he had learned as a mountain man, Indian fighter and Crow subchief, including customs such as horse-thievery, which folks thereabout were not inclined to put up with. Jim rode out of California in 1854, just ahead of the vigilantes."[26]

Nor this: "In the Sacramento Valley, ranchers grew edgy over raids by horse-thieves. Remembering old Jim's background, they talked of direct action. Beckwourth knew better than to try to convince an armed posse of his innocence. He moved on to Denver."[27] The date is 1852!

Local tradition has it that Jim outsmarted himself:

Jim was doing pretty well for himself at his little trading post snuggling in the hills and overlooking the broad, fertile Sierra Valley, until he decided he wasn't doing well enough.

His book doesn't contain the story, but pioneers recount the incident:

"Jim started making books on a footrace between a Negro boy and an Indian. He bet all his horses, guns, blankets and everything on the race, which was to be over a mile course.

159

"Jim really had two Negro boys of the same size. One hid in a clump of willows at the half-way point and darted out from them in a fresh burst of speed as his teammate entered—but the Indian outran the relay team and won. Jim went broke and soon left the country."[28]

As a matter of fact, he did not leave California finally until after November 10, 1858, for on that day Charles DeLong visited with him in Marysville: ". . . had Chief Jim Beckwourth in the office and listened to a long set of storie's [sic] of his."[29]

Somehow, Jim found himself back in Missouri. His route is unknown, but no doubt he took the old familiar trail to Santa Fe and visited some of his Indian friends along the way. Once back in civilization, Jim could not go long unnoticed, and he is soon appearing once again in the newspapers—to say nothing of the courts.

Eastward Again

The now-famous pioneer first turns up in the St. Louis press on August 24, 1859. The writer noted that Jim was at that time in Kansas City and that he had not been "within the settlements" for twenty years—a slight exaggeration, since he had carried dispatches to Fort Leavenworth in 1848.[1]

A month later, still in Kansas City, Jim received further notice in a paper there:

> This morning one of the oldest, perhaps the oldest, mountaineer now living, leaves this city for the Rocky Mountains. We refer to Mr. James Beckwith, whose autobiography has already been written and published, by the Messrs. Harper's and Bros. Mr. Beckwith goes out with the train of Dr. Lee, as a guest of the doctor. The train consists of ten wagons, loaded with miners' merchandise and is destined for Auraria.[2] These wagons also contain 1,600 pounds of material for the Rocky Mountain News, and 5,000 pounds of drugs. A large quantity of freight is left behind for the doctor's train, that will leave here sometime in March next.
>
> James Beckwith, the mountaineer referred to, has been a mountain man for the last forty years, and is well known as the "great western" guide and interpreter, being familiar with nearly all the Indian dialects, and speaking the English, French and Spanish languages with equal fluency. In 1837 he held a captain's commission in a muleteer company, under Col. Zac Taylor. . . .
>
> He has been stopping in this city for several weeks, making his headquarters at the house of Col. E. M. McGee.[3] This morning or tomorrow he leaves with Dr. Lee, intending to reach his ranch upon the Feather River, in California, some-

time next spring. He proposes during the winter to pay the Crows a visit, having formerly been in this nation for a number of years. A correspondence embracing the particulars of this trip to California, written by himself, will appear in this paper at an early date.[4]

Unfortunately, the very next day, the paper was obliged to report that the old "Mountaineer" had suffered an accident: he had been riding bareback and was thrown, with resultant severe bruises. The injury was not serious and the "old war horse" was expected to be ready for service again in a few days.[5] Jim's accident lost him the chance to travel with Dr. Lee. But meanwhile an old friend at Westport, Louis Vasquez, had been in touch and he now hired Jim to take a train to Denver and act as agent-trader there, in company with A. Pike Vasquez, a nephew of Louis.[6]

Beckwourth's arrival in Jefferson Territory on November 16, received immediate attention from "Observer," who wrote his paper that

> Jim Beckwith, the well-known mountaineer and formerly chief of the Crow Indians, arrived. He got a little jolly on his arrival the first night, perhaps, because, as he said, he just come to one of his old camping grounds, and he might be d—d if he knew an individual in it!—that he was an "honest Indian" and heretofore kept "ahead of the hounds," but now, by George, we have stole a march on him and passed his time![7]

In closing, "Observer" had a local joke to relate: "Colorado City is growing and extending itself so fast that humorous folk say they must either take steps to stop its growth or cut away the mountain ridges! They believe Leavenworth and St. Joe are 'right smart places' but are altogether too far away from this place to ever amount to much."[8]

A call on William N. Byers, editor of the Rocky Mountain News, resulted in a lengthy and laudatory column:

> We had formed the opinion, as has, we presume, almost

everyone, that Captain Beckwourth was a rough, illiterate back-woodsman, but were most agreeably surprised to find him a polished gentleman, possessing a fund of general information which few can boast. He is now sixty-two years of age, but looks scarce fifty, hale, hearty and straight as an arrow. . . . For some years he has resided in California, in what is universally known as Beckworth Valley, from whence he returned only a few months since. He visited St. Louis—which he had not seen for twenty-two years—again greeted his friends and relations after an absence of half an ordinary life-time; "but," says the veteran, "I could find *no* St. Louis, I got lost in the streets and had to get a *guide* to lead me to my brother's house."

He soon tired of the great city, and moved up the river to visit his old friend, and comrade on many a bloody field, Col. Vasquez, of Westport, Mo. . . .

On the second of October, he set out for this place with A. P. Vasquez & Co.'s train, and its safe arrival, after running the gauntlet of hostile Indians, is, no doubt, in a great measure due to his experience. When coming up the Arkansas, he met with Cheyennes, whom he had not seen for over twenty years; but he was instantly recognized, his presence telegraphed for many miles to the scattered bands, who came rushing to meet and welcome him, whom they consider the "Big Medicine" of all the white men of the plains. He says he feels like prosecuting the settlers, who are encroaching, and building cities on his hunting grounds. We hope he may live to see a great city, and a greater State here, where, no doubt, he did not dream of seeing a white man, except for his fellow trappers and traders.

We look forward to many pleasant hours in listening to the stories of the old hero, and hope to be able to interest our readers likewise.[9]

The *Daily Kansas City Journal of Commerce* picked up the Byers article and reprinted it with the comment that it would be read with "great interest, as the 'Old Mountaineer' is well known by nearly every chick and child in this city, he having . . .

remained in our city for several months, as the guest of his old mountain friends, and in particular of his oldest and warmest friend, Col. Vasquez."[10] Jim was in town as a trader, and he and A. Pike Vasquez lost little time in making it known; they ran the following:

NEW ADVERTISEMENT

Just Arrived
for
A. P. Vasquez & Co.
their
Winter Supply of Goods

Consisting, in part, of
Nails, from 4 pennies up to 10's, Window Glass and Glass Dishes, a large assortment of Queensware, (no longer any necessity of eating out of tin,) containing rare and curious pieces, new in this country. . . .

In addition, they advertised "Groceries, Candles, Champaign & Catawba Wines (in lieu of strychnine whiskey), Dried and Preserved Fruits, Pickles, Sugar and Fresh Flour . . . Good, Warm Winter Clothing . . . Dressed Deer Skins, . . . all of which they would exchange for the 'glittering ore,' or coin would be taken sooner than miss a sale."[11]

Queensware and "champaign"! A far cry from the foo-fa-rah the mountain men once offered the ladies of their acquaintance.

Shortly after his arrival in Denver, Jim bought property in what is now North Denver, but then and for many years after known as the "Town of Highland," in Jefferson Territory.[12] He settled down to storekeeping, but he was not out of touch with his former friends, the Cheyennes; they depended upon him to represent them in their relations with the settlers. William N. Byers provided an avenue of communication for the Indians through his newspaper. Jim had come to him with the story of an encounter with several bewildered and hungry Cheyennes who had arrived in town and found their welcome something less than hearty:

"My chief, we are glad to see you—although we do not like to see you among the pale faces. In passing through our hunting grounds, many a pale face has been lost, but never has one come to a Cheyenne lodge without getting plenty to eat, and being set on the right road to his people. Last night I arrived here; have not eaten a mouthful, and pale-face has not asked me to eat. Chief, I am hungry." Whereupon, the Captain took them to his boarding house, where they partook of a hearty meal.

After this the Captain counselled them to "go to their lodge, rest today, and tomorrow return to their tribe." They expressed a wish that the Captain would apply for appointment as their agent, thinking their former companion would better know their wants, and be more capable of administering to them, than anyone else. The Captain told them that they should return to their tribe, consult with them, and if agreeable to them let him know next moon, when he would do all in his power to consummate their wish.[13]

This was not the only time Jim tried to stir up the public conscience through the newspapers. Someone must have taken his dictation, for Beckwourth could not spell correctly. He could speak eloquently, however, as this letter testifies.

Justice to the Indians—an article they seldom obtain—and security to my fellow citizens, compel me to seek your columns to redress one of the greatest outrages ever perpetrated in this, or any other country; and I am charitable enough to believe that a majority of the whites would assist in punishing severely the perpetrators were they known.

On Saturday last a band of Cheyenne and Appache Indians visited our city in compliance with a promise made to me in January last. While on my way to the States, I met them, and gave them an invitation to visit us and trade their robes, which they agreed to, as soon as their hunt was over.

On their arrival they called upon me in a body, requesting me to show them a camping place—I done so. After dark a lot of *drunken devils* and "bummers" went to the lodges, took the Indian women and girls forcibly out, committing acts of violence, which in any other country would condemn the perpetrators to ignominy and shame; age was not respected—the gray hairs of John Poisel's old Indian wife could not protect her; she was taken from her husband's side in bed; but before they succeeded in their hellish work, crippled as he is, compelled them by threats with his pistol, to release her.[14] The same night three mules were stolen from the Indians, taken off some ten miles and fettered, but the thieves could not *steal the trail*; the red man found his mules. . . .

The Indians are as keenly sensible to acts of injustice as they are tenacious of revenge, and it is more humiliating to them to be the recipients of such treatment *upon their own lands*, which they have been deprived of, their game driven off and they made to suffer by hunger, and when they pay a visit, abused more than dogs. My advice is, that municipal regulations be made preventing the sale of intoxicating drinks to them, with such penalties as would make the law respected. And all emigrants who are on their way here, ought to, most religiously, refrain from giving Indians whiskey, or trading it it to them for their horses, for if he sells his pony, he will steal one from the next white man that comes along. All our Indian troubles are produced by the imprudent acts of unprincipled white men. . . .

I am to meet them next moon, to let them know if our citizens will suffer or permit such outrages to go unnoticed.[15]

This letter, aided by editorial comments from the *Rocky Mountain News* resulted in a "Public Meeting," for the purposes of inquiring into the outrages upon the Indians. The chairman of the meeting appointed a committee of five, including James

Beckwourth, "whose duty it should be to ascertain the authors, and all connected with it, and report. . . ."[16]

The committee apparently learned the name of only one man:

> Capt. Beckworth stated that he had gone to John Poisel's lodge, after he had been called upon by the Indians with their complaint, and asked him who had perpetrated the outrages. Poisel told them that Phil Gardner[17] and others were the perpetrators, but refused [out of concern for Jim's safety] to give him the names, stating that . . . he would be at the meeting, and make his own report, even though he were compelled to crawl on his hands and knees to reach the hall. [Beckwourth] supposed his increased infirmities were the only reason for his being absent.

Ultimately, these meetings resulted in the appointment of Jim Beckwourth as "local agent" to take charge of the Indians during their visits, to note all depredations committed on either side, and to transact all business with the Indians. He was also to call all necessary meetings.

A committee member moved that an attempt be made to secure, from Washington, Beckwourth's appointment as the stationary Indian agent. After some discussion, Jim announced that he was not seeking the office and gave it as his opinion that Colonel A. G. Boone, who had already been appointed and was on his way to Jefferson Territory, was an excellent choice.[18]

On yet another occasion, Beckwourth, as Acting Indian Agent, used his authority to address the public:

> Captain Beckwith requests us to give notice to all persons that each and every man detected in selling or giving liquor or ammunition to Indians will be punished and the Indians protected against outrage or insults from the Whites.
> Five hundred of the Cheyenne and Arapahoe warriors have joined the Kiowas, and ammunition will be immediately forwarded to them to prosecute their warfare against the troops or white settlers. It may be well to state here that one or two

James P. Beckwourth in citizen dress (From T. D. Bonner, *James P. Beckwourth*, 1856 edition)

persons are known to have sold whiskey to Indians, and if persisted in they will most assuredly be punished without respect as to personal standing.[19]

Jim married yet again; this time the ceremony was quite formal and legal, apparently, for at least two newspapers carried

168

the notice: "Married—on the 21st of June 1860, by A. C. McGrew, Esq., Mr. James Beckwourth and Miss Elizabeth Lettbetter, of Denver."[20]

As far away as Atchison City, Kansas, the marriage was publicly announced—with considerably less dignity: "The noted Jim Beckwourth, ex-chief of the Crow Indians, has once more committed matrimony. At one time in his life he had eight wives and a separate lodge for each. Last week he took to his bosom a paleface whom he has lately wooed and won."[21]

It has been said that Elizabeth was Spanish; that she was a Negress;[22] and that she was a "paleface," as noted above. It will probably never be known what her nationality was. At least one child was born of this marriage, for its death in infancy was announced in the press: "Died—This morning, at half-past five, Julia L. Beckwourth, daughter of James P. Beckwourth, aged one year, eight months and eight days."[23]

Nolie Mumey says that a son of Jim Beckwourth was killed in a riding accident in 1875, but earlier sources have it that this man was a nephew of Jim's.[24] In any case, he could not have been the son of Elizabeth Lettbetter, since any child of hers and Jim's could not have been more than fourteen years of age in 1875 and this man had been carrying mail for a number of years on the Western Slope when he was fatally injured. He may have been a brother of the Edward Beckwith who talked with Francis Cragin in Colorado Springs.[25]

Shortly after his marriage, Jim is said to have entertained a distinguished visitor—General William Larimer, who had attained that rank with the Pennsylvania State Militia. The visit was for the purpose of "eating possum," at the invitation of the Beckwourths.[26] On the face of it this news speaks poorly for Jim's social and financial status, and it is only fair to examine the rest of the tale:

Jim Beckwith was another frontiersman with whom I became acquainted in those days . . . Beckwith was a negro. I called on Jim and his bride in their cabin on the banks of the Platte River, a few miles up the river from Denver, in 1860. Jim had invited me there to eat possum with them. Jim had passed through many adventurous experiences, of which perhaps none was more thrilling or more dangerous than that of his sixteenth year. It was at the "Massacre of the Alamo"— that tragic event in the history of our southwest. It is said that only seventeen escaped from the Alamo that fateful Sunday morning.

Here General Larimer launches into a long account of what happened to the supposed various survivors of the Alamo, then remembers that he should be talking about Jim Beckwourth:

> The negro, a 16-year-old valet to Colonel Travis, who went out behind Mrs Dickinson on the horse, became afterwards the chief of the Crow tribe of Indians in the Crow nation, and was known throughout all the Western country by the name of Beckwith.
>
> For a number of years he left the tribe and went to a place on Clear Creek near the present site of Denver. It was here that he married a colored woman and built him a house, but afterwards returned to his old tribe, and remained until his death, about 1883. His widow Candelaria, at the extremely advanced age of 107 years, in 1892 still lived in her little adobe house in Mexican San Antonio.[27]

Jim Beckwourth, who was never anywhere near the Alamo, would have been at least thirty-six years of age at the time of that tragedy. According to the simplest calculations, his wife, if she were 107 in 1892, must have been seventy-five years old in 1860, the year of the general's visit. Yet we are expected to believe that Jim and "his bride" invited him to dine on 'possum, this detail being given, of course, to reinforce the statement that Jim was a Negro. It is but charitable to point out that the general was recalling events that had occurred fifty-eight years previously and that he lived in a period when racists were perfectly open in stating their prejudices.

Despite his having become a responsible citizen, property-owner, husband, and father, Jim was not destined to be a "city man." After the death of his daughter, his marriage began to break up; he and Elizabeth sold some of their property in July, 1864.[28] Jim was soon living with a Crow wife, Sue. They spent their time farming and trapping, sometimes entertaining the Indians clustered around them on the South Platte. In 1862, Beckwourth worked as an army guide with E. L. Berthoud, of the Colorado Second Infantry.[29]

But even these diversions proved too restrictive. Jim moved away from Denver City and camped at Monument Creek for a while in the winter of 1865–66;[30] later he took a trapping party to the Green River. It met with disaster:

> Adventures of Jim Beckwourth—Almost as long ago as we can remember we read a book with the above title. We little expected then to listen to almost as startling new adventures of this old mountaineer and trapper from his own lips. He got back yesterday from his winter's trapping excursion away over on the headwaters of Green River, and reports losing all his horses and men. Three of them, Burns, Williams and Dave Clayton, were killed by Indians, which he thinks were his old enemies of the Blackfoot tribe. These same Indians also stole his horses. The last one, John Simmons, was drowned between Pratt's and St. Vrain's Forks of the Green River; he lost all his traps at the same place, and everything else, except 280 fine Beaver skins; these he cached, and went into Pass Creek Station for horses, and brought them in. Jim has almost material enough for another book of adventures.[31]

Jim's time was almost gone and, although tenacious of life, he must have felt a certain longing for release and repose, for Jim Beckwourth had, meanwhile, been through a long series of other unhappy experiences.

The Last Trail

Storekeeping had engaged most of Beckwourth's time in 1860 and well into 1861. During an absence in the East, A. Pike Vasquez placed Jim in charge of the store on Ferry Street; later, a farm belonging to Vasquez and Company was given over to his management.[1] Jim's business associates trusted him and relied upon his judgment. When Louis Vasquez wanted his partnership with Pike dissolved he appointed Beckwourth his "true and lawful attorney," empowering him to make all necessary settlements and collect and hold all moneys due to Louis.[2]

Carefully, Beckwourth reported the goods on hand and their value. The accountant who rendered the inventory may have had some of Jim's problems with figures—as when he computed two-thirds of $149.33 as being $112 (owed to Louis Vasquez), thus doing A. Pike out of some $13. This particular item gave trouble still later with the account of "mdze J. B. Beckwourth Ranch a/c $149.33 ⅓ 37.33"—an error of nearly $13 again.[3] Aside from such minor mistakes, the accounts seem sound and straightforward.

An old acquaintance, Jim Bridger, kept in touch with Beckwourth by letter. He (or his agent) wrote once in May and again in December, 1860, at which time he thanked Jim for "yours of the 8th;" it had given "agradill" of pleasure to the recipient.[4] Bridger was later employed by A. P. Vasquez and Company (May 12, 1861 to May 19, 1862) at $25 a month, whereas Jim Beckwourth's "sallery" was $75. Bridger, as had Louis Vasquez, demonstrated his faith in Jim by giving him power of attorney to dispose of some of "Old Gabe's" property in Denver.[5]

Despite all this, Beckwourth's life in Denver was a contradiction of all that was most important to him: yearning for the freedom and the challenge implicit in the life of a mountain man, he had no capacity for adaptation, except to nature. Inevitably, he clashed with the new mode of life rapidly being imposed on the West he had known. Now the high adventures were reduced to sordid encounters with local courts: there was a charge of theft from the army, another of manslaughter.[6] From both of these charges Jim emerged as "not guilty," but they were nevertheless signals of the new era—there was a time when these affairs could have been settled without legal repercussions.

The manslaughter case occurred just two weeks after the death of Beckwourth's infant daughter. Jim was lying ill in bed when a notorious Negro blacksmith, known as "Nigger Bill" Payne, came to the Beckwourth home in a quarrelsome mood. The sequel is described by the *Rocky Mountain News* in an account that can scarcely be called impartial:

The following is the substance of the coroner's inquest held on Saturday night at James P. Beckwourth's ranch and saloon, a few miles up the Platte. Payne went up to Beckwourth's on Saturday evening; talked with his wife or woman who was then stopping with Mrs. Beckwourth; tried to force a ring off her finger; she cried and alarmed the house; Beckwourth, who was sick and sleeping on the bed, arose and remonstrated with Payne, ordering him out of the house; hard words and a scuffle ensued; both ran for a double barreled gun, loaded and lying in a corner of the bar-room, which gun both grabbed and wrestled over. Two white men, N. A. Fairchilds and John McGuire, who happened to be present, took the gun away from both of them and put it away, putting Nigger Bill out of the house. Bill immediately started to break in again to go for Beckwourth, who, seeing that, took up the gun and defended himself by firing at Bill as he was just approaching him, at the door. Bill walked in through the bar-room and into the dining room, after which, without speaking, he fell in or near the fire-place and instantly died, from the effects of two discharges of shot in his neck and shoulder. There was an inquest held in an hour after, during which the evidences of Maria A. Payne, and those two white men concurred in the evidence as above, "That Wm. Payne came to his death by reason of gun-shot wounds received at the hands of James P. Beckwourth."

This Payne came out here as a slave with some persons connected with the old Express Company, and did blacksmithing here most of the time since. He was considered a savage and dangerous character always and by almost all of our citizens, having killed a fellow negro here in cold blood a few years since. He was large and strong of muscle and a rough case. Old Capt. Beckwourth was arrested and is in jail awaiting his examination today. The unanimous voice of the people is that he did a good job, and will be at once cleared. Indeed this sentiment was so universal yesterday on the street, from the various old and new circumstances of cases, that you would hear of nothing but "bully for Beckwourth, if he ever runs for Indian chief again, we sign his papers of recommendation." Also the expression, "a Payneful funeral," there was a "black berrying" party today at the graveyard, etc., were in many men's mouths, who are noted for principles of charity, justice, right and order.[7]

The subpoena and a lengthy, dull indictment, along with various other official papers relating to this case, are available, but the newspaper account gives a far more colorful picture of the outcome:

Jim Beckwourth.—This "old chief" had his trial in U. S. Court on Tuesday, for the shooting of "Nigger Bill," in self defence. After a few minutes the jury rendered a verdict of "not guilty," thus letting Jim go rancheward on his way rejoicing. James M. Cavanaugh was the Cap's counsel.[8]

Not long afterward, Jim's participation in the "Sand Creek

Massacre" cast a dark shadow over his long friendship with the Cheyenne Indians and must have left him with a deep sense of shame and regret.

In August, 1864, John Evans, Governor of Colorado Territory, had been authorized to establish the Third Regiment of Colorado Volunteer Cavalry ("100-days men") for the protection of citizens of Denver, who were in a state of panic following reports of Indian depredations and murders in the outlying settlements. The commander of this regiment was Colonel John M. Chivington, a former Methodist minister turned avenger; his avowed aim was the annihilation of the Cheyennes. On August 23, the *News* announced that Colonel Chivington had proclaimed martial law in order to stimulate enlistments in his forces.[9]

Jim Beckwourth, who was hired as guide and interpreter by Colonel George L. Shoup, may have been coerced by the popular mood as well as by the military rule of the day. In his later testimony he implied that he feared for his life should he refuse. It is difficult to credit any willingness on his part to move against the Cheyennes, particularly since these Indians had been peaceful for months.[10]

Chief Black Kettle's people, encamped at Sand Creek northeast of Fort Lyon, believed that they were under the protection of troops stationed at that post, under the command of Major Scott Anthony of the Colorado First Regiment. On the contrary, Major Anthony was merely biding his time until the arrival of Colonel Chivington. Although Major Anthony fully approved the attack on the unsuspecting Cheyennes, several of his and Colonel Chivington's officers did not; their reluctance to commit "murder" failed to halt the indiscriminate slaughter of women and children, along with their warrior-defenders—a mere prelude to disgraceful atrocities and mutilation of bodies.[11]

Colonel Chivington's forces attacked the Cheyennes on the morning of November 29, 1864. It was not long before a military commission[12] (the third official group to investigate this matter) was asking questions. Parts of Jim Beckwourth's testimony are of great interest:

Question. Were you present at Sand Creek at the time of attack upon Black Kettle's camp, by Colonel Chivington?

Answer. Yes, I was present.

Question. Previous to the attack on Black Kettle's village, did you hear Colonel Chivington give any orders or make any remarks to his command?

Answer. His remark, when he halted us in the middle of Sand creek, was this: "Men, strip for action." He also said, "I don't tell you to kill all ages and sex, but look back on the plains of the Platte, where your mothers, fathers, brothers, sisters have been slain, and their blood saturating the sands of the Platte."[13]

. . . .

Question. During the last fourteen years have you passed through the Cheyennes or Arapahoes villages?

Answer. Yes. Have been in them frequently since.

Question. Have you any acquaintance with the chiefs of the Cheyennes and Arapahoes, and their people?

Answer. Yes.

. . . .

Question. Were all those Indians killed on Sand Creek warriors?

Answer. There were all sexes, warriors, women, and children, and all ages, from one week old up to eighty years.

Question. What proportion of those killed were women and children?

Answer. About two-thirds, as near as I saw.

. . . .

Question. Did any of the Indians make an attempt to reach Colonel Chivington's command at the time of the attack?

Answer. Yes, one Indian.

Question. Do you know his name? If so, state it, and what he did[.]

Answer. The name he went by with the Indians was Spotted

James P. Beckwourth in the 1860s (Courtesy Western History Department, Denver Public Library)

View of Beckwourth Peak and Valley (Photograph by Elinor Wilson)

Beckwourth's Trading Post, Ramelli Ranch (Courtesy Mrs. Guido Ramelli)

Seth Ward, sutler at Fort Laramie in 1866 (Courtesy
Wyoming State Historical Department)

$93.00
700.00

Fort Laramie W.T. August 13th 1866

On demand I promise to pay S E
Ward or order Ninety three 70/100 Dollars, for
value received James Buchanan 7th

$00—
6.50
100

James Buchanan

Note to Seth Ward, sutler at Fort Laramie (Courtesy Wyoming
State Historical Society)

Auraria and Pikes Peak, 1859 (Courtesy Western History Department, Denver Public Library)

Sue Beckwourth, James P. Beckwourth's last wife
(Courtesy State Historical Society of Colorado)

Denver May The 18 1864

I here by give & bequeth all of My Property in Colerado Terri tory to My wife Elisabeth Beckwoth after My Depts Dews & Demands is paid I appoint her as my Administrators, to settle all of my & Gardean to settle all of my fast depts depts I here by Place My hand & seal

Witnes N. C. Fairchild Lizie Williams (Seal)
" " James H. Williams (Seal)
before witnesses I assign My hand & seal

James P. Beckwourth (Seal)

Beckwourth's Will (Courtesy Clark Library, Brigham Young University)

Antelope, and by the whites, White Antelope. He came running out to meet the command at the time the battle had commenced, holding up his hands and saying "Stop! stop!" He spoke it in as plain English as I can. He stopped and folded his arms until shot down. I don't know whether the colonels heard it or not, as there was such a whooping and hallooing that it was hard to hear what was said.

Question. Was any attention paid to White Antelope as he advanced toward the command?

Answer. None, only to shoot him, as I saw.

.   .   .   .

Question. Was any person shot in Colonel Chivington's camp after the battle with the Indians?[14]

Answer. Yes.

Question. State who it was.

[J. M. Chivington objects. Objection not sustained.]

Answer. It was a half-breed, who went by the name of Jack Smith, John Smith's son. He was sitting in the lodge with me; not more than five or six feet from me, just across the lodge. There were ten to fifteen soldiers came into the lodge at the time, and there was some person came on the outside and called to his [Jack's] father, John Smith. He, the old man, went out, and there was a pistol fired when the old man got out of the lodge. There was a piece of the lodge cut out where the old man went out. There was a pistol fired through this opening and the bullet entered below his right breast. He sprung forward and fell dead, and the lodge scattered, soldiers, squaws, and everything else. I went out myself; as I went out I met a man with a pistol in his hand. He made this remark to me; he said, "I am afraid the damn son of a bitch is not dead, and I will finish him." Says I, "Let him go to rest; he is dead." That is all that occurred at that time. We took him out and laid him out of doors. I do not know what they did with him afterwards.[15]

This was the very Jack Smith whose infantile temper tantrum Lewis Garrard had witnessed in 1846:

Smith's son Jack took a crying fit one cold night, much to the annoyance of four or five chiefs, who had come to our lodge to talk and smoke. In vain did the mother shake and scold him with the severest Cheyenne words, until Smith, provoked beyond endurance, took the squalling youngster in hands; he shu-ed, and shouted, and swore, but Jack had gone too far to be easily pacified. He then sent for a bucket of water from the river, and poured cupful after cupful on Jack, who stamped, and screamed, and bit, in his puny rage . . . again and again the cup . . . was replenished and emptied. . . . At last, exhausted with exertion and completely cooled down, he received the remaining water in silence, and, with a few words of admonition, was delivered over to his mother, in whose arms he stifled his sobs, until his heart-breaking grief and cares were drowned in sleep.[16]

When Garrard took final leave of John Smith and his squaw, he recorded: "Little Jack had contributed much to my happiness; for, although he could not talk American, the sight to me was an oasis in the desert. Among rough men, and no kind words, Jack, at least, was not devoid of childish affection, and to amuse and talk to him recalled home and cheerful retrospections."[17]

The child was, when Garrard knew him, about three or four years old; in 1864, therefore, he was not more than twenty-two years of age. Jack Smith remembered the lessons of his infancy well; when threatened by one of the Colorado Volunteers, he retorted that "he did not give a damn; that if he wanted to kill him, shoot him."[18]

Jim Beckwourth must have known this young man as an infant in the Cheyenne camps, at Bent's Fort, or at the Pueblo. That he did not attempt to assist him on this occasion seems strange, until it is remembered that there were some fifteen soldiers in the lodge, all of them there for the purpose of seeing that Jack Smith did not leave it alive. At a time when the popular mood was for total annihilation of the Plains Indians, it would have been suicide for Beckwourth to defy the implicit and explicit orders of Colonels Chivington and Shoup to "take no prisoners."[19] Jim was too old for heroics.

Conscience ridden, Jim Beckwourth made one last and futile attempt to reconcile his position with that of the Cheyennes. Alone, he set out in early January, 1865, to find their camp. The Indians had been on the warpath since the tragedy of Sand Creek and it was not difficult to learn their whereabouts. The Commission investigating the Sand Creek affair wanted to know the results of his visit:

Question. When and where did you see [the Cheyennes]? Answer. I saw them between the 9th and 12th of January, on the White Man's Fork. I went into their village in the night. The White Man's Fork heads in the vicinity of the Smoky Hill. It used to be called the Box Elder by the trappers.

Question. How large a village was it? Answer. There were about one hundred and thirty or one hundred and forty lodges. They were then traveling north.

· · · · · · · · · · · · · · · ·

Question. While in the camp of the Indians on White Man's Fork, did you have any conversation with them in reference to Sand Creek? Answer. Yes. Question. What was said? [Objection by J. M. Chivington. . . . Objection overruled.] Answer. I went into the lodge of Leg-in-the-water. When I went in he raised up and he said, "Medicine Calf, what have you come here for; have you fetched the white man to finish killing our families again?" I told him I had come to talk to him; call in your council. They came in a short time afterwards, and wanted to know what I had come for. I told them I had come to presuade [sic] them to make peace with the whites, as there was not enough of them to fight the whites, as they were as numerous as the leaves of the trees. "We know it," was the general response of the council. But what do we want to live for? The white man has taken our country, killed all of our game; was not satisfied with that, but killed our wives and children. Now no peace. We want to go and meet our families in the spirit land. We loved the whites until we found out they lied to us, and robbed us of what we had. We have raised the battle-axe until death.

They asked me then why I had come to Sand Creek with the soldiers to show them the country. I told them if I had not come the white chief would have hung me. "Go and stay with your white brother, but we are going to fight till death." I obeyed orders and came back, willing to play quits.

It was a sad and humiliating defeat for a man whose counsel had once been eagerly sought by these same Indians. Now there was little reason for Jim Beckwourth to remain in Denver and none at all for him to visit the Cheyenne Indian camps he once knew. Attempts at trapping, such as the recent one on Green River, had met with no success. He turned to scouting for the army, and was employed at Fort Laramie in this capacity for a brief period in August, 1866.[20] At that time, a young soldier discovered Jim in an unaccustomed role:

One day in Fort Laramie, some time before our departure for Platte Bridge, on entering the quarters, I found sitting in my bunk a big man with a huge head bearing a thick, glossy shock of intensely black hair, which inclined to curl, showing some negro ancestry. His knees were pulled up towards him, and upon them rested many sheets of paper, these supported by a board, forming an improvised desk. He was laboriously writing, or trying to write; anyway it did not seem to come easy. His heavy swarthy features had a peculiar puzzled expression. He was an entire stranger to me. He wore a fringed buckskin coat, beaded and somewhat ornamented, as were his moccasins, the latter more elaborately; his leggins were similarly decorated. His costume was certainly not the work of white man or woman. The men about the quarters apparently took no notice of him, as though he were a frequent visitor.

His pistols hanging from the belt were lying on the gray army blanket beside him on the bed. I was looking fixedly at him and wondering who he could be, when suddenly he raised his head and asked:

"Son, is this your bunk?"

A few more words were exchanged and I presently found myself sitting beside him. He explained that he was writing his autobiography. This was the manner in which I first met that well-known old guide and scout, Jim Beckwith. . . . He was frequently, in fact almost constantly, retained by the Government as guide in tracking marauders or hostile bands. This he performed with a skill and knowledge that seemed uncanny.[21]

It is possible to trace Jim Beckwourth's movements fairly closely in the last few months of his life. After leaving Fort Laramie, he worked for Colonel Henry B. Carrington, who had built Fort Phil Kearny. At this time, Jim was once again a partner of Jim Bridger: "Besides the visits of Bridger to the other bands of Crows along the route from Big Horn to the Upper Yellowstone, James Beckwith, the now famous mulatto of the plains, who had also lived among the Crows as an adopted chief, and had several Crow wives, was employed as an assistant guide, and was sent to their villages, where he subsequently sickened and died."[22]

Jim's death was the proper stuff for legend building. No sooner had word been received that Beckwourth was dead than the storytellers enlarged upon the mystery of his last visit to the mountains and conjecture took the place of any serious effort to learn what had happened. For years afterward, those "who knew" passed around such tales as this:

In 1876 [sic], he was back on the Big Horn river in Montana with Captain John W. Smith, post-trader at Fort C. F. Smith. Beckwith had regained some of his former influence among the Crows. As soon as the troops came to the fort, Smith sent him to the river to bring up a large party of Crows that was camped there for the purpose of trading with them. Beckwith who was getting old, was mounted on a spirited cavalry horse and seeing a small herd of buffalo he determined to kill one. His companions tried to persuade him not to attempt to run buffalo on such a horse, but he would not listen to them and started in pursuit. He soon was in the midst of the buffalo herd. His frightened horse became unmanageable, plunging and rearing among the running buffalo, and the old man was thrown and seriously injured. Some Indian women picked him up and placing him on a travois started with him for camp, but he died before reaching it. He was buried on the Big Horn in the hunting grounds of his adopted people.[23]

William N. Byers, who had known Beckwourth in Denver, in later years listened a little too avidly to the fabrications of Oliver Perry Wiggins and filled up lengthy columns of his *Encyclopedia of Biography of Colorado* with fantastic stories of Jim's life. As to his death, Byers had this to say:

Early in the '60s, while engaged in business and enjoying the comforts of domestic life, one of the most singular circumstances conceivable occurred to Beckwourth. The Crows, who had removed as far north as the headwaters of the Missouri, had not forgotten nor lost their affection for their whilom chief. They had even kept track of him through all these years, and when they were finally apprised of his situation in Denver they sent envoys to persuade him to make them a visit. He yielded to the influence and went to the encampment of the Crows. They entertained him with all the honors an Indian can bestow. During the time they used every means and argument to persuade him to again become their chief. Upon his final refusal and his preparation to return to his home, the Indians honored him with a great farewell dog feast. The meat that was served to him was poisoned and he died on the spot. The Crows freely acknowledged the crime, saying, "He has been our good medicine. We have been more successful under him than under any chief." Their excuse was that if they could not have him living it would be good medicine to them to have him dead. A locality in the Sierra Nevadas was named Beckwourth's pass.[24]

Today much is known of the circumstances of Jim Beckwourth's death, thanks to the Templeton Diaries in the Newberry Library of Chicago.[25] Lieutenant Templeton was stationed at Fort C. F. Smith, in the heart of the Crow hunting grounds. His entries for September and October are revealing:

Sept 1st [1866] . . . In the evening were somewhat surprised to see a mulatto ride into camp. He proved to be the redoubtable "Jim Beckwith" formerly chief of the Crows.

13th . . . About 20 indians came down off the hills on the other side of the river. . . . I didn't like their looks at any time but the officers and Beckwith said they were Crows &c. Beckwith & myself went down to the ferry. . . . Beckwith . . . wanted to go over to them. . . . as soon as [he] had a few words of conversation . . . he whispered to me that they were Sioux. . . . He . . . felt quite safe and wanted to talk. I stood it about 10 minutes until I saw some coming around on the right and left and then told "Jim" that "he must cut his talk short. . . ." We had not much more than got into our canoe, before they rode off about 200 yds from where we had talked and killed a miner. . . .

18th Beckwith says there is something bad going to happen as his medicine did not act right last night. he has some of the indian ideas of premonition and dreams, and a good deal more of cunning. He has undoubtedly imposed greatly on the Crows with whom he lived The day passed without our knowing anything of anything bad having taken place. . . .

29th . . . Bridger saw the Crows on Clarks Fork . . . They are anxious to see Beckwith[.]

Oct. 1st . . . I forgot to say that Beckwith and Thompson of

D. Co. went out by themselves at dark night before last intending to go to the Crow village.

10 . . . There is no sign of Beckwith yet.

20th . . . Lt. B. met a few Crows, who told him that there were
two white men in their village from this Post. I presume they
are Beckwith and Thompson[.] I am glad to hear that there is
any sign of their being alive. I had about given them up as
dead[.]

24th   The camp was all astir again about 2 p.m. by the
appearance of three indians on the other bank of the river. . . .
They all came over and told us that Beckwith and Thompson
were in the village and that the village would be here in five
nights.

30th   The Crows to the number of about 50 or 60 came in,
in the evening. "Shane" the interpreter and Thompson who
went with Beckwith came with them. We misunderstood the
indian who came in in reference to Beckwith; they wished to
tell us that he was dead, as we found much to our sorrow to
be the case. Thompson says that he complained of being sick
on the same evening that he left here, and soon after commenced bleeding at the nose. On his arrival at the village he
and Thompson were taken into the lodge of "The Iron Bull"
and were his guests while they remained. There Beckwith died
and was burried by his host. It seems strange that he should
die among the indians with whom he spent the better part of
his life. He was, with all his faults, certainly a man of some
talent, and was what might be called decidedly smart. I was
very sorry to hear of his death as he was a very pleasant man
and one who would interpret for the best interests of the government, and would fight besides. He told the Crows that he
wanted 100 young men of them to go next spring to fight the
Sioux. They seemed perfectly willing. In addition I had antici-
pated much pleasure in learning the Crow language from
him.[26]

It was not long until old friends in Denver were reading once again about James P. Beckwourth:

> This venerable and celebrated mountaineer, who was as famous in the peculiar life he had chosen as any man who ever lived, is no more. He has gone to the happy hunting grounds of the savage race whose customs of life he had, to such a great degree, adopted. Of the exact time, place or manner of his death we have yet no particulars, but it is reported as having occurred in the North Platte country, where he has been trapping and trading during the greater portion of the last two years. It is probable that his death was occasioned by old age, and the gradual wearing out of his once remarkable constitution and powerful physical frame. His age was probably about seventy years, though we believed he claimed to be ten or twelve years older. . . .

> In later years, when Government began exploring this western country, Beckwourth cut loose from his Indian friends and became a guide, interpreter and hunter, for various expeditions. In this capacity he served almost every one of the early explorers of any celebrity. At length California was discovered; or rather its wealth became known. Beckwourth took up his home there in a valley deeply hidden in the Sierra Nevadas, which took his name. He remained there for several years— the first settled home he seems ever to have had . . . .

> In wild western life and adventure, he was the compeer of the Choteaus, the Bents, the Sarpys, the Vasquezs, the Meeks, Bridger, Jack Hays, Kit Carson, Bill Williams, and a host of others who have become famous in their way, and among whom none excelled him in wild and daring adventure, or peculiar characteristics in mode of life. We know that many looked upon him as a bad man. We have heard since his death such words as these: "No loss to the country," "It was time," and other similar remarks. He doubtless had his faults, and who has not? Certainly he was not worse than any of us would likely have been with such a beginning, and such surroundings through a long and eventful life. If any one can point to a

felony of his we have yet to know it. At any rate, now that he is dead, let us spread the mantle of charity over his faults, and remember him only as one who marched in the van-guard of the great army which moves ever toward the setting Sun: one of that heroic and devoted band of pioneers, who blazed the pathway to the giant West, whose exhaustless wealth and unexampled prosperity we now enjoy.[27]

Still another newspaper gave its farewell:

JIM BECKWITH is dead. At last the adventurous old mountaineer has succumbed to the penalty we all must pay, sooner or later. His life has been one continuous chain of adventures, the history of which has filled may [sic] a page in the semi-fashionable yellow covered literature of the day. His last campaign settled him forever down among the mountains he had so often traversed as scout, guide and chief. He laid down to die at a point somewhere between North Platte and Fort Garland. *Requiescat in pace.*[28]

Jim's words to Bonner had been prophetic:

The attachments I had formed during my savage chieftianship still retained some hold upon my affections, and it was barely possible I might return to them, and end my days among my trusty braves. There at least was fidelity, and, when my soul should depart for the spirit land, their rude faith would prompt them to paint my bones, and treasure them until I should visit them from my ever-flowering hunting-ground, and demand them at their hands.[29]

One can only hope that George Templeton's version of Jim's death was the correct one, and that he did not die a lonely death on the trail, as Lockwood believed. For surely "Enemy of Horses" deserved the final solace of being surrounded by old and admiring friends; certainly "The Medicine Calf" should have had one last opportunity to play the chief and to harangue the young warriors before his restless soul departed to seek reunion with comrades of a happier time.

The Language of Beckwourth

It is impossible to make a serious study of T. D. Bonner's *Life and Adventures* without coming to a recognition of James P. Beckwourth's mastery of languages. He spoke English with amazing correctness and at times with a poetic quality; French with an ease that threw Bonner off almost entirely on French names; Spanish perhaps not so well, but surely he understood that language. He is said to have known the Indian dialects extremely well—so much so that Dame Shirley reported that "this man . . . can make himself understood in almost any language. . . ."[1]

Throughout the book foreign phrases occur and there is no evidence that T. D. Bonner alone supplied them. On the contrary, Bonner rendered names phonetically; St. Vrain, for example, is "Saverine." In French, the name would sound something like "Sah Vren," with only a slight "n" sound in the first syllable. Had Bonner known French, he would have immediately recognized these sounds and written "St. Vrain." Similarly, Portage des Sioux becomes "Portage *de* Soix": it is a common error to give the "day" sound of *des* to the simple *de*. How Bonner arrived at his spelling of Sioux is less easy to explain.

Other foreign names and words occur: "manes" (Latin: man-ās, the appeased spirit of a dead person); "Comble de bienfait" (French: the greatest blessing) are examples. "Provost" is rendered "Provo," and "Gervais" as "Jarvey," a sure sign that Beckwourth pronounced these names correctly.

Beckwourth's gift for vivid dramatic description is apparent throughout the book. An example comes to mind with his use of another French word, given by Bonner as "Poo-der-ee," a label

187

for a peculiar kind of snowstorm. (One can hear T. D. Bonner saying, "How do you spell that?" And Jim's ponderous sounding-out of a phonetic version is easy to imagine.)

These storms have proved fatal to great numbers of trappers and Indians in and about the Rocky Mountains. They are composed of a violent descent of snow, hail, and rain, attended with high and piercing wind, and frequently last three or four days. The storm prevented our seeing the object for which we were directing our course. We all became saturated with the driving rain and hail, and our clothing and robes were frozen stiff; still we kept moving, as we knew it would be certain death to pause on our weary course. The winds swept with irresistible violence across the desert prairie, and we could see no shelter to protect us from the freezing blast.[2]

Compare this graphic description with that of Edwin T. Denig:

People are frozen to death in crossing these prairies. . . . The sun is invisible and even other objects are hidden at a distance of from 50 to 100 paces by the particles of snow being whirled through the air by the wind. This is called pouderie, which leaves but two alternatives to the traveler—to ramble on at hazard in hopes of keeping himself warm by walking and stumbling on timber, or to lie down and let the snow blow over him. . . . Both these methods are often resorted to by the Indians and traders. . . . Both sometimes fail, sometimes succeed.[3]

Each of these paragraphs describes a phenomenon well known to those familiar with Colorado and Wyoming winters. Beckwourth conjures up sensations of fear and wonder at nature's force; one can almost feel the sudden violence of the attack. Denig's description falls short of Beckwourth's in emotional impact; the former conveys a more practical picture of the storm and its dangers.

The poetic qualities of Beckwourth's language are nowhere

better shown than in his rendition of Porcupine Bear's diatribe against the use of alcohol in trading (p. 102).[4] If Jim Beckwourth improvised this speech as he sat reminiscing in a lonely cabin in the Sierras, he displayed a rare talent for depicting exotic scenes. If he was quoting from memory, he was equally gifted in recall, after such a lapse of time. This facility in the use of language has kept the book alive and interesting for a century and a quarter.

Another striking example of Beckwourth's peculiar ability to produce powerful emotional responses occurred in his testimony before a military commission investigating "the conduct of the late Colonel J. M. Chivington . . . in his recent campaign against the Indians."[5] In this instance we are fortunate in having a document that presumably records Beckwourth's speech verbatim and that, of course, permitted no editing or revision.

Beckwourth was present in an Indian lodge at Sand Creek when young Jack Smith was murdered by a soldier of Colonel Chivington's Third Regiment of Colorado Volunteer Cavalry. As Beckwourth went out of the lodge, he ". . . met a man with a pistol in his hand. He made this remark to me: he said, 'I am afraid the damn son of a bitch is not dead, and I will finish him.' Says I, 'Let him go to rest; he is dead.' "[6] The restrained simplicity of this admonition conveys a weariness and disillusionment that paragraphs could not equal; the sadness and finality of death are there, and the compassion of the old for the young—all embraced in eight words.

The speech mannerisms of Jim Beckwourth occur both in his book and in his testimony: the archaic "I know not," instead of "I do not know," is an example. Occasional lapses of grammar ("Not as I know of." "The threats was made by soldiers. . . .") are balanced by correct usage in other instances ("By whom I know not." "I was intimately acquainted with him.").

Jim Beckwourth left to his countrymen a tale of adventure and exploration that is still informative, exciting, and amusing. While not a humorist, he frequently reveals his sense of fun and occa-

189

sionally speaks with a dry wit. In one instance, a repentant
Cheyenne, desiring to make peace following his quarrelsome
behavior of the day before, came to Jim with an offering of robes.

> "Take those robes [the Indian pleaded] and hereafter you
> shall be my brother, and I will be your brother. Those robes
> will make your heart right, and we will quarrel no more."
> I took the robes with me, ten in number, and found my
> heart perfectly mollified.[7]

In this mood, Jim looked back upon some of his experiences
as a lonely courier traveling down the Arkansas on his way to the
"settlements." His accounts of narrow escapes on these sojourns
take on more of the ludicrous ("and as for the Camanches, I
could beat them off with 'black soup'")[8] and less of the dramatic
and heroic tone that characterized some tales of his earlier life.

Beckwourth enjoyed playing upon the naïveté of the tender-
foot army officers for whom he worked. He played a joke on
Lieutenant Colonel Willock, who had engaged Beckwourth as
spy, interpreter, and guide after the occupation of New Mexico.
Beckwourth volunteered to go out from camp and kill an antelope; the colonel, doubting that any existed in that area, engaged
to pack on his back all that Jim could kill. It was not long until
Beckwourth saw the tracks of three antelope; saying nothing, he
went on a few yards, then threw back his head and began to sniff.

> "What the dickens are you sniffing so for?" asked the colonel.
> "I am sure that I smell an antelope," said I.
> "You smell antelope!" and the colonel's nostrils began to
> dilate; "I can smell nothing."
> [Craftily, Jim sent the colonel up one hollow, taking the
> other side himself. Jim found the animals on his own course,
> and promptly shot one of them.]
> The Colonel . . . came running at his best speed. There was
> the very beast, beyond all dispute, to the utter astonishment
> of the colonel, who regarded for some moments first the game
> and then the hunter.

"And you smelled them!" he pondered; "well, I must confess, your olfactory nerves beat those of any man I ever yet fell in with. Smell antelope! Humph! I will send my boy to carry him in."

"But that was not the bargain, colonel," I said. "You engaged to pack in on your back all I should kill. There is your burden; the distance is but short."

But the colonel declined his engagement. . . . He never could get over my smelling antelope, and we have had many a hearty laugh at it since.[9]

And so have we all.

The Beckwourth Valley, Ranch, and Trail

Beckwourth's enchantment with the valley he discovered is easy to understand. The area where his trading post and hotel stood is still today a place of exquisite beauty. The cattle graze in grass "up to their eyes" and the little Big Grizzly Creek sparkles as freshly as ever. Tall pines tower on the hillsides and in the fall brilliant hues of poplar and oak trees add a magic touch.

The ranch is the property of Mrs. Guido Ramelli and has been owned by her late husband's family since the early 1900s. In the ranchhouse, Mrs. Ramelli has a table, measuring about twenty-four by thirty inches, that came from Beckwourth's trading post. It is believed that Beckwourth made it himself. In this table is a cash drawer, about six inches below the top. But the unique feature is that the entire top lifts off, revealing a hidden area above the cash drawer. Evidently intended as a "safe," this secret drawer is divided into sections of different sizes to accommodate various denominations of coins and papers.

Beckwourth's old trading post still stands near the Ramelli ranchhouse (see photograph, taken in 1928, presented to the author by Mrs. Ramelli). It is a one-room structure having double doors and three windows facing southeast across the meadows toward Beckwourth Peak. Built of logs and heavily chinked, it is still sturdy and has served as the foreman's house for many years. A photograph of a similar but larger structure nearby has been published as being Beckwourth's trading post.[1] It is actually the dairy house built in 1917, according to Mrs. Ramelli.

Although the historic old Beckwourth Trail has long since

been abandoned, it is possible to follow it on maps of the period and to approximate it on today's maps. A secondary graveled highway (County B1) from Oroville to Quincy generally follows the route used by Beckwourth. The trail at no time touched the North Fork of the Feather and it should not be confused with the fabulous Feather River Highway of today (State 70).

State 70, leading to Portola from Quincy, lies generally to the south of Beckwourth Trail. From Portola the road passes the old Beckwourth Ranch near the confluence of Grizzly Creek and the Middle Fork of the Feather. About fifteen miles due east lies the pass. When Jim brought in the first wagons he had gone on to the Humboldt Sink, probably through an easy valley southward by way of what is now Interstate Highway 395. He followed the Truckee westward a few miles, beyond the Stone and Gates Crossing, then known as Glendale.[2]

The best description of the route has been given by A. W. Keddie:

Beginning at Beckwourth Pass, on the main summit of the Sierra Nevada Range, which is the divide between the Pacific and the Great Basin, the Beckwourth Trail went due west through the northern edge of Beckwourth Valley—now called Sierra Valley—to its outlet at the Beckwourth Ranch. Thence the Trail turned slightly to the right, went up Grizzly Valley to the summit of Grizzly Valley and Genesee Valley; then turned to the left, and went down the hill to Spring Garden Valley; then followed Spring Garden Creek to American Valley; thence to the American Valley Ranch, now Quincy. From Quincy the trail turned to the right, and went in a northwesterly direction across American Valley to Elizabethtown; thence westerly, up Emigrant Hill and on to Snake Lake Valley; where it turned to the left and reached the summit east of Buck's Ranch, by way of what is now known as the Edman mine. From the summit east of Buck's Ranch the trail—as near as I can determine—followed about the line of the present traveled wagon road through Buck's Ranch, Buckeye, Mountain House, and on to Oroville.

The Beckwourth Ranch was at the lower end of Beckwourth (Sierra) Valley, where Beckwourth had a log house near the outlet of Grizzly Creek.[3]

Today's Interstate Highway 80 has become the busiest east-west route in northern California. The beauty of the Feather River country justifies the interested tourist in taking the slower route to the north.[4] In an effort to retain the historical essence of the area, the Native Daughters of the Golden West erected a monument at the pass, but nevertheless drew back at naming "the discoverer." The inscription reads:

Dedicated To The Discoverer And To The
Pioneers Who Had Passed Along This Trail
By The Las Plumas Parlor No. 254
N.D.G.W., May, 1937

No desert waste nor red skins bold could swerve them from the western strand—Naught could their courage e'er dismay in onward trudging day by day.

A. W. WERN

A far more fitting monument has at last been raised to the memory of James P. Beckwourth. It stands beside the highway overlooking the old ranch and the valley of Big Grizzly Creek. Beyond it Beckwourth Peak towers over the rich meadows and the sleek cattle grazing there. The bronze plaque reads:

James P. Beckwourth

Ranch And Trading Post

Beckwourth, A Mountaineer,
Trader And Crow Chief,
Discovered And Promoted

This Emigrant Trail In
1852, Near This Site. He
Established The First
Waystop For Emigrants
Between Here And
Salt Lake City,
Imogen Parlor No. 134
Native Daughters Of The
Golden West
September, 1970.

Jim Beckwourth would have been pleased, also, to know that a town nearby is named for him, although for many years it was known as "Beckwith." The first post office was established at this village in 1870 and it was not until July, 1932, that the spelling was officially changed to honor the area's first pioneer.[5]

Publishing History

1856. *The Life and Adventures of James P. Beckwourth, Mountaineer, Scout, Pioneer and Chief of the Crow Nation*, written from his own dictation by T. D. Bonner. First edition. Harper and Bros., New York. Preface unsigned, but attributed to T. D. Bonner. xii, 537 pp. Illustrations not listed.

1856. First English edition. The same. Sampson Low, Son and Company, London. (All relevant records destroyed during World War II.) Bernard De Voto, 1931 Knopf edition, noted a copy dated 1858." Except for the date, it does not differ from the 1856 printing."

1892. New English edition. Edited, with Preface, by Charles G. Leland ("Hans Breitmann"). T. Fisher Unwin, London. New illustrations from "reproductions of the portraits painted by Catlin during his stay among the North American Indians." xxvii, 440 pp. A handsome volume.

1931. Edited, with Preface and Introduction by Bernard De Voto, Alfred A. Knopf, Inc., New York. Introduction is highly literary and entertaining, but it and the notes suffer from lack of documentation. Frontis., xl, 404 pp.

1932. Preface by Harry Carr. The U.S. Library Association, Inc., Westwood Village, Los Angeles, Calif. A brief introduction by Carr is titled *The Smiling Pioneer*, a heading continued for the remainder of the book. The introduction contains no new information. This version is a severe abridgement, embracing Chapters 32 through 36 of the original. A most attractive little book. 87 pp.

1950. Edited by Joseph Arnold Foster, published by Scripps College, Claremont, Calif. A 3" x 5" booklet containing a few highlights from Beckwourth's autobiography as written by Bonner. The editor selected some of the more exciting episodes and made no editorial comment other than a brief and unilluminating opening paragraph. One of the few known copies is at William Andrews Clark Memorial Library, University of California, Los Angeles. Foster's booklet is a Beckwourth editorial curiosity. 26 pp., wrappers.

1965. Reprint, 1,500 copies. Ross and Haines, Inc., Minneapolis. Introduction by Stan Nelson, who largely follows standard sources. No notes. Original illus. First indexed edition, a helpful addition. 547 pp.

It has often been said that the *Life and Adventures* was serialized in a London newspaper prior to the first edition. The British Museum, Bibliographical Information Service, can find no evidence of such serialization.

Notes

1. T. D. Bonner, *The Life and Adventures of James P. Beckwourth*, Ross and Haines edition, 1965. Unless otherwise noted, all references to the *Life and Adventures* will be to this edition.

2. "What [Meredith T.] Moore Saw of Beckwourth in California," Connelley Papers, *Kansas State Historical Society*. The physical descriptions of Beckwourth in this chapter are all drawn from this source.

3. Francis Parkman, *The Oregon Trail*, 124–25.

4. Bonner, *op. cit.*, Knopf edition, 1931, xix. "Moore says there was no appearance whatever of the negro in Beckwourth, yet all the old trappers and plainsmen called him a nigger," according to William E. Connelley in "What Moore Saw of Beckwourth in California."

5. H. H. Bancroft, *Pioneer Index*, vol. II, 53.

6. Hiram M. Chittenden, *The American Fur Trade of the Far West*, II, 689–90.

7. Dale L. Morgan, *Jedediah Smith and the Opening of the West*, 156.

8. William E. Connelley, "Centennial Celebration at Pike's Pawnee Village," *Kansas State Historical Society Collections*, X (1907–1908), 117–19.

9. Charles Christy, "The Personal Memoirs of Capt. Chas. Christy," *The Trail*, Vol. I (October, 1908), 16–18. The Francis W. Cragin Notebooks, Pioneers' Museum, Colorado Springs, contain references to Jim Beckwourth's youth: "Mr. Ben Spencer says Mr. Jim Beckwourth was a slave of O'Fallon, who first brought Jim west fr. St. Louis when Beckwourth was a mere boy" [XX–5]. "Jac. Beard says Jim Beckwourth was a slave of the Sublette family, in St. Louis" [I–10].

10. *Ibid.*, 18. There were at least two steamboat captains named Beckwith on the rivers in the years 1823–27, at which time Jim Beckwith would have been twenty-three or more years of age; neither captain was named Jim. If there were any Captain Beckwiths in presteamboat days, their names have not been found.

11. Connelley, *loc. cit.*, 117.

12. William E. Dellenbaugh, *Fremont and '49*, 118.

13. Connelley, *loc. cit.*, 119.

14. Henry Inman, *The Old Santa Fe Trail*, 338.
15. Lewis H. Garrard, *Wah-to-yah and the Taos Trail*, 237.
16. Bonner, *op. cit.*, 490.
17. W. F. Hynes, *Soldiers of the Frontier*, 59.

CHAPTER II:
Sir Jennings and "Miss Kill"

1. A. C. Beckwith, *Marvin Beckwith and His Wife*, 5–6. See also "The Hunter Papers," Missouri Historical Society.
2. William Armstrong Crozier, ed., *Virginia County Records*, V, 72.
3. Sir Edmund Jenings to Richmond County Justices, Richmond County Deed Book, No. 5, 68.
4. Paul E. Beckwith, *The Beckwiths*, 56. The Barnes Papers, Duke University Library, Manuscripts Division, indicate that he was living in 1779, in which year he was ninety-two years of age. He died in 1780.
5. Beverly Fleet, *Virginia Colonial Abstracts*, Vol. XIII, 34.
6. Barnes Papers, Depositions of John Ryner and Rheuben Settle, December 30, 1786. The Barnes Papers are used by kind permission of Duke University Library.
7. *Ibid.*, Deposition of Rhueben Settle.
8. W. G. S[tanard], "Racing in Colonial Virginia," *Virginia Magazine of History*, Vol. II, 1895, 300–301.
9. "An Inventory and Appraisement of the Estate of Sir Jonathan Beckwith . . . bearing date February, 1797," Richmond County Court Records.
10. Richmond County Order Book, No. 18, 1776–84.
11. Delmont R. Oswald, "James P. Beckwourth," in LeRoy R. Hafen, ed., *The Mountain Men*, VI, 38.
12. Paul E. Beckwith, *op. cit.*, 57.
13. Richmond County Will Book, No. 6, 1753–67.
14. George H. S. King, *Marriages of Richmond County, 1668–1853*, 13.
15. Richmond County Deed Book, No. 17 (1793–1802), 10, 71–73, 364.
16. Probate Court Records, St. Louis, Missouri, "Applications for Letters and Appointments of Administration and Executors, 1805–1815," 22.
17. Other letters for Jennings were advertised in the *Missouri Gazette* on July 11, 1811; October 11, 1811; January 5, 1820; and *Missouri Republican* January 9, 1823; October 10, 1825; October 6, 1826.
18. Clarence E. Carter, *The Territorial Papers of the United States, Louisiana-Missouri Territory, 1806–1814*, XIV, 382, 383, 391. On the latter, the name of "Jenings" Beckwith, as signer. The textual portion of the memorial was printed in the *Louisiana Gazette*, January 11, 1810.

19. Deed Record B, Recorder of Deeds Office, St. Charles County, St. Charles, Missouri. Jennings was a party to numerous land transactions; they are recorded in the following St. Charles Deed Books: B,105; C,364; C,428; D,111; D,238; G,546; S,196.

20. All known relevant Virginia records are listed in the bibliography.

21. Paul E. Beckwith, *op. cit.*, 57.

22. *Missouri Republican*, November 26, 1823; April 19, 1824; April 11, 1825; November 14, 1825; May 17 and May 31, 1827; October 4, 1827. The *Missouri Gazette*, October 9, 1818; January 12, 1820; April 10, 1818. The 1818 census of St. Charles County gives the name of Lott Beckwith as head of a family in St. Charles Township.

23. Malbeth (Malbis for Malebisse?) Beckwith's name appears in the 1818 census of St. Charles County, in Portage des Sioux. Lawrence Butler built and lived in "Soldier's Retreat," in Frederick (now Clarke) County, Virginia.

24. Paul E. Beckwith, *op. cit.*, 57.

25. Jennings Beckwith's will, Richmond County Court Unrecorded and Unproved Will File.

26. Francis W. Cragin Papers, Western History Department, Denver Public Library.

27. James Haley White, "St. Louis and Its Men Fifty Years Ago." Incomplete typescript, Missouri Historical Society.

28. St. Charles, Missouri, Circuit Court Records, 1810–1811: Risdon H. Price won a judgment against George Casner of $72.99.

29. St. Louis, Missouri, Circuit Court Archives, Book I, 278.

30. St. Louis, Missouri, Recorder of Deeds, Deed Z2, 211, Julia C. Soulard to Winey Beckwith. This deed carries a stricture against erecting a "slaughter house a Powder magazine a Powder mill or a Graveyard."

31. St. Louis, Missouri, Circuit Court Archives, Book 4, 365.

32. Nolie Mumey, *James Pierson Beckwourth, 1856–1866*, 174. See Beckwourth's will and his note to Seth Ward.

33. His land appeared on delinquent tax lists August 31, 1816, and again on November 1, 1827. (See *Missouri Gazette* and *Missouri Republican* on these dates.) Some of his land was sold at public auction in 1817 by the sheriff of St. Charles County.

34. St. Louis, Missouri, Circuit Court Archives, Book III, 400 (July 13, 1824); Book IV, 116 (July 15, 1825); Book IV, 365 (June 24, 1826). The last named is indexed as given, but no papers have been found to confirm the item.

35. *Richmond* (Va.) *Enquirer*, December 1, 1835. The same paper, on November 30, 1835, said, "Died, at Mt. Airy, Richmond County, the 14th of November, Sir Jennings Beckwith, in the 73rd year of his age."

CHAPTER III:
A Youth in Missouri

1. T. D. Bonner, *Beckwourth*, 13.
2. Frederick County (Va.) Land Tax Lists, Virginia State Library, Richmond.
3. Frederick County (Va.) Personal Property Tax Rolls, 1798–1806, Virginia State Library, Richmond.
4. A Jennings Beckwith enlisted in the United States Army from Maryland in 1813, but no other records of residence there have been found. Heitman, *Historical Register*, 205.
5. Bonner, *op. cit.*, 18.
6. J. T. Scharf, *History of St. Louis*, I, 824–25. See also *Heritage of St. Louis*, St. Louis Public Schools ed., 51–56.
7. *Missouri Gazette*, February 3, 1819.
8. *Montana Post*, February 23, 1867, as cited by Leland, 1892 edition of T. D. Bonner, *Life and Adventures of James P. Beckwourth*.
9. *The Weekly Butte Record*, July 21, 1866, Oroville, Calif.
10. Bonner, *op. cit.*, 15.
11. Clarence E. Carter, *The Territorial Papers of the United States, Louisiana-Missouri Territory, 1806–1814*, 384. "Hard is the fate of the claimant (and the orphan children of those) . . . who from fear of *the savage tomahawk* [were prevented from developing their lands]." Emphasis in original.
12. "Indian Troubles in St. Charles County," *St. Charles Bicentennial Historical Program Book*, 13. The names of the victims are listed.
13. Clark Papers, Records of the United States Superintendency of Indian Affairs, St. Louis, Roll 3, Vol. XI, 48 pages, Kansas State Historical Society, Topeka.
14. "Indian Troubles in St. Charles County," *St. Charles Bicentennial Program Book*, 13–14.
15. Clark Papers, Records of the United States Superintendency of Indian Affairs, Roll 1, Vol. II, 3, 12, 18, 20.
16. *Missouri Gazette*, October 2, 1812, "Copy of a letter dated Sept. 15, 1813, from Ramsey's Creek from General Howard to Governor Clark," Emphasis added.
17. Bonner, *op. cit.*, 5.
18. *Missouri Gazette*, October 2, 1812.
19. Carter, *op. cit.*, 391. Samuel Griffith's name is one removed from Jennings Beckwith's on the 1810 Memorial cited, note 11. Beckwith sold land to Daniel Griffith in 1823 (St. Charles Deed Book, Record G-546, St. Charles County, St. Charles, Missouri).
20. "Indian Fighter Tells of Adventures," *St. Charles Bicentennial Program Book*, 16. Van Burkleo says the area was called "Petit Coat," his rendering of Les Petites Cotes.

21. *Ibid.*
22. Bonner, *op. cit.*, 18–20.
23. Moses Meeker, "Early History of the Lead Region of Wisconsin," *Wisconsin Historical Collections,* Vol. VI (1872), 271–296.
24. Richard M. Johnson was later U.S. Senator from Kentucky and Vice President under Martin Van Buren (1837–41). Richard G. Hobbs, *Glamorous Galena,* 21, says, "Thomas January and his wife arrived [in 1820] so Mrs. January was the first white woman to set foot in the new settlement." James Kennerly and his brother George were both active in Indian trade. The treaty is noted in *General Laws Regulating Indian Affairs,* Part I, 57th Congress, Sess. 1, Res. 24, 1902, 122–23.
25. Meeker, *loc. cit.,* 273.
26. *Ibid.,* 280.
27. Bonner, *op. cit.,* 22.
28. Walter Havighurst, *Upper Mississippi, A Wilderness Saga,* 94.
29. E. Littré *Dictionnaire de la Langue Française.* The river was known as Fevre as late as 1834 (see Mitchell's Guide, 164).
30. Bonner, *op. cit.,* 22–23.

CHAPTER IV:

Mountain Man

1. Harrison C. Dale, *The Ashley-Smith Explorations,* 115.
2. Louise Barry, "Kansas Before 1854: A Revised Annals, (Part Four, 1821–1822)," *Kansas Historical Quarterly,* Vol. XXVII, 516–17.
3. *Ibid.,* 517.
4. Dale L. Morgan, *Jedediah Smith and the Opening of the West,* 79–80.
5. *Ibid.,* 156.
6. Barry, *loc. cit.,* 516–17.
7. T. D. Bonner, *Beckwourth,* 32.
8. Dale L. Morgan and Carl I. Wheat, *Jedediah Smith and His Maps of the American West,* 56–57.
9. Dale, *op. cit.,* 92.
10. *Ibid.,* 116–17.
11. Bonner, *op. cit.,* 37–39.
12. Dale, *op. cit.,* 119–20.
13. Bonner, *op. cit.,* 43.
14. Dale L. Morgan, ed. "The Diary of William H. Ashley." *Missouri Historical Society Bulletin,* Vol. XI (October, 1954), 27, 31.
15. Dale, *op. cit.,* 123–24.
16. Bonner, *op. cit.,* 42.
17. Warren Angus Ferris, *Life in the Rocky Mountains,* 43. Ferris, a Quaker, was born at Glen Falls, New York, December 26, 1810. Educated

as a civil engineer, he joined the American Fur Company at the age of nineteen. He remained in the mountains from 1830 to the close of 1835. His work has enjoyed no such popularity as Beckwourth's.

18. Bonner, *op. cit.*, 51–52.

19. Morgan, "Diary of Ashley," 33. Bonner, *op. cit.*, 53.

20. Morgan, "Diary of Ashley," 34. Bonner, *op. cit.*, 62. James C. Clyman was one of the Ashley men of 1823. He came close to losing his life to the Aricara but escaped to take part in a series of dangerous adventures before being reunited with Ashley's party. His reminiscences can be read in *James Clyman, Frontiersman,* ed. by Charles L. Camp. Zacharias Ham is little known, but Hams Fork, Wyoming, is named for him. Dale L. Morgan, "The Ashley Diary," 30, says he went to California with the Wolfskill party in 1830–31 and was supposed to have been drowned in the Colorado River in 1832.

Thomas Fitzpatrick was a famous mountain man, guide, and Indian agent throughout his adult life. A good brief biography of him appears in Morgan and Harris, *op. cit.*, 300–307.

21. Don Berry, *A Majority of Scoundrels,* 108.

22. Bonner, *op. cit.*, 64–65.

23. Francis Parkman, *The Oregon Trail,* 123.

24. Bonner, *op. cit.*, 117.

25. Alonzo Delano, *Life on the Plains and Among the Diggings,* 327–30. Also, *Alonzo Delano's California Correspondence,* 75–77.

26. Bonner, *op. cit.*, 74–85, 93, 96–98.

27. Morgan, *Jedediah Smith,* 406. Étienne Provost was one of the earliest traders in Santa Fe. He roamed the Rockies for many years, both as a free trapper and in the employ of various companies. When he met Ashley he was in partnership with one François Léclerc. A detailed biography appears in Morgan and Harris, *op. cit.*, 343–51.

28. Bonner, *op. cit.*, 105. Morgan, *Jedediah Smith,* 298.

29. Bonner, *op. cit.*, 106.

30. Morgan, *Jedediah Smith,* 298.

31. Jedediah Strong Smith is becoming perhaps more famous as a mountain man and explorer than even Jim Bridger, thanks to the exhaustive researches of Dale L. Morgan, who claims that Smith is "an authentic American hero."

CHAPTER V:

Domestic Bliss Among the Crows

1. T. D. Bonner, *Beckwourth,* 151.

2. Sublette Papers, Missouri Historical Society.

3. Dale L. Morgan, *Jedediah Smith and the Opening of the West,* 305–306.

4. Bonner, *op. cit.*, 143–44.

5. *Ibid.*

6. *Ibid.*, 151.

7. *Ibid.*, 152.

8. *Ibid.*, 150.

9. *Ibid.*, 148. The frequent Biblical, classical and historical allusions may be attributable to T. D. Bonner.

10. George Catlin, *Letters and Notes on the North American Indians*, I, 46, 50; Edwin T. Denig, *Five Indian Tribes*, 155; and Charles Larpenteur, *Forty Years a Fur Trader*, 37. All comment on the handsomeness of the Crow men, but none has anything good to say of the appearance of the women. Denig paints an especially appalling picture.

11. Bonner, *op. cit.*, 202.

12. Bonner, *Beckwourth*, 1931 Knopf ed., xxiv. "The chaste Pine Leaf . . . is straight from the novels of Emerson Bennett." Howes' *U.S. IANA* says of Emerson Bennett's *The Prairie Flower*: "It seems probable that this romance was really written by Sidney W. Moss, who accompanied Hastings to California in 1842, so some of the incidents may be factual."

13. Denig., *op. cit.*, 196–97.

14. *Ibid.*, 198.

15. *Ibid.*, 196. Berdêche: homosexual or invert. Denig says Woman Chief was "tolerably good looking."

16. Robert H. Lowie, *The Crow Indians*, 215.

17. *Ibid.*, 335.

18. Denig, *op. cit.*, 191.

19. *Ibid.*

20. Bonner, *Beckwourth*, Ross and Haines ed., 157–58. Lowie, *op. cit.*, 48, briefly describes this custom.

21. Denig., *op. cit.*, 149, 152, and Lowie, *op. cit.*, 49, 56, 128–29. Denig found their behavior totally disgusting. Lowie takes a more detached attitude, but grants a universal "philandering."

CHAPTER VI:

Indian War Chief

1. Robert L. Lowie, *The Crow Indians*, 216.

2. *Ibid.* See also *Narrative of the Adventures of Zenas Leonard*, ed. Milo M. Quaife, 233–34.

3. T. D. Bonner, *Beckwourth*, 155.

4. Annie Heloise Abel, *Tabeau's Narrative of Loisel's Expedition to the Upper Missouri*, 157.

5. *James Clyman, American Frontiersman*, ed. Charles L. Camp, 21.

6. John C. Ewers, "When Red Men and White Men Met," *The Western Historical Quarterly*, Vol. II (April, 1971), 134.

7. Francis Parkman, *The Oregon Trail*, 190–91.

8. American Fur Company Ledger T382 shows that Beckwourth was in debt (July, 1832) "to note due 22d November, 1830, $225.00." Missouri Historical Society.

9. Kenneth McKenzie to Samuel Tulloch, January 8, 1834. McKenzie wanted no more "apichamores, pieces of lodge & mean wolf skins . . . they will bring nothing in St. Louis." See also McKenzie to Pierre Chouteau, Jr., June 30, 1834. Pierre Chouteau Collection, Fort Union Letter Book, Missouri Historical Society.

10. Charles Larpenteur Papers: Manuscript Autobiography, microcopy, Vol. 5, Minnesota State Historical Society. This description is sufficiently different from Eliot Coues' rendition ("the great mulatto brave") to deserve comment. See Larpenteur, *Forty Years a Fur Trader*, 88.

11. "Sand Creek Massacre," *Report of the Secretary of War*, Senate *Exec. Doc. 26.* 39th Cong., 2nd Sess. Washington, D.C. 1867, 76.

12. American Fur Company Ledgers, T382; W245, Missouri Historical Society.

13. Letter of Jacob Hall to Manuel Alvarez, February 1, 1852. Alvarez Papers, State Records Center and Archives, Santa Fe.

14. Edwin T. Denig, *Five Indian Tribes of the Upper Missouri*, 142. George Catlin, *Letters and Notes on the North American Indians*, I, 47. Leonard, *op. cit.*, 228. Osborne Russell, *Journal of a Trapper, 1834–1843*, 55, says that "one village is called 'Long Hair's Band' after their chief whose hair is eleven feet six inches long."

15. George R. Brooks, ed. "The Private Journal of Robert Campbell," *Missouri Historical Society Bulletin*, Vol. XX (October, 1963), 11.

16. Leonard, *op. cit.*, 236–38.

17. Bonner, *op. cit.*, 190.

18. *Ibid.*, 193.

19. Leonard, *op. cit.*, 241–43. Leonard writes in a context of 1834, but other circumstances seem to support the date of 1833. There has been much conjecture about the identity of this man. Dr. W. F. Wagner thought he was Edward Rose, a Negro interpreter among the Crow Indians, but Rose had died the previous winter.

20. Bonner, *op. cit.*, 194–95.

21. Leonard, *op. cit.*, 245.

22. Bonner, *op. cit.*, 198.

23. *Ibid.*, 190.

24. Charles Kelley and Dale L. Morgan, eds., *Old Greenwood, The Story of Caleb Greenwood*, 192, citing Lewis Henry Morgan, *The Indian Journals, 1859–62.*

25. James H. Bradley, "Affairs at Fort Benton from 1831 to 1869," *Contributions to the Historical Society of Montana*, Vol. III, 255.

26. *Trinidad* (Colo.) *Daily News*, June 18, 1882.

27. Catlin, *op. cit.*, I, 47.

28. Lloyd McFarling, *Exploring the Northern Plains*, 255ff.

29. Mae Reed Porter and Odessa Davenport, *Scotsman in Buckskin*.

30. *Ibid.*, 72.

31. See the famous letter of Kenneth McKenzie to Samuel Tulloch, January 8, 1834, in which he tells Tulloch to *sell* the skins back to their original owners. Pierre Chouteau Collection, Fort Union Letter Book, Missouri Historical Society.

32. Two letters dated November 13, 1833, from "Hams Fork." Sublette Papers, Missouri Historical Society.

33. Kenneth McKenzie to David Mitchell, January 21, 1834. Pierre Chouteau Collection, Fort Union Letter Book, Missouri Historical Society.

34. Kenneth McKenzie to Samuel Tulloch, March 11, 1834. Pierre Chouteau Collection, Fort Union Letter Book, Missouri Historical Society.

35. Letter to General William Clark, dated July 26, 1833. National Archives, Record Group No. 75, Letters Received, St. Louis.

36. Bonner, *op. cit.*, 253–56.

CHAPTER VII:

Farewell to Ap-sa-ro-kee

1. T. D. Bonner, *Beckwourth*, 370–71.

2. Kenneth McKenzie to Samuel Tulloch, January 8, 1834. Pierre Chouteau Collection, Fort Union Letter Book, Missouri Historical Society. All letters cited in this chapter are from this source.

3. *Ibid.*, March 11, 1834.

4. *Ibid.*

5. Bonner, *op. cit.*, 361.

6. Kenneth McKenzie to Samuel Tulloch, January 8, 1834.

7. *Ibid.*, April 22, 1834.

8. Bonner, *op. cit.*, 304.

9. Kenneth McKenzie to Pierre Chouteau, Jr., June 30, 1834.

10. Bonner, *op. cit.*, 360.

11. *Ibid.*

12. J. Archdale Hamilton to Samuel Tulloch. February 23, 1835.

13. J. A[rchdale] H[amilton] to Samuel Tulloch, April 6, 1835.

14. D. L. (Daniel Lamont) to Samuel Tulloch, April 6, 1835.

15. Bonner, *op. cit.*, 364–68.

16. Charles Larpenteur, "Original Journal of Charles Larpenteur, Fort Union, 1834–37," Minnesota Historical Society, St. Paul. Since he obviously was not talking about Jim's courage, this is an important instance of Beckwourth's having been called a mulatto by a contemporary. It is also the earliest known variant in the spelling of his name.

17. Annie Heloise Abel, ed., *Chardon's Journal at Fort Clark, 1834–1839,* 429.

18. *Ibid.*, 429n identifies this man as Antoine Garreau, interpreter.

19. William G. D. Carson, *The Theatre of the Frontier*, 180.

20. Bonner, *op. cit.*, 384.

21. *Ibid.*, 386.

22. *Encyclopedia of the History of St. Louis,* II, 811–12.

23. *St. Louis Directory for the Years 1836–1837.*

24. Frances F. Victor, *River of the West*, 231–32.

25. Osborne Russell, *Journal of a Trapper,* 89; J. Cecil Alter, *James Bridger*, 178; Stanley Vestal, *Joe Meek*, 221.

26. Bernard Pratte, Jr., "Reminiscences," *Missouri Historical Society Bulletin,* Vol. VI (October, 1949), 68–69.

27. Samuel Allis, "Forty Years Among the Indians . . . ," *Nebraska State Historical Society Collections,* Vol. II (1887), 149.

28. American Fur Company Ledger X490, Missouri Historical Society.

29. Larpenteur, "Original Journal of Charles Larpenteur, Fort Union, 1834–37."

30. Hiram M. Chittenden, *Fur Trade,* II, 623–25.

31. Larpenteur, "Original Journal of Charles Larpenteur, Fort Union, 1834–37."

32. *Ibid.*

33. Chittenden, *op. cit.*, 626

34. Kenneth McKenzie, Order on Pratte Chouteau & Co., to pay James Beckwith, dated July 21, 1836. Chouteau-Papin Collection, Missouri Historical Society.

35. American Fur Company Ledgers 425; X473; X475; X476; AA 211. Missouri Historical Society.

CHAPTER VIII:

Renown in the Everglades

1. T. D. Bonner, *Beckwourth*, 303–304.

2. Minnie Moore-Willson, *The Seminoles of Florida,* 6.

3. Osceola was born in 1804. He was arrested by order of General T. S. Jesup and taken to Fort Moultrie, Charleston, South Carolina. Thomas Sidney Jesup began his army career as second lieutenant, 7th Infantry, May 3, 1808, and within ten years was brigadier general; brevet major general, May 8, 1828. He died in June, 1860. Heitman, *Historical Register,* 573.

4. Edwin C. McReynolds, *The Seminoles,* 128ff. General Wiley Thompson, a native of Virginia, served as militia officer in the war of 1812, rising to the rank of major general. He served six consecutive terms in the U.S. House of Representatives and was an advocate of Indian removal. See also Moore-Willson, *op. cit.*, 16. Major Francis Langhorne Dade began his

army career as third lieutenant, 12th Infantry; brevet major, December 24, 1828; he was killed December 8, 1835. Heitman, *Historical Register*, 350.

5. Bonner, *op. cit.*, 405. General Edmund P. Gaines began his army career as ensign March 3, 1799, rose steadily through the ranks to brigadier general, March 9, 1814; brevet major general, August 15, 1814; died June 6, 1849. Heitman, *Historical Register*, 442.

6. Moore-Willson, *op. cit.*, 271. The Seminole name of "Sam Jones" was Ar-pe-i-ka. "Alligator" was Al-la-pa-taw. Alligator's Indian name is sometimes given as "Halpatter."

7. Bonner, *op. cit.*, 1931 Knopf edition, xxv–xxvi. The Missouri Volunteers were mustered in at Columbia, not St. Louis. The majority of Morgan's Spies were Delaware and Osage Indian scouts.

8. Reports of Persons and Articles Hired (1818–1905), Major Brant's Reports, Record Group 92, National Archives. Joshua B. Brant began his army career as a private, February 26, 1813, and rose to sergeant major by July, 1814; at that time he became an ensign and rose steadily in rank to major, December 28, 1832. He resigned November 7, 1839. Heitman, *Historical Register*, 241.

9. *Ibid.*, Major Brant's "Monthly Records."

10. William Richard Gentry, Jr., "Full Justice," *The Columbia, Missourian*, October 2, 1924, 5. Richard Gentry "served as an officer with the state troops of Kentucky, served in the War of 1812, and later held commissions with the state troops of Missouri, attaining the rank of major-general."

11. Gentry, *loc. cit.*, 8.

12. *Ibid.*, 9.

13. Beckwourth says his ship was on a reef for twelve days. He is very close to Gentry's mark; here, for once, Jim is not exaggerating.

14. Gentry, *loc. cit.*, 10. Letter dated December 2, 1837. By this date, Gentry had lost more than two-thirds of his men, many of whom had thought better of it and had departed for home before the ships left New Orleans.

15. Letters Received, Office of the Adjutant General, Main Series (1822–1860) Microcopy 567, National Archives. This contains the voluminous testimony heard by the Missouri General Assembly in its investigation of the matter.

16. Gentry, *loc. cit.*, 14.

17. Bonner, *op. cit.*, 411. Newton Straight, *Alphabetical List . . . ,* 101, says there were twenty-six Americans killed, 111 wounded. Gentry sets the number at twenty-seven killed, 143 wounded. Beckwourth says "more than a hundred," all told.

18. Moore-Willson, *op. cit.*, 237–38.

19. Gentry, *loc. cit.*, 23.

20. *Ibid.*, 20. See also Microcopy 567, cited in fn. 15 above.

21. Bonner, *op. cit.*, 412.

22. Gentry, *loc. cit.*, 25.
23. Thomas Hart Benton to Richard H. Gentry, dated Senate Chamber, March 10, 1838. (Used by the kind permission of the State Historical Society of Missouri.) *The Columbia, Missourian,* October 2, 1924, says "This position [as postmistress] she held for thirty consecutive years. Mrs. Ann Gentry was the first woman ever appointed to a government office in the United States."
24. Bonner, *op. cit.*, 413–14.
25. *Ibid.*, 417.
26. Moore-Willson, *op. cit.*, 31–33.
27. Bonner, *op. cit.*, 417.

CHAPTER IX:
The Santa Fe Trail

1. LeRoy R. Hafen, "Early Fur Trade Posts on South Platte," *Mississippi Valley Historical Review,* Vol. XII (June, 1925 to March, 1926), 338. Beckwourth merely names "Sublet" without using a given name. Hafen believes him to have been Andrew.
2. *Ibid.* Also see David Lavender, *Bent's Fort,* 172.
3. Dale L. Morgan and Eleanor T. Harris, *The Rocky Mountain Journals of William Marshall Anderson,* 362–63.
4. T. D. Bonner, *Beckwourth,* 422.
5. *Ibid.*, 497–98.
6. *Ibid.*, 422–23.
7. Hafen, "Fort Vasquez," *The Colorado Magazine,* Vol. XLI (Summer, 1964), 8. A restoration of Fort Vasquez was undertaken by the WPA in the 1930s. Recent excavations show the existence of at least eight rooms inside the walls. See also *Rocky Mountain News,* July 20, 1969, "Fort Vasquez Unearthed."
8. Bonner, *op. cit.*, 426.
9. Bernard De Voto, *Beyond the Wide Missouri,* 30. Also see Lauren C. Bray, "Louis Vasquez, Mountain Man," Kansas City Westerners *The Trail Guide,* Vol. III (December, 1958), 7–8.
10. Bonner, *op. cit.*, 428.
11. *Ibid.*, 433. At the time of writing this, both Bonner and Beckwourth were probably drinking steadily. A letter pasted in the back of The Bancroft Library's second copy of the *Life and Adventures* asserts that much of the money advanced to the two men by citizens of Quincy and by Joseph L. Davis, went for whisky. Bonner is described as an inebriate. C. G. Goodwin [Charles Carroll Goodwin?] to Miss Maud E. Wilson, May 2, 1917.
12. Lavender, *op. cit.*, 184, says that they realized seven hundred robes and four hundred buffalo tongues.

13. Bonner, *op. cit.*, 455. Beckwourth, in connection with the Crow robbery of Fitzpatrick, called this man "Charles A. Wharfield." Lavender, *op. cit.*, 217, says that Warfield "had been around the mountains and in Santa Fe before [1843]."

14. Bonner, *op. cit.*, 457.

15. Two "Lees" appear in the chronicles: Stephen L., sheriff under Governor Charles Bent, who died with him in the Taos massacre, and Elliot, a relative of Stephen, who was severely injured at the time Charles Towne lost his life to the Apaches.

16. Bonner, *op. cit.*, 459.

17. George Bird Grinnell, *The Cheyenne Indians*, I, 354–56.

18. Bonner, *op. cit.*, 461.

19. *Ibid.*, 464. The Archdiocese of Santa Fe refused permission to study the microfilmed marriage records of the diocese.

20. *Ibid.* Emphasis added.

21. Chauncey P. Williams, *Lone Elk, The Life Story of Old Bill Williams*, 21–22.

22. Alpheus H. Favour, *Old Bill Williams, Mountain Man*, 21. "William Sherley Williams was born in 1787."

23. Leroy R. Hafen, "Mountain Men Who Came to California," Los Angeles Corral of the Westerners *Fifth Brand Book*, 21–27.

24. Lavender, *op. cit.*, 214. Letter dated January 1, 1843.

25. Hafen, "Mountain Men," mentions several who were still living there in the late 1840s. See Wilbur F. Stone, "Early Pueblo and the Men Who Made It," *The Colorado Magazine*, Vol. VI (November, 1929), 200–201. "In 1854 a band of Ute warriors made a sudden attack on the fort, massacred the inmates and pillaged and dismantled the buildings."

26. H. H. Bancroft, *History of California*, IV, 453.

27. Morgan and Harris, *op. cit.*, 296–97, on Fallon; 281, on Robidoux. Arthur Woodward, "Trapper Jim Waters," *Los Angeles Corral of the Westerners* Publication No. 23, n.d., 10–11, for several others.

28. Bancroft, *op. cit.*, II, 53. Who actually led this horse-stealing raid is a matter of controversy.

29. Bonner, *op. cit.*, 474–75.

30. *Ibid.* John Brown, Sr. later moved to California and settled in San Bernardino, where he became prominent in civic affairs. He was intrigued by spiritualism and wrote an odd little book called *The Mediumistic Experiences of John Brown, the Medium of the Rockies*. See also John Brown, Jr., *History of San Bernardino and Riverside Counties*, 1130–32.

31. *Santa Fe Republican*, September 17, 1847.

32. Woodward, *loc. cit.*, 10.

33. Ralph E. Twitchell, *The History of the Military Occupation of the Territory of New Mexico*, 122ff. Also Lavender, *op. cit.*, 249–50. Steve Lee may have been Jim Beckwourth's former partner; Lavender refers to his "stillhouse" and to his store.

34. Although there is no documentary proof of this, it is probable that Towne would have gone to the public hostelry, since most of the public officials were absent, if not, in fact, already dead.

35. Bonner, *op. cit.*, 485.

36. Twitchell, *op. cit.*, 128–29.

37. *Santa Fe Republican*, February 12, 1848.

38. *Warsaw* (Mo.) *Saturday Morning Visitor*, July 29, 1848.

CHAPTER X:

"Most Terrible Tragedy"

1. Dale L. Morgan, ed., "The Diary of William H. Ashley," *Missouri Historical Society Bulletin*, Vol. XI (January, 1955), 170.

2. The Diary of Orville C. Pratt, 1848. Used by permission of The Beinecke Library, Yale University.

3. Jim was called "Beckworth" as early as 1836; this seems to be the earliest instance of the "full style."

4. T. D. Bonner, *Beckwourth*, 500.

5. Pratt Diary, entry of August 29, 1848.

6. *Ibid.*, entry of August 30.

7. *Ibid.*, entry of September 3.

8. LeRoy R. Hafen and Ann W. Hafen, eds., *The Far West and the Rockies Historical Series, 1820–1875*, Vol. I, 358–59.

9. Rand McNally *Pioneer Atlas*, 47.

10. "Dictation." C–E 201. "Incomplete abstract of book, in the handwriting of Walter M. Fisher." A resumé of T. D. Bonner's *The Life and Adventures of James P. Beckwourth*, The Bancroft Library.

11. William T. Sherman, "Old Times in California," *North American Review*, Vol. 148 (March, 1889), 269–71. Captain William Goodwin Dana of Boston, Massachusetts, married Maria Josepha Carillo. Their beautiful old adobe—Casa de Dana—on the mesa just south of Nipomo, is gradually being vandalized and destroyed. See H. H. Bancroft, *History of California*, II, 774, for an amusing sketch of Dana.

12. Bancroft, *op. cit.*, V, 690.

13. Bonner, *op. cit.*, 504.

14. *Ibid.*

15. "California's Mission San Miguel Arcangel," *The Franciscan Fathers*, 14–16. Another Rios dwelling, known as "Caledonia," was built later, about a quarter of a mile from Mission San Miguel. It, like the Dana house, is badly in need of restoration.

16. "Recuerdos Historicos de California," por la Senora Caterina Avila de Rios, Santa Clara, June 20, 1877. Manuscript in The Bancroft Library, with whose kind permission this material is used. Translation by the author.

17. Francis Z. Branch came to California with Wolfskill's party in 1831.

He remained and opened a store and boardinghouse at Santa Barbara, often engaging in hunting and trapping. He married Manuela Carlon in 1835, was given a grant of a rancho at San Luis Obispo, and died in 1874. John M. Price came to California in 1836, living in the Monterey district. He was exiled in 1841, but returned and in 1848 was alcalde in San Luis Obispo. (Bancroft, *op. cit.*, Vol. IV, 784). Myron Angel, *History of San Luis Obispo County*, 304, says that John M. Price and F. Z. Branch reported the crime, but Angel is incorrect as to the date and the name of "Read."

18. *California Star and Californian*, October, November, and December, 1848, *passim*.

19. Bancroft, *History of California*, V, 691. See also Harlan W. Jacob, *California '46 to '88*, 134–36; Don Augustin Janssens, *Life and Adventures*, 142–43; and Annie L. Morrison and John H. Haydon, *History of San Luis Obispo County and Environs*, 66.

20. Sherman, *loc. cit.*, 271–73.

21. *California Star and Californian*, December 16, 1848, Vol. II, No. 28.

CHAPTER XI:

The Forty-Niner

1. Colonel Richard Barnes Mason left Monterey in February, 1849. Jim may have lost his job at that time. It no doubt would have surprised both men to know that Beckwourth's father and Colonel Mason's mother were first cousins. Richard Barnes was their grandfather (see Chapter II).

2. T. D. Bonner, *Beckwourth*, 507. See Victor M. Berthold, *The Pioneer Steamer California, 1848–1849*, 60–62. The *California* arrived at Monterey on February 24, 1849 and departed three days later for San Francisco. Beckwourth could not have gone to Stockton on the *California*—her crew deserted, and she did not leave the bay until May.

3. See "Gold Rush Country," *Sunset Discovery Books*, 24–25, 43, and "Guide to the Mother Lode Country," *Automobile Club of Southern California*, 10–11.

4. John F. McDermott, ed., "Gold Fever: The Letters of 'Solitaire,' Goldrush Correspondent of '49," *Missouri Historical Society Bulletin*, Vol. VI (October, 1949), 34–35.

5. John M. Letts, *California Illustrated*, 92. All italics are in the original.

6. Letts, *op. cit.*, 93–94. Tracy's initials were "J. C." He came from Santa Fe in company with "Schillinger and Hicks."

7. *Ibid.*, 93.

8. *Ibid.*, 94.

9. *Ibid.*, 99.

10. *Ibid.*, 99–100. There is a hint from Alonzo Delano that Jim continued for some time to carry dispatches: "He is now in California, and I am

told is waiting for the snows to melt on the mountains, when he starts as a bearer of dispatches to some of the distant inland posts." (*California Correspondence*, Letter dated Yateston, June 14, 1850.)

11. John Brown, Jr., *History of San Bernardino and Riverside Counties*, 1131.

12. Bonner, *op. cit.*, 509. "Chapineau" was the son of Toussaint Charbonneau and Sacajawea. He was the protegé of William Clark, who took him to St. Louis and provided his education.

13. James H. White, Incomplete Typescript, Missouri Historical Society, 3.

14. *Ibid.*

15. H. H. Bancroft, *History of California*, III, 766.

16. Bonner, *op. cit.*, 513–14.

17. Boutwell Dunlap, "Some Facts Concerning Leland Stanford . . . ," *California Historical Society Quarterly*, Vol. II (October, 1923), 204–205. "James P. Beckwourth was at El Dorado Canyon, adjoining Michigan Bluff, in 1850. His story was in part taken down by Philip Stoner and was finished later by Bonner."

18. *History of Placer County*, 373.

19. Bonner, *op. cit.*, 515–16.

20. *Illustrated History of Plumas, Lassen, and Sierra Counties*. See also George C. Mansfield, *History of Butte County*, 80, and A. M. Fairfield, *Pioneer History of Lassen County*, 11, 16, 17.

21. John M. Steele, *In Camp and Cabin*, 151.

22. *Ibid.*, 165.

23. *Ibid.*, 173.

24. *Ibid.*, 177.

25. Jerry McKevitt, " 'Gold Lake' Myth Brought Civilization to Plumas County," *Journal of the West*, Vol. III (October, 1964), 489.

CHAPTER XII:

Jim Meets the "Squire"

1. Manuel Alvarez Papers, State Records Center and Archives, Santa Fe, New Mexico. Emphasis added.

2. Manuel Alvarez Business Papers, State Records Center and Archives, Santa Fe, New Mexico.

3. Prior to 1854, two California sites were known as Grass Valley. This one was just south of Onion Valley.

4. *Marysville* (Calif.) *Herald*, June 3, 1851.

5. Dr. S. M. Miles was the first mayor of Marysville; also the third. The town was incorporated February 5, 1851. The council was composed of eight aldermen.

6. No records reveal the names of the men who helped to clear the route.

7. *Oroville* (Calif.) *Mercury Register*, August 13, 1939. A report of a luncheon speech given by Miss Coolbrith in San Francisco, 1927. See George Wharton James, *Heroes of California*, Chapter XIV, for another account of Ina Coolbrith's journey into California.

8. Charles Morgan, "A Mountain Man Writes a Book," *Frontier Times*, June 26, 1965, 22–23.

9. T. D. Bonner, *Beckwourth*, 518. The fire actually occurred on August 31, 1851. Eighty buildings, which with their stocks were valued at $500,000, were destroyed.

10. Proceedings, Minutes of the City Council, Marysville, September 1, 1851, 54. Marysville City Library.

11. H. H. Bancroft, *History of California*, VI, 464. See also *Marysville* (Calif.) *Appeal*, December 6 and 9, 1903, quoting *Marysville Herald* of August and September, 1851. The fire of September 10 burned twenty-five buildings. It was estimated that the two fires destroyed three-fourths of the business section of the town.

12. Proceedings, Minutes of the City Council, Marysville, May 9, 1853, 224. Marysville City Library.

13. Her full name was Louise Amelia Knapp (Smith) Clappe. Her husband, whom she later divorced, was a physician. See Lawrence Clark Powell, "California Classics Reread," *Westways*, Part I, December, 1969, for her life.

14. There is no evidence for this, but Jim does say he tried to get in touch with Frémont at Mariposa and failed. He may have been hoping for a job as guide or dispatch carrier.

15. Louise A. Clappe, *The Shirley Letters from the California Mines, 1851–1852*, Carl I. Wheat, ed. Letter the Eighth, 68. Also Letter the Ninth, for references to the "Squire."

16. *Ibid.*, 70.

17. John Francis McDermott, ed. "Gold Fever, The Letters of 'Solitaire,' Goldrush Correspondent of '49," *Missouri Historical Society Bulletin*, Vol. VI (October, 1949), 35.

18. Clappe, *op. cit.*, 71.

19. *Ibid.*

20. *Illustrated History of Plumas, Lassen and Sierra Counties*, 208.

21. *Ibid.*, 209.

22. Copy at American Antiquarian Society, Worcester, Massachusetts.

23. J. E. A. Smith, *History of Pittsfield, Berkshire County, 1800–1876*, 680–81.

24. Josiah Gilbert Holland, *History of Western Massachusetts*, I, 469.

25. "The Berkshire Hills," *The Historic Monthly*, September, 1901. A holding of the Berkshire (Mass.) County Historical Society.

26. Copy at American Antiquarian Society, Worcester, Massachusetts.

27. The discovery by Alexander Summers of a copy of the 1847 "Mountain Minstrel" in the Powell Library, University of California, Los Angeles, provided the necessary key to other materials relating to T. D. Bonner's life.

28. Pittsfield, (Mass.) *New England Cataract*, August 29, 1844. No complete files of this paper are known to exist.

29. *Ibid.*

30. Samuel L. Clemens, *Huckleberry Finn*, Chapter 17.

31. T. D. Bonner, *Mountain Minstrel*, 33.

32. *Ibid.*, 47. O. Whittlesey contributed yet another poem, "respectfully dedicated to Gen. T. D. Bonner." No explanation for the military title has been determined.

33. Pittsfield, Massachusetts Public Library, Genealogical Records.

34. H. H. Bancroft, *History of California*, VI, notes Burch briefly, as a claimant against Frémont for supplies, 1846.

35. Kimball Webster, *The Gold Seekers of '49*, 116–17.

36. *Illustrated History of Plumas, Lassen and Sierra Counties*, 208.

37. *Ibid.*

CHAPTER XIII:
"My Pleasant Valley"

1. *Marysville* (Calif.) *Herald*, as cited by *Alta California*, May 6, 1852.

2. Sister M. Benilda Desmond, O.P., *History of the City of Marysville, California, 1852–1859*, 22. See also *Oroville* (Calif.) *Daily Butte Record*, summer and fall of 1856, *passim*.

3. T. D. Bonner, *Beckwourth*, 519. See Appendix B for details of the ranch today.

4. *Ibid.*, 523.

5. Granville Stuart, *Forty Years on the Frontier*, 52–53.

6. Elisha Brooks, *A Pioneer Mother of California*, 33.

7. Bonner, *op. cit.*, 526.

8. Harriet Sherrill Ward, *Prairie Schooner Lady*, 163.

9. *Ibid.*, 164–65.

10. *Ibid.*, 162.

11. *Ibid.*, 165. Beckwourth and Bonner had evidently already made a verbal agreement to produce their book.

12. *Ibid.*, 166.

13. Plumas County (Calif.) Record of Bills of Sale and Agreements, I, 9.

14. By Nolie Mumey, in *James Pierson Beckwourth, 1856–1866*, 27–28. A copy of the "Davis Contract" is in the Huntington Library. The original is on page 15 of the Plumas County records cited above.

15. Memorandum of an Agreement between Harper & Brothers and

T. D. Bonner, June 21, 1855. Used by kind permission of Harper and Row, Publishers, Inc.

16. "Story of James P. Beckwourth," *Harper's New Monthly Magazine*, Vol. XIII (June to November), 1865, 455.

17. The City Clerk's Office of Lynn, Massachusetts, has no record of Bonner's death.

18. Letter from Donald E. Nutting, Office of the Clerk of the Courts, County of Essex, Salem, Massachusetts, to the author. Dated March 16, 1970.

19. Proceedings, Minutes of the City Council, Marysville, January 19, 1856, 159; February 4, 1856, 161.

20. Bonner, *op. cit.*, 519.

21. *Ibid.*, 529–30.

22. *Ibid.*, 532.

23. Dorothy V. Jones, "John Dougherty and the Pawnee Rite of Human Sacrifice: April, 1827," *State Historical Society of Missouri Bulletin*, Vol. LXIII (April, 1969), 293–316. See also John Willard Schultz (Apikuni), *Blackfeet and Buffalo*, 358–68.

24. John E. Sunder, ed., "Report of a Journey to the Rocky Mountains," *Missouri Historical Society Bulletin*, Vol. XI (October, 1954), 46.

25. Obed G. Wilson, *My Adventures in the Sierras*, 195–96. It is noteworthy that no visitor to the ranch referred to Beckwourth as a "mulatto," nor did "Dame Shirley" or Ina Coolbrith.

26. Charles Morgan, "A Mountain Man Writes a Book," *Frontier Times*, June 26, 1965, 22–23.

27. Don Baxter, "Beckwourth Pass," *Gateways to California*, 35.

28. *San Francisco Chronicle*, August 1, 1937. Mrs. Guido Ramelli, present owner of "Beckwourth's Ranch," confirms this old tale as a bit of folklore often repeated by her late husband.

29. Carl I. Wheat, ed., "California's Bantam Cock, the Journals of Charles E. DeLong, 1854–1863." *California Historical Society Quarterly*, Vol. IX, 345.

CHAPTER XIV:

Eastward Again

1. *Missouri Gazette*, August 24, 1859.

2. Present "West Denver."

3. Elijah Milton McGee owned a farm west of Kansas City and kept a small tavern in a two-story frame house, according to Joseph Snell, Kansas State Historical Society. One of Mr. Snell's sources noted that "he was a very hospitable man, and always kept a decanter of whiskey on the table in the hotel office, and invited every one who called to take a drink."

4. *Kansas City* (Mo.) *Daily Journal of Commerce*, September 28, 1859.
5. *Ibid.*, September 29, 1859.
6. LeRoy R. Hafen, "Early Fur Trade Posts on the South Platte," *Mississippi Valley Historical Review*, Vol. XII (June, 1925 to March, 1926), 338. "A. Pike Vasquez was most probably a son of the interpreter [A. F. Baronet Vasquez] who accompanied Lieutenant Pike on his southwestern expedition in 1806–1807. Pike calls him 'Baroney.' . . ."
7. Letter from "Observer" to *Missouri Republican*, November 30, 1859, as cited in LeRoy R. Hafen and Ann W. Hafen, *The Far West and the Rockies Historical Series, 1820–1875*, Vol. XIII, 215.
8. *Ibid.*
9. *Rocky Mountain News*, December 1, 1859. All references to the *Rocky Mountain News* were copied from files of the State Historical Society of Colorado, unless otherwise noted.
10. *Kansas City* (Mo.) *Daily Journal of Commerce*, December 13, 1859.
11. *Rocky Mountain News*, December 1, 1859, cited in Nolie Mumey, *James P. Beckwourth, 1856–1866*, 57.
12. Mumey, *op. cit.*, 97.
13. *Rocky Mountain News*, April 4, 1860.
14. Janet LeCompte, "John Poisal," in LeRoy R. Hafen, ed. *The Mountain Men and the Fur Trade of the Far West*, VI, 353–58, for a good account of this man.
15. *Rocky Mountain News*, April 18, 1860.
16. *Rocky Mountain News*, April 25, 1860.
17. Hafen, "Charles Gardner, 'Big Phil, the Cannibal,'" in *The Mountain Men*, 147.
18. *Rocky Mountain News*, May 2, 1860; May 23, 1860.
19. *Ibid.*, May 23, 1860.
20. *Rocky Mountain News*, June 21, 1860.
21. *Atchison City* (Kansas) *Freedom's Champion*, July 2, 1860, as cited by Mumey, *op. cit.*, 103.
22. *Montana Post*, February 23, 1867. See "Jim Beckwourth, Noted Mountain Character," *Riverton* (Wyo.) *Review*, April 6, 1928, and "Beckwourth, Colorful Fur Trader," *Wyoming State Tribune*, Section 3, July 23–26, 1940.
23. *Rocky Mountain News*, April 29, 1864.
24. Sidney Jocknick, *Early Days on the Western Slope of Colorado*, Chapter XI.
25. Cragin Papers, Western History Department, Denver Public Library.
26. Hafen, "Last Years of James P. Beckwourth," *Colorado Magazine*, Vol. V (August, 1828), 137.
27. Herman S. Davis, ed., *Reminiscences of General William Larimer and of His Son, William H. H. Larimer*, 208–209.

28. Mumey, *op. cit.*, 96.
29. Cragin Papers, Western History Department, Denver Public Library, statement of E. L. Berthoud, 1903.
30. *Ibid.* Statement of Amos Welty, 1902.
31. *Rocky Mountain News*, June 27, 1866.

CHAPTER XV:
The Last Trail

1. Nolie Mumey, *James Pierson Beckwourth, 1856–1866*, 91.
2. *Ibid.*, 74.
3. *Ibid.*, 80.
4. *Ibid.*, 71.
5. *Ibid.*, 72–77.
6. *Ibid.*, 105–111.
7. *Rocky Mountain News*, May 16, 1864.
8. Official documents relating to this charge are at the Library, State Historical Society of Colorado. The newspaper item is attributed to the *Rocky Mountain News Weekly*, August 17, 1864, Vol. 6, No. 18, and also to "Daily of Tuesday, 16th." Colorado State Historical Society.
9. Morse H. Coffin, *The Battle of Sand Creek*, 9. See also Lynn I. Perrigo, "Major Hal Sayr's Diary of the Sand Creek Campaign," *The Colorado Magazine*, Vol. XV (March, 1938), 43, 45, 49n.; and Stan Hoig, *The Sand Creek Massacre*, 83. The titles of these works represent the varying points of view of the authors.
10. Hoig, *op. cit.*, 126–27, 141–43.
11. *Ibid.*, 177–92 *passim*.
12. *Ibid.*, 169. The report of this commission is known as "The Sand Creek Massacre," *Report of the Secretary of War*, Senate Exec. Doc., No. 26, 39 Cong., 2 Sess. All testimony quoted in this chapter is from this source and appears on pages 68–74.
13. Coffin, *op. cit.*, 19. Coffin recalled that Colonel Chivington, "during this two or three minute halt [turned] to the command [and said] 'Boys, I shall not tell you what you are to kill, but remember our slaughtered women and children,' or words similar, and I think the above is correct, nearly word for word." See also William M. Breakenridge, *Helldorado*, 28–30.
14. Coffin, *op. cit.*, 29. "I have received from a friend a version which differs slightly [from still another account that agrees with Beckwourth's]. This man Smith was shot by a soldier of the Colorado Ist and that the man who shot him was sitting down in the midst of a crowd of soldiers who had collected per agreement and a space was left by the boys standing for the pistol ball to pass through."

15. Hoig, *op. cit.*, 156n. "Major Sayr tried to say that Jack Smith was killed accidentally when looking at a gun, but he admits that 'some of the boys dragged the body out onto the prairie and hauled it about for a considerable time.'" Jack Smith was believed to have been the leader of a band of Cheyennes that murdered a white father and his children and then raped the mother, who later hanged herself. "The story may or may not have been completely true, but all Colorado believed its truth. The furies engendered by it and similar tales of atrocities had much to do with what followed" (David Lavender, *Bent's Fort*, 356). See also Hoig, *op. cit.*, 107.

16. Lewis H. Garrard, *Wah-to-yah and the Taos Trail*, 58–59.

17. *Ibid.*, 263.

18. Hoig, *op. cit.*, 155–57.

19. Coffin, *op. cit.*, 29. "I have never, as I remember, heard an opinion other than that the killing was intentional, and also that he deserved what he got.... Col. Shoup in his official report of the battle mentioned young S. being taken violently ill, and died before morning.... Neither Col. Chivington nor Col. Shoup (not to mention others) have been honest in [these matters]."

20. Mumey, *op. cit.*, 163. Statement undocumented.

21. W. F. Hynes, *Soldiers of the Frontier*, 50–51.

22. Margaret Carrington, *Ab-sa-ra-ka*, ed. by M. M. Quaife, 151–52n. Ironically, the record has been confused by Mrs. Carrington herself: "December 9, 1866. Lieutenant Grummond conducted the Masonic services, assisted by Mr. Weston, Mr. Saunders, Mr. Beckwourth and others, while Chaplain White conducted the religious portions" (225–26). It is puzzling that Mrs. Carrington should not have known of Beckwourth's death two months prior to this date.

23. Granville Stuart, *Forty Years on the Frontier*, 53. The editor adds that "this story was apparently told Mr. Stuart by Tom H. Irvine, one time sheriff of Custer County, Montana."

24. William N. Byers, *Encyclopedia of Biography of Colorado*, 20–21. For comments on O. P. Wiggins, see Lorene and Kenny Englert, "Oliver Perry Wiggins, Fantastic Bombastic Frontiersman," *The Denver Westerners Roundup*. Vol. XX (February, 1964), 3–14 and Harvey Lewis Carter, *Dear Old Kit*, 20–27.

25. Another account in a rare book (also in the Newberry) corroborates much of the Templeton version: James D. Lockwood, *Life and Adventures of a Drummer-Boy*, 156–61.

26. George Templeton, Transcript of Manuscript Diary, 1866. Used by permission of the Newberry Library, Chicago.

27. *Rocky Mountain News*, February 6, 1867.

28. *Daily Miners' Register*, February 2, 1867.

29. T. D. Bonner, *Beckwourth*, 371.

APPENDIX A:

The Language of Beckwourth

1. Louise A. Clappe, *The Shirley Letters*, 68.
2. T. D. Bonner, *Beckwourth*, 288–89.
3. Edwin T. Denig, *Five Indian Tribes*, 9.
4. Also see Bonner, *op. cit.*, 459–61, for the complete speech.
5. "Sand Creek Massacre," *Report of the Secretary of War*, Sen. Exec. Doc. 26, 39th Cong., 2nd Sess., Washington, G.P.O. 1867, 2.
6. *Ibid.*, 71.
7. Bonner, *op. cit.*, 453.
8. "Black soup" was coffee, a beverage the Indians enjoyed.
9. Bonner, *op. cit.*, 490–92.

APPENDIX B:

The Beckwourth Valley, Ranch, and Trail

1. Effie Mona Mack, *Nevada, A History of the State*.
2. *Ibid.*, 118. Miss Mack mistakenly says that the trail followed the main Feather River: "There was not a great deal of travel over this route because the Feather River canon was very hazardous." *Ibid.*, 121.
3. George C. Mansfield, *History of Butte County, California*, 51.
4. In 1858, George H. Baker, a Sacramento artist, exhibited an oil painting of Beckwourth's ranch. He won a prize for "originality." California State Agricultural Society: Transactions during the year 1858, Sacramento, 1859.
5. Walturh Frickstad, *A Century of California Post Offices*, 122.

Bibliography

Manuscripts and Unpublished Materials

American Fur Company. Index to Ledgers. Also, Ledgers X490; 425; X473; X475; X476; AA211; T382. Missouri Historical Society.

Arapahoe County (Colo.) District Court Records. The People vs. James P. Beckwourth. Indictment, May 14, 1864; Subpoena, August 13, 1864; Verdict of the Jury filed August 13, 1864. State Historical Society of Colorado.

Barnes Papers. Duke University Library, Manuscripts Division.

Beckwith, Jennings. Recommended to Appointment as Captain. Richmond County (Va.) Order Book (1776–1784), No. 18.

———. Records of land transactions, Richmond County (Va.) Deed Books, Nos. 5, 17, 19, 21. Virginia State Library.

———. Records of land transactions, Recorder of Deeds Office, St. Charles, Missouri. Deed Books B105; C364, 428; D111, 238, G546; S196.

———. Appointment as appraiser. St. Charles, Missouri, Probate Court Records. Marked "All Territory of Louisiana, St. Charles, Missouri." Held in "Applications for Letters and Appointments of Administration and Executors, 1805–1815."

———. Deed of Manumission to James Beckwith. Book 3, 440; Book 4, 116; Book 4, 365. St. Louis, Missouri, Circuit Court Archives. Civil Courts Building.

———. Deed of Manumission to Lurana Beckwith. Book 4, 365. St. Louis, Missouri, Circuit Court Archives. Civil Courts Building.

———. Deed of Manumission to Winey Beckwith. Book I, 278.

St. Louis, Missouri, Circuit Court Archives. Civil Courts Building.

———. Last Will and Testament. Richmond County (Va.) Court Unrecorded and Unproved Will File.

———. Last Will and Testament Ordered to lie for proof. Richmond County (Va.) Court Order Book, No. 28.

Beckwith, Jonathan. "An Inventory and Appraisement of the Estate of Sir Jonathan Beckwith . . . bearing date February, 1797." Richmond County (Va.) Court Records.

Beckwith, Malbis. Listed. Census of St. Charles County, Missouri, 1818.

Beckwith, Winey. Deed from Julia Soulard. Deed Record Z2, 211. St. Louis, Missouri Recorder of Deeds.

Beckwourth, James P. Note to Smith, Jackson and Sublette, January 6, 1829. Sublette Papers, Missouri Historical Society.

———. Two Contracts with T. D. Bonner. Plumas County Record of Bills of Sale and Agreements, Vol. I. Plumas County Court House, Quincy, California.

———. Note to Seth Ward, dated August 3, 1866. Wyoming State Archives, Cheyenne.

———. Will. Beckwourth Collection, Clark Library, Brigham Young University.

Benton, Thomas Hart. Letter to Richard H. Gentry, dated Senate Chamber, March 10, 1838. State Historical Society, Columbia, Missouri.

Bonner, T. D., Jr. Record of death, 1845. Genealogical Records, Pittsfield (Mass.) Public Library.

Brant, Joshua B. Reports of Persons and Articles Hired, 1818–1905. Record Group 92, National Archives.

Butler, Beckwith. Last Will and Testament. Frederick County (Va.) Will Book, No. 9.

Casner, George. Suit against Risdon H. Price. St. Charles, Missouri Circuit Court Records, 1810–1811.

Clark, William. Papers. Superintendency of Indian Affairs. Microfilm, Roll I, Vols. 1–4; Roll III, Vols. 9–13. Kansas State Historical Society.

Cragin, Francis W. Notebooks. Pioneer Museum, Colorado Springs, Colorado.

———. Papers. Western Historical Manuscripts Department, Denver Public Library.

Fisher, Walter M. "Dictation." C-E 201. "Incomplete abstract of book, in the handwriting of Walter M. Fisher." A resume of T. D. Bonner's *The Life and Adventures of James P. Beckwourth.* The Bancroft Library.

Fitzpatrick, Thomas F. Letter to William Sublette, dated Ham's Fork, November 13, 1833. Sublette Papers, Missouri Society.

———. Letter to Wm. H. Ashley, dated Ham's Fork, November 13, 1833. Sublette Papers, Missouri Historical Society.

Frederick County (Va.) Land Tax Records (1797–1810). Virginia State Library.

———. Personal Property Tax Rolls (1798–1806). Virginia State Library.

Goodwin, C. G. Letter to Miss Maude E. Wilson, dated May 2, 1917. The Bancroft Library.

Hall, Jacob. Letter to Manuel Alvarez, dated February 1, 1852. Alvarez Collection. State Records Center and Archives, Santa Fe, New Mexico.

Hamilton, J. Archdale to Samuel Tulloch, April 6, 1835. Fort Union Letter Book. Missouri Historical Society.

Hunter Family Papers. Missouri Historical Society.

Jenings, Sir Edmund. Letter to Justices of Richmond County Court. April 25, 1709. Richmond County Deed Book, No. 5.

Lamont, Daniel. Letter to Samuel Tulloch, dated April 6, 1835. Fort Union Letter Book. Missouri Historical Society.

Larpenteur, Charles. Papers. 1834–1871. Microfilm, 5 vols. Minnesota Historical Society, St. Paul.

Letters Received by the Office of the Adjutant General, Main Series (1822–1860). Microcopy No. 567, File B69, 1840, Roll

202. National Archives. Testimony relating to service of Missouri Volunteers in Florida.

McCoy, Waldo and Co. Receipt to James Beckwith, January 1, 1851. Manuel Alvarez Business Papers. State Records Center and Archives, Santa Fe, New Mexico.

McKenzie, Kenneth. Order on Pratt, Chouteau and Co., to pay James Beckwith, July 21, 1836. Chouteau-Papin Collection, Missouri Historical Society.

————. Four Letters: to Pierre Chouteau, April 23, 1834; to Samuel Tulloch, April 23, 1834; to Samuel Tulloch, March 11, 1834; to Samuel Tulloch, January 8, 1834. Fort Union Letter Book. Missouri Historical Society.

Memorandum of an Agreement between Harper & Brothers and T. D. Bonner, June 21, 1855.

Miskell, Henry. Will. Richmond County Will Book, No. 6. Virginia State Library.

Nutting, Donald E. to Elinor Wilson, Report of the Office of the Clerk of the Courts, County of Essex, Salem, Mass.

Oswald, Delmont. "Unpublished Master's Thesis." Brigham Young University.

Pratt, Orville C. Diary, 1848. Yale University, Beinecke Library.

Proceedings: Minutes of the City Council, Marysville, California. September 1, 1851; May 9, 1853; January 19, 1856; February 4, 1856. Marysville City Library.

"Recuerdos Historicos de California," por la Señora Caterina Avila de Rios, Santa Clara, June 20, 1877. The Bancroft Library.

Sanford, John F. A. to William Clark, St. Louis, July 26, 1833. National Archives, Record Group No. 75. Letters Received, St. Louis.

Templeton, George. Diary, 1866. The Newberry Library, Chicago.

White, James H. "St. Louis and Its Men Fifty Years Ago." Incomplete typescript. Missouri Historical Society.

Newspapers

Atchinson City (Kansas) *Freedom's Champion.*
California Star and Californian.
Central City (Colo.) *Daily Miners' Record.*
The Columbia, Missourian.
Cheyenne, *Wyoming State Tribune.*
Denver (Jefferson Territory) *Rocky Mountain News.*
Denver (Colo.) *Rocky Mountain News.*
Kansas City (Mo.) *Daily Journal of Commerce.*
Marysville (Calif.) *Herald.*
Marysville (Calif.) *Appeal.*
Montana Post
New Orleans, *Louisiana Gazette.*
Oroville (Calif.) *The Daily Butte Record.*
Oroville (Calif.) *Mercury Register.*
Oroville (Calif.) *The Weekly Butte Record.*
Pittsfield (Mass.) *New England Cataract.*
Richmond (Va.) *Enquirer.*
Riverton (Wyo.) *Review.*
St. Louis, *Missouri Gazette.*
St. Louis, *Missouri Republican.*
St. Louis, (Mo.) *Globe-Democrat.*
San Francisco (Calif.) *Chronicle.*
Santa Fe (N. Mex.) *Republican.*
Trinidad (Colo.) *Daily News.*
Warsaw (Mo.) *Saturday Morning Visitor.*

Books

Abel, Annie Heloise, ed. *Chardon's Journal at Fort Clark, 1834–1839.* Pierre, S.D., 1932.
———. *Tabeau's Narrative of Loisel's Expedition to the Upper Missouri.* Norman, 1968.
Alter, J. Cecil. *Jim Bridger.* Norman, 1967.

Angel, Myron. *History of San Luis Obispo County*. Reprint of Thompson's and West's edition. Berkeley, 1966.

Ashley, William H. Letter to Thomas Hart Benton dated January 20, 1829. 20th Cong., 2nd Sess., *Senate Documents 67*. (Serial 181.)

Bancroft, Hubert Howe. *Works*. San Francisco, 1884–86.

———. "California Pioneer Register and Index, 1542–1848." Extracted from *History of California*. Baltimore, 1964.

Beckwith, A. C. *Marvin Beckwith and His Wife, Abigail Clarke*. Elkhorn, Wisconsin, 1899.

Beckwith, Paul E. *The Beckwiths*. Albany, 1891.

Bell, Major Horace. *Reminiscences of a Ranger*. Santa Barbara, 1927.

Berry, Don. *A Majority of Scoundrels*. New York, 1961.

Berthold, Victor M. *The Pioneer Steamer California, 1848–1849*. New York, 1932.

Boddie, John Bennett. *Historical Southern Families*. Vol. 3. Redwood City, Calif., 1959.

Bonner, T. D. *The Life and Adventures of James P. Beckwourth*. Reprint. Minneapolis, 1965.

———. *The Life and Adventures of James P. Beckwourth*, edited and with an introduction by Bernard De Voto. New York, 1931.

———. *The Life and Adventures of James P. Beckwourth*, edited, with preface by Charles G. LeLand. London, 1892.

———. *The Mountain Minstrel*. Concord, New Hampshire, 1847.

———. *The New England and New York Cataract Songster*. Pittsfield, Mass., 1845.

———. *The Temperance Harp: A Collection of Songs*. Northampton, Mass., 1842.

Breakenridge, William M. *Helldorado: Bringing the Law to the Mesquite*. Glorieta, New Mexico, 1970.

Brooks, Elisha. *A Pioneer Mother of California*. San Francisco, 1922.

Brown, Dee. *Fort Phil Kearny, An American Saga*. New York, 1962.

Brown, John, Jr. *History of San Bernardino and Riverside Counties*. Chicago, 1922.

Brown, John, Sr. *The Mediumistic Experiences of John Brown, the Medium of the Rockies*. San Francisco, 1892.

Bryan, William and Robert Rose. *A History of the Pioneer Families of Missouri*. St. Louis, 1876.

Byers, William N. *Encyclopedia of Biography of Colorado*. Chicago, 1901.

Carrington, Margaret Irvin. *Ab-sa-ra-ka, the Home of the Crows*. Chicago, 1950.

Carson, Wm. G. D. *The Theatre on the Frontier: The Early Years of the St. Louis Stage*. Chicago, 1932.

Carter, Clarence E. *The Territorial Papers of the United States, Louisiana–Missouri Territory, 1806–1814*. Vol. 14. Washington, 1949.

Carter, Harvey Lewis. *"Dear Old Kit," The Historical Kit Carson*. Norman, 1968.

Catlin, George. *Letters and Notes on the North American Indians*. 2 vols. New York, 1841.

Chittenden, Hiram Martin. *The American Fur Trade of the Far West*. Stanford, 1954.

Clappe, Louise Amelia. *The Shirley Letters from the California Mines, 1851–1852*, with an introduction and notes by Carl I. Wheat. New York, 1949.

Clemens, Samuel. *Huckleberry Finn*. New York, 1960.

Clyman, James. *James Clyman, American Frontiersman*, edited by Charles L. Camp. Portland, Oregon, 1960.

Coffin, Morse H. *The Battle of Sand Creek*, edited and with notes by Alan W. Farley. Waco, Texas, 1965.

Crozier, William A. *Virginia County Records*. Vol. V. New York, 1908.

Dale, Harrison C. *The Ashley-Smith Explorations*, rev. ed. Glendale, 1941.

Davis, Herman S. *Reminiscences of General William Larimer and of His Son, William H. H. Larimer*. Lancaster, Pa., 1918.

Delano, Alonzo. *Life on the Plains and Among the Diggings*. Ann Arbor, 1966.

———. *Alonzo Delano's California Correspondence*. Being Letters Hitherto Uncollected from the Ottawa (Illinois) *Free Trader* and the New Orleans *True Delta, 1849–1852*. Sacramento, 1952.

Dellenbaugh, William E. *Frémont and '49*. New York, 1914.

Denig, Edwin T. *Five Indian Tribes of the Upper Missouri*. Norman, 1961.

Desmond, Sister M. Benilda, O.P. *History of the City of Marysville, California, 1852–1859*. Dominican Sisters, San Jose.

De Voto, Bernard. *Across the Wide Missouri*. Boston, 1947.

———. *The Year of Decision: 1846*. Boston, 1943.

Ellison, William and Francis Price, eds. *The Life and Adventures in California of Don Agustín Janssens, 1834–1856*. San Marino, 1953.

Eubank, H. Ragland. *Authentic Guide Book of the Historic Northern Neck of Virginia*. Colonial Beach, Va., 1934.

Fairfield, Asa Merrill. *Fairfield's Pioneer History of Lassen County, California*. San Francisco, 1916.

Favour, Alpheus H. *Old Bill Williams, Mountain Man*. Norman, 1962.

Ferris, Warren Angus. *Life in the Rocky Mountains*. Salt Lake City, 1940.

Fleet, Beverley. *Virginia Colonial Abstracts*. Baltimore, 1941.

Frémont, John Charles. *Report of the Exploring Expedition to the Rocky Mountains in the Year 1842, and to Oregon and North California in the Years 1843–44*. Washington, 1845.

Frickstad, Walturh. *A Century of California Post Offices*. Oakland, 1955.

Garrard, Lewis H. *Wah-to-yah and the Taos Trail,* ed. by Ralph Bieber. Glendale, 1938.

———. *Wah-to-yah and the Taos Trail.* Norman, 1966.

General Laws Regulating Indian Affairs, Part I, 57th Cong., 1st Sess., Res. 24, 1902.

Grinnell, George Bird. *The Cheyenne Indians.* 2 vols. New York, 1962.

Hafen, LeRoy R. *The Far West and the Rockies Series, 1820– 1875,* Vol. I. Glendale, 1954.

——— (ed.). *The Mountain Men and the Fur Trade of the Far West,* Vol. VI. Glendale, 1968.

Harlan, Jacob W. *California '46 to '88.* Oakland, 1896.

Havighurst, Walter. *Upper Mississippi, A Wilderness Saga.* New York, 1944.

Hayden, Horace E. *Virginia Genealogies.* Washington, D. C., 1931.

Heitman, Francis B. *Historical Register and Dictionary of the United States Army from Its Organization September 29, 1789 to March 2, 1903.* Washington, D.C., 1903.

History of Placer County. Oakland, 1882.

History of Northern California. Chicago, 1891.

Hoig, Stan. *The Sand Creek Massacre.* Norman, 1961.

Holland, Josiah Gilbert. *History of Western Massachusetts,* Vol. I. Springfield, Mass., 1855.

Hoover, M. M., H. E. Rensch, and E. G. Rensch. *Historic Spots in California,* 3rd ed., rev. by William N. Abeloe. Stanford, 1966.

Howes, Wright. *U.S. IANA* (1650–1950). New York, 1962.

Hyde, William and Howard L. Conard. *Encyclopedia of the History of St. Louis,* Vol. IV. New York, 1899.

Hynes, W. F. *Soldiers of the Frontier.* Privately printed, n.d.

Illustrated History of Plumas, Lassen and Sierra Counties. San Francisco, 1882.

Indian Affairs: Laws and Treaties, Vol. II. Washington, D.C., 1903. 57th Cong., 1st Sess.

Inman, Henry. *The Old Santa Fe Trail*. New York, 1897.

James, George Wharton. *Heroes of California*. Boston, 1910.

Jocknick, Sidney. *Early Days on the Western Slope of Colorado*. Denver, 1913.

Kelly, Charles and Dale L. Morgan, eds. *Old Greenwood, The Story of Caleb Greenwood*. Georgetown, Calif., 1965.

King, George H. S. *Marriages of Richmond County, Virginia, 1668–1853*. Fredericksburg, 1967.

Larpenteur, Charles. *Forty Years a Fur Trader*. Chicago, 1933.

Lavender, David S. *Bent's Fort*. New York, 1954.

Leonard, Zenas. *Narrative of the Adventures of Zenas Leonard*. Chicago, 1934.

Letts, John M. *California Illustrated*. New York, 1852.

Littré, Emile. *Dictionnaire de la Langue Française de Emile Littré*. Editions Universitaires, 1958.

Lockwood, James. *Life and Adventures of a Drummer Boy*. Albany, 1893.

Lowie, Robert H. *The Crow Indians*. New York, 1956.

McDonald, Rose M. E. *Clarke County, A Daughter of Frederick*. Berryville, Va., 1943.

McFarling, Lloyd. *Exploring the Northern Plains*. Caldwell, Idaho, 1955.

Mack, Effie Mona. *Nevada: A History of the State*. Glendale, 1936.

McReynolds, Edwin P. *The Seminoles*. Norman, 1966.

Mansfield, George C. *History of Butte County, California*. Los Angeles, 1918.

Mitchell's United States. Mitchell and Hinman, Philadelphia, 1834.

Moore-Willson, Minnie. *The Seminoles of Florida*. Kissimmee, Florida, 1928.

Morgan, Dale L. *Jedediah Smith and the Opening of the West.* Lincoln, 1967.

—— and Carl I. Wheat. *Jedediah Smith and His Maps of the American West.* San Francisco, 1954.

—— and Eleanor T. Harris, eds. *The Rocky Mountain Journals of William Marshall Anderson.* San Marino, 1967.

—— *Overland in '46.* 2 vols. Georgetown, Calif., 1963.

Morrison, Annie L., and John H. Haydon. *History of San Luis Obispo County and Environs.* Los Angeles, 1917.

Mumey, Nolie. *James Pierson Beckwourth, 1856–1866.* Denver, 1957.

Murray, Charles A. *Travels in North America.* 2 vols. London, 1854.

Parkman, Francis. *The Oregon Trail.* 6th ed., rev. Boston, 1877.

Petersen, William J. *Steamboating on the Upper Mississippi.* Iowa City, 1968.

Porter, Mae Reed, and Odessa Davenport. *Scotsman in Buckskin.* New York, 1963.

Richardson, A. D. *Beyond the Mississippi.* Hartford, 1867.

Russell, Osborne. *Journal of a Trapper, 1834–1843.* Lincoln, 1968.

St. Louis, Missouri *Directory for the Years 1836–1837.* St. Louis, 1836.

"Sand Creek Massacre," *Report of the Secretary of War, Senate Exec. Doc. 26.* 39th Cong., 2nd Sess. Washington, D.C., 1867.

Scharf, John T. *History of St. Louis City and County,* Vol. I. Philadelphia, 1883.

Smith, J. E. A. *History of Pittsfield, Berkshire County, 1800–1876.* C. W. Bryan and Co., 1876.

Steele, John M. *In Camp and Cabin.* Chicago, 1928. Published with General John Bidwell's *Echoes of the Past.*

Stewart, George R. *The California Trail.* New York, 1962.

Strait, Newton A. *An Alphabetical List of Battles, 1754–1900.* Washington, D.C., 1905.

McDermott, John F., ed. "Gold Fever: The Letters of Solitaire. . . ." *Missouri Historical Society Bulletin*, Vol. VI (October, 1949).

McGroarty, W. B. "Champe of Lamb's Creek." *Virginia Magazine of History*, Vol. 44, 1936.

McKevitt, Jerry. " 'Gold Lake' Myth Brought Civilization to Plumas County." *Journal of the West*, Vol. III (October, 1964).

Meeker, Moses. "Early History of the Lead Region of Wisconsin." *Wisconsin Historical Collections*, Vol. VI, 1872.

Morgan, Charles. "A Mountain Man Writes a Book." *Frontier Times*, June 26, 1965.

Morgan, James Robert, and John L. Roselius. "The Death of James Bowie: A Historical Enigma." *San Diego Westerners 2nd Brand Book*, 1971.

Morgan, Dale L., ed. "The Diary of William H. Ashley." *Missouri Historical Society Bulletin*, Vol. XI (October, 1954; January, 1955).

Perrigo, Lynn I. "Major Hal Sayr's Diary of Sand Creek Campaign." *The Colorado Magazine*, Vol. XV (March, 1938).

Powell, Lawrence Clark. "California Classics Reread." *Westways* (December, 1969).

Pratte, Bernard, Jr. "The Reminiscences of General Bernard Pratte, Jr." *Missouri Historical Society Bulletin*, Vol. VI (October, 1949).

Rauch, Theodosia. "Les Petites Cotes." St. Charles, Missouri. n.d.

Rosenstock, Fred A. "Small Miracles in My Life as a Book Hunter." *Monthly Round-Up, The Denver Westerners*, Vol. XXII (January, 1966).

Sherman, William T. "Old Times in California." *North American Review*, Vol. 148 (March, 1889).

S[tanard], W. G. "Racing in Colonial Virginia." *Virginia Magazine of History*, Vol. II, 1895.

Stone, Wilbur F. "Early Pueblo and the Men Who Made It."

Address at Pueblo July 4, 1876. *The Colorado Magazine.* Vol. VI (November, 1929).

Sunder, John E., ed. "Report of a Journey to the Rocky Mountains." *Missouri Historical Society Bulletin,* Vol. XI (October, 1954).

Van Burkleo, William. "Indian Fighter Tells of Adventures." St. Charles (Missouri) *Bicentennial Historical Program Book,* 1969.

"When This Was Indian Land." St. Charles (Missouri) *Bicentennial Historical Program Book,* 1969.

Woodward, Arthur. "Trapper Jim Waters." *Los Angeles Corral, The Westerners,* No. 23. n.d.

Maps

Fisher, Richard Swainson. "Johnson's New Illustrated Family Atlas." New York, 1863.

Jackson, Captain W. A. "Map of the Mining Districts of California." Published by John Arrowsmith, 1851.

Rand-McNally Indexed Atlas of the World, Vol. I, 1907.

Rand-McNally Pioneer Atlas, 1869. Reprint, 1969.

Richmond County Primary and Secondary Highway Systems, January 1, 1967.

Tunnison, H. C. "Tunnison's Peerless Universal Atlas of the World." Jacksonville, Ill., 1893.

Index